To Mary dear
with warm affection
and prayers.
Fr. Cronan Regan C.P.

SIGNPOST

by Cronan Regan

FRANCISCAN HERALD PRESS
Chicago, Illinois 60609

SIGNPOST: Questions about the Church and Religion You Always Wanted Answered, by Cronan Regan, C.P. Library of Congress Catalog Card Number: 70-169056; ISBN: 8199-0432-5. Copyright © 1972 by Franciscan Herald Press, 1434 West 51st Street, Chicago, Illinois 60609. Made in the United States of America.

ꞁꝫꝫꝫꝫꝫꝫꝫꝫꝫꝫꝫꝫꝫꝫꝫꝫꝫꝫꝫꝫꝫꝫꝫꝫꝫꝫꝫꝫꝫꝫꝫꝫꝫꝫꝫꝫ

IMPRIMI POTEST:
Very Rev. Flavian Dougherty, C.P.
Provincial Superior
Province of St. Paul of the Cross

NIHIL OBSTAT:
Rev. William F. Hogan
Censor Librorum

IMPRIMATUR:
✝ Most Rev. Thomas A. Boland, S.T.D.
Archbishop of Newark

October 14, 1971

To my Father and Mother

who now know

all the answers

CONTENTS

4. THE OTHER CHURCHES

5. QUESTIONS OF BELIEF

8. CHRISTIAN MISCELLANY

PREFACE

Somewhere in his voluminous writings, Christopher Dawson has said: "Man and Christ face each other as the question and the answer, the desire and the fulfillment."

Man in every age is a living question mark. He is always reaching out restlessly to grasp the meaning of his own truth. He is plagued by basic questions: Who am I? Where did I come from? Where am I going? How do I get there? What waits for me around the next corner? Human existence itself is so inseparable from restlessness and search that most of us can feel a kinship with the mood, if not the melody, of a song like "What's It All About Alfie?".

When *SIGN* Magazine celebrated its golden jubilee recently, the editors went back and paged through fifty volumes to select some representative pieces from each decade of its history. They discovered that everything in *SIGN* finally focused on two questions: (1) what does it mean to be really human? (2) How does the Good News of Christ help us to achieve Christian humanism? And a pictorial review of some of the triumphs and the tragedies, the hopes and frustrations of our era made the editors find new cogency in the words of the Second Vatican Council: "All human activity, constantly imperiled by man's pride and deranged self-love, must be purified and perfected by the power of Christ's cross and resurrection."

Christ and His cross are at the core of God's revelation to man. If we want to know what God thinks about the meaning of man, we cannot separate our question from the presence of Christ in human history and the answer given by a cross of death and an empty tomb. The Paschal mystery wrought in the human flesh of God made man is the central event in the history of mankind.

The centrality of this event has given unity and cohesiveness to whatever has been written for *SIGN* for more than fifty years.

But nowhere is this truth more evident than in "Signpost" — a timeless feature that never grows old or stale, because the questioning spirit is always alive and squirming and tantalizing within the human heart.

Over a period of fifty years, some eight or ten theologians have filled the role of editor of "Signpost." None of them faced the challenge of this assignment at a more turbulent moment in the life of the Church than Cronan Regan, Passionist.

In our post-Vatican II world, there is the anguish of imperative change. The people of God are suffering from growing pains. The liturgical renewal, with its emphasis upon a sense of community in worship, has made older forms of piety seem outdated or even subtly selfish. The new catechetics have created questions in parents' minds about how their children are learning the faith. Ecumenical overtures to Churches other than our own have made some faithful Roman Catholics feel that their old certainties and even their awareness of being uniquely enriched by the providence of God are slipping through their fingers. The downgrading of speculative thinking in the study of theology has made large segments of younger Catholics impatient with the complexity of religious education. The emergence of situation ethics and the new stress upon the primacy of love in moral theology have disturbed an older generation of believers who were more comfortable in a moral universe of easily verified demands concerning right and wrong.

All of this, and much more, has made the faithful of Christ more than ever aware of being bombarded by questions rising up in their own hearts. The questions are good questions. And only a man with a good mind and a real talent for humane exposition of his own convictions can answer them well.

Father Cronan Regan has brought an enviable combination of gifts to this task. He seems to have a passion for clearness. He is his own harshest critic of the adequacy of an answer. He does not attempt to do more than a believer can promise to do when confronting the mysteries of faith. He is not a simplistic answer man. He is a theologian who has steeped himself in the best of traditional theology and has meditated enough upon the mysteries of faith to avoid the pitfall of becoming a mere spouter of words. And perhaps most important of all, he has developed a humane compassion that enables him to feel the anguish of unanswered questions, whether they are prompted by the doubts of the troubled, the anger of the belligerent, or the disappointment of people who are just hurting.

His book is a good priest's gift to people who have asked good questions.

AUGUSTINE P. HENNESSY, C. P.
EDITOR—*The Sign*

ACKNOWLEDGMENTS

For permission to include copyrighted material in this volume, the following acknowledgments are gratefully made: to The America Press for excerpts from *The Documents of Vatican II* edited and translated by Walter M. Abbott, S.J., and Joseph Gallagher © 1966 by The America Press; to the National Center of Religious Education for Scripture quotations from *The New American Bible* © 1970 by Confraternity of Christian Doctrine; to Farrar, Straus & Giroux, Inc. for excerpts from *Shalom: Peace, The Sacrament of Reconciliation* by Bernard Haring © 1967, 1968 by Bernard Haring; to Doubleday & Company, Inc. for excerpts from *The Jerusalem Bible* © 1966 by Darton, Longman & Todd, Ltd. and Doubleday & Company, Inc.; and also to my longtime associates and religious family for permission to reprint material that first appeared in *Sign, National Catholic Magazine* © 1968-1971 by the Passionist Missions, Inc.

Grateful acknowledgment is also made to Miss Mary Alice Slater of St. Anthony Guild Press for her careful editorial help, and to Miss Marcia B. Goodman for compiling the index.

1
The Anxiety
of
Change

Prayers or Prayer

My little brother is in the first grade. He doesn't know the Our Father that was taught by God himself. He said his Sister doesn't teach them that or the Hail Mary. The kids who made their first Holy Communion came down the aisle hand in hand swinging to the music. Mom said she just wonders what our heavenly Father thinks of us, with all these changes in the Church.

The one thing we are sure of is what our heavenly Father thinks of us. Our Lord told us: "God so loved the world that he gave his only Son" (John 3:16). The Psalmist puts it beautifully: "Merciful and gracious is the Lord, slow to anger and abounding in kindness. . . . Not according to our sins does he deal with us, nor does he requite us according to our crimes. . . . As a father has compassion on his children, so the Lord has compassion on those who fear him. For he knows how we are formed; he remembers that we are dust" (Psalm 103: 8, 10, 13-14). God has not changed. He cannot change. He is always Love pouring itself out, calling sinful men to be transformed and enter into union with him. Even when we're being silly or selfish or stupid, God still reaches out to us to call us to that change which will be maturity and love and true religion.

True religion. That's the problem. It is your problem, and I'm sorry it is upsetting you so much as you see changes in liturgy and deportment that seem to you to be destroying true religion. But I don't think it's fair to say that the changes in the Church are creating the problem. It is because the problem was crowding in on them that the bishops of the Church came to see that we would have to change. And that change is helping to make the problem stand out more sharply, even more painfully, so that we can deal with it more effectively.

For years, the Church in America had a marvelous formula. It came in with the immigrants. It provided a center of stability for them in a new land. It acted as a bridge with the culture of the new land, educating their children, fighting for their dignity. It min-

istered God's gifts of the word and the sacraments and provided
the place of prayer, worship, and social life. The formula of parish,
school, and Baltimore Catechism worked wonderfully well. It met the
people right at the level of their needs and helped many to become
grand men and women radiating a true religious sense.

But times change, and the needs of people change. Yet our formula
did not change. As the population grew, we built bigger churches,
and the individual became more anonymous and more alienated
from the parish community and the act of worship. We provided
education in Catholic institutions for anywhere from eight to sixteen
years. We found that we had well-informed Catholics, perhaps even
more committed Catholics than would otherwise have been the case.
But we also discovered, with appalling frequency, that Catholicism
had no real ultimate meaning for many we had indoctrinated. We began to ask ourselves some pointed questions. They had learned their
prayers; had they learned to pray? They had learned about God;
did they know God? They knew all the virtues and could recite their
theology; had they been helped to grow in virtuous unselfishness?
Missals were no mystery to them, but could they join with Christ and
make the Mass their grateful worship?

And so we're going through the painful process of trying to change.
Some of the change is going badly. We have to help one another
through this awkward phase, like cheerful invalids who trust in the
work of the Holy Spirit. Some of it is, however, going very well indeed.

This is a very roundabout way to get to the problem of your
little brother. I think that Sister is trying to teach him to pray — to
pray as a six-year-old prays. He should not get the idea that talking
to God means using big words he doesn't understand. Nor that praying is just for very solemn times that aren't very pleasant. I'm sure
that he will learn the Our Father as soon as he can handle words
like "art," "hallowed," "come," and "trespass." Is it wise to delay
things that long? I'm not sure. But when he does learn his prayers,
I hope that he will already have learned how to pray and will like
to pray.

Was the Past So Wrong?

**Foremost in my mind is this question: What is wrong now with all
we were taught, all we learned and believed in the past? There
must have been something entirely wrong; else, why the numerous**

changes? Why are there no prayer books now, no litanies, no examination of conscience, no thanksgiving after Holy Communion, no weekly confession? Were all of these things wrong in past years?

This is *the* problem. Are you being asked to reject everything that you've ever learned, everything that you have lived for, everything that you loved in the past? Sometimes it feels that way, doesn't it? But this is a misunderstanding.

As I understand it, the changes that have been made and that are being made are intended to help make the face of our holy Church more recognizable for men who belong to this century. This implies a judgment that some of the external and changeable aspects of the Church's life were out of date. They were no longer feeding the faith and devotion and the charity of today's people as they had nourished our grandparents and the generations that preceded them. This is not the same thing as saying that these things were wrong in the past. They worked in the past, and they worked wonderfully well. Through the changes that the Church is encouraging she is hopeful of finding modes of expressing the one faith that will work at least as well in the present.

At the same time, there are some scatterbrained people talking about change who are distorting the intentions of the Church as she makes a heroic effort to speak to the men of the twentieth century. It is these people who would eliminate prayer, examination of conscience, prayerful communion with our Lord after receiving the Eucharist, regular confession. There is nothing in the Vatican Council that authorizes us to downgrade these things. There is no one in high places in the Church who is anxious to do away with any of these things. In fact, the whole direction of the changes shows that the intention of the Church's leaders is to keep these central acts of Catholic religious life even more alive for the people of our generation.

Unfortunately, in any time of transition, it is those who are on the fringe who are often the most vocal. But those in the mainstream of change in the Church are not extremists, nor are they emptying our faith of its central riches.

For myself, I find it wonderful to be able to understand the Mass perfectly as it is celebrated in my own language. I think it is valuable to find a renewed appreciation of the complex thing the Mass is: a banquet with our blessed Lord as well as a sacrifice that is the memorial of the Passion of the Lord. I'm very happy to see Catholics becoming concerned about questions of peace and poverty — a Christian who is following his Lord in the Gospel ought to be preoccupied with these great problems of mankind more than with the anxieties of following the laws of fast and abstinence. And yet all of these concerns will be enduring and valuable only if they are fired by a spirit of penance and of prayer and of faith and of genuine love of God and loyalty to the Church. These are the things that were so right in the past. They are still absolutely right in the present. And if they are declared out of date, it will not be a help for renewing the Church; it will be an apostasy from Christ.

What Is the Truth?

In one of your columns you refer to a position as a ". . . distortion of the Catholic truth. . . ." What, please, is "Catholic" truth? If it differs from plain, vanilla truth, then it is not truth but is itself distortion. Please explain.

Thank you for deflating semantic pomposity. "Catholic" truth does not differ from "plain, vanilla" truth. Truth is the way things really are. When I affirm that Jesus Christ is indeed God and man, my judgment is true if this is the way things really are. And if it is true, then it is true not merely for Catholics or for men of a certain era. It is always and everywhere true. Another man may be perfectly sincere in disagreeing with me — but, judged against the bar of the way things really are, if one of our positions is true, the other will be false. The true statement will not be the whole truth, however; that is, Jesus *is more* than my single statement can affirm. He is also a male of Palestinian origin, he is risen, et cetera. We can grasp the truth only in a fragmentary way. Each of our true statements expresses no more than a facet of "the way things really are."

Why do we sometimes say things like "Catholic truth"? For the same reason that we might speak of "scientific truth" or "mathematical truth." That is, because of the way in which we arrive at the certain judgment that this is the way things are. There are two principal ways of arriving at the truth. One is by way of evidence. When a housewife smells a pungent odor and lifts the cover from a smoking saucepan, she has the evidence that permits her to make the true judgment that the string beans are burnt. The other way is that of testimony. Long after the evidence has been destroyed and the mess cleaned up, her husband may come to make a similarly true judgment, when he hears the lament from the one qualified witness of the minor disaster, because he believes her.

The only way that we can arrive at the truth of our faith is through testimony: God must open something of his mysterious self to us. In most cases, this testimony is mediate. It comes to us through the testimony of the Church and the Scriptures. The term "Catholic truth" is a kind of awkward shorthand. It means that we have come to this certainty through the testimony of God which is communicated to us through those who hold the office of teacher in the Catholic Church — the pope and the bishops.

The Dutch Catechism

Could you please define for me, if you can, the points I should know in reading "A New Catechism" — the 1967 copy that did not meet with the approval of Pope Paul. It has been a source of information to me the year and a half I've had it, and I have enjoyed it thoroughly. Still, it bothers me not to know precisely the reasons it is not on our reading list in my college religion course.

There is no reason why the so-called Dutch Catechism should not be on your reading list, unless it be that your harried professor can't include every good book on a single list.

The catechism was published in Holland in 1966 with the backing of the Dutch bishops. It was written as an adult expression of the faith designed to meet the conditions of the Church in the Netherlands. It tends to avoid using traditional religious expressions in favor of those more intelligible to modern man and to downplay those parts of Catholic conciliar and papal teaching most apt to jar Protestant sensibilities.

The Vatican objected strongly that these tendencies and silences made the text unsatisfactory as it stands. Among the problem areas were these: original sin, Christ's atoning satisfaction and sacrifice, the sacrificial character of the Mass, the priestly nature of the ordained ministry, the Church's teaching authority, angels, Our Lady, et cetera. Basically, the objection was more about what the catechism did not say than about what it said.

While the matter was under discussion, the Dutch bishops asked foreign publishers to delay issuing translations, and the imprimatur of the American edition was withdrawn. In spite of this, the catechism was published here and in England. Undoubtedly, there were economic reasons pressuring the publishers to get the book on the market — they already had a great deal invested in the translation.

However, many groups thought this move ill-conceived.

A committee of cardinals studied the book and finally issued a report in October, 1968, recommending corrections in the text. As the result of a compromise between Rome and Holland, the original text remains unchanged and a supplement, written in the spirit of the cardinals' recommendations, is appended to all new editions of *A New Catechism*. It is now included in the American edition of the book.

New Theology?

I recently heard a young priest give a lecture that absolutely stunned me. He said such things as: the Ten Commandments are pre-Mosaic and were only tribal law; we don't turn to the Scripture to learn how to live; right conduct is determined by our conscience, not by the commandments; to sacrifice a person for the sake of law is the great offense (isn't this what the Church has always done?). It looks like a whole new ball game to me. Please comment.

If your reporting of his lecture is accurate, I think that the pitcher in your new ball game should spend a couple more seasons in the bush leagues. It sounds like another example of the kind of thing that has disturbed me very much in the years since the Vatican Council closed — a self-styled apostle of renewal who seems to deal in half-truths for their shock value. We find it too often with religion teachers who have taken a couple of courses in theology. How many youngsters come home with the impression that the story of Adam and Eve is fictional and therefore unimportant? What these teachers fail to do is to show their students that the inspired fiction conveys the profound truths of man's dependence on God, his destiny of a life with God, the dignity of every man, the reality of sin, the religious foundations of marriage, et cetera.

There are many new insights and attitudes that have come to the fore in recent years. It is the job of the teacher and the popular lecturer to present this newness accurately and to attempt to bridge the gap between the old and the new harmoniously. None of the new threatens the substance of our faith.

From the items you report, I gather that your lecturer was trying to bring his audience from an impoverished view of Christian morality to a richer view of the responsibility of the Christian person. This is a wonderful goal. Too many religious people have been moralistic rather than loving. Too many have thought of the Christian's life as one lived in rigid external conformity with the book, with little concern for personal motives and growth. Too often, all the rules seemed equally important. It is this kind of horrible distortion (so easy to caricature) that has made it easier for a new generation to turn off religion as something irrelevant and dehumanizing.

But the remedy for this situation is not to undermine the importance of every norm of human behavior except that of the autonomous conscience. Commandments exist to instruct a person, to inform his conscientious judgment. He cannot abdicate his own responsibility in the name of the commandments. But neither can he ignore them without falling into moral anarchy. And when commandments or laws have God's sanction, they bind one's conscience in a uniquely firm way.

Now for a brief word about the facts you report. It is true that the Hebrews shared much of a common heritage with their neighbors in the Middle East. It is likewise true that these other people recognized the binding wisdom of the fourth to the tenth commandments before the Chosen People did — the prohibition of murder did not come down as a new revelation from Mount Sinai. But it is not true that the Ten Commandments are merely the social rules of primitive tribes. In fact, scholars generally agree that the religious formulation of the Ten Commandments is Israel's distinctive contribution to legal lore. And Christians see the new commandment of love as the transforming soul of the ten, not as their abolition (see I John 2:3-11).

Again, it makes no sense to speak of a *right* conscience or *right* conduct unless rectitude is measured by norms. Conscience and commandments are correlatives, not enemies.

It is true that to destroy a person for the sake of a law is a horrible thing. Whether the Church has ever done this, I leave to the judgment of God. But this has never been a policy she can be comfortable with. Her whole reason for existence is to bring human persons to the full development that they can find only in God and ultimately in the Resurrection. However, this does not mean that the Church should permissively encourage everyone to do his "own thing" regardless of commandment, law, or right order. If it is possible to fail Christ by crushing a person under an unreasonable burden of human law, it would also most certainly be failing Christ and the person if he were encouraged to express that self which feels cramped by God's commandments or society's laws. There are times when the greatest help a person can receive is to be confronted with the law that reminds him of his personal responsibility. Then it is that some will say that the person is being sacrificed for the sake of a law. But might it not be that only then is he beginning to become his true self, though the way of growth is a way of the cross?

Changing and Changeless

About twenty-five years ago, when I was about to be married, I asked my pastor for the name of an acceptable book on the sexual side of marriage. He said the only ones were written in Latin and that the Church forbade reading books available in English as it was a mortal sin to do so. Today, Catholic magazines and newspapers are recommending books on the sexual side of marriage in English. If the Church has changed her teaching on this subject from being a mortal sin to a meritorious act, what assurance is there that other things she now considers mortal sins will not be approved in another twenty-five years?

Men can make mistakes. Don't you think that either your pastor was mistaken or that you misunderstood him? A thing can hardly be wholesome in Latin and mortal sin in English. There never has been a teaching of the Church that declared it a mortal sin for Catholics to seek information on the sexual intimacies of marriage in a language they can understand.

Yet there are different pastoral emphases at different times and in different situations. There was a time when many well-meaning people equated silence with modesty, and ignorance with innocence. The "marriage manuals" of this era were considered suspect. A number of them were indeed unbalanced. They tended to reduce the rich reality of married love to something that could be measured solely in terms of successful sensual transports. Twenty-five years ago, many reacted by trying to keep people away from such questionable material. Recently the effort has been more realistic — provide the young people with the information they genuinely need, and provide it in the context of a book that treats of married love in all its dimensions. This is a real, practical shift of emphasis. It is not a doctrinal change.

Do we have any guarantee that the Church will not some day approve of things she now considers mortal sins? Yes and no. The Church is the divinely appointed interpreter of God's designs for human living. In its fundamental principles, this design is clear and unchanging. The Church can never teach that it has become good to hate one's neighbor. But in its application, God's design often emerges from the changing patterns of human society and from the development of man's self-understanding. Years ago, for example, it was taught in many areas that it was seriously sinful to send your children to public schools or to attend non-Catholic services. Today these actions are no longer considered sinful and are often encouraged. The values remain the same. The religious education of children is a high priority obligation, and fidelity to the Catholic profession of faith is required for salvation. It is now seen that these values need not be jeopardized or repudiated by the aforementioned actions and that other important values may be fostered by them. This is a change. But it is not an arbitrary one. In the next quarter century we will probably see more changes of this kind.

"... The Kingdom the Power and the Glory"

The closing phrases of the Our Father now include "The kingdom, the power and the glory." For years and years, I heard the good holy nuns, later the priests, and also our fine Catholic periodicals, explain that this Protestant ending of the Lord's Prayer, while beautiful, is not used by the Catholic Church because the Our Father is the prayer given us by Christ himself and this ending was never part of his words. I have accepted the disappearance of the altar rail and some horrible translations of the Scriptures into our modern English — but I will await with interest your explanation of this innovation.

An explanation which is given often depends on the kind of question that is asked and the religious climate in which it is asked. I remember the day when Catholics spearheaded the fight to eliminate Bible reading and prayer from the public schools because the Protestant versions and forms were used. Their effort at that time was to protect their children from what they thought was a form of proselytizing. Today, many Catholics deplore the Supreme Court decision that effectively eliminates this prayer and Bible reading, because they fear a godless secularization. The positions of the concerned Catholics of both eras are apparently totally opposed — but, then, the situations are totally different.

The approach your teachers took some forty years ago was good, as far as it went. But it was not the whole picture.

The Lord's Prayer appears in the New Testament. But it is given in two quite different forms in Matt. 6:9-13 and in Luke 11:2-4. Both are the word of God, part of the inspired Scriptures. While both versions surely derive from what our Lord taught about how the Christian is to pray, both seem to have been reworked in a rhymed style for use in public worship *before* the Evangelists included them in their versions of the Gospel. This is a normal phenomenon. We have the same kind of thing in the four different versions of our Lord's words at the Last Supper instituting the Blessed Eucharist (Matt. 26: 26-28; Mark 14: 22-24; Luke 22: 19-20 I; Cor. 11:23-26).

The Christian churches, both East and West, have used the Matthean form of the Lord's Prayer in their liturgies. In many of the Greek manuscripts of St. Matthew's Gospel, the text of the Lord's Prayer continues with the beautiful doxology, "For thine is the kingdom," et cetera. However, in many other Greek manuscripts of this Gospel, including those that present-day scholarship considers more reliable, this passage is not included as part of the text.

In accordance with the first family of manuscripts, the Eastern Churches, both Catholic and Orthodox, use this formula to conclude the Lord's Prayer in their liturgical services.

The Latin Rite of the Catholic Church uses the form of the prayer that was given in the Latin Version of St. Matthew's Gospel. By happy chance, St. Jerome had one of the manuscripts we now consider more authentic when he made his Latin translation — and so our tradition does not use the concluding prayer of praise as an integral part of the Lord's Prayer.

How did the conclusion get into the Greek texts in the first place? Very likely some early Christian communities, before the year 100, followed the Jewish practice of concluding their special prayer with a formal doxology. A copyist who was familiar with the way the Church was praying the Lord's Prayer, probably nodded and added the liturgical formula to the copy of the Gospel. It was a thoroughly understandable error and could easily have been repeated when the next copy of the Gospel was made by hand.

Is our present usage a drastic innovation? I don't think so. If you will look carefully at the Roman Missal, you will see that we have always followed the Lord's Prayer with an expanded conclusion: "Deliver us. . . ." This prayer extends the concluding petition and makes it more particular. In the present Mass prayers, this addition has been a bit shortened and the doxology " . . . the kingdom, the power and the glory . . . " concludes this petition;

it does not conclude the Lord's Prayer. The doxology is a beautiful addition to the Mass prayers; it is not an addition to the Lord's Prayer.

As our Holy Father has insistently reminded us, the changes in the prayers of the Mass are an enrichment of our prayer life; in no wise are they an abandonment of our belief or our tradition.

2
Understanding
the
Bible

Understanding the Bible

During Lent I decided to read five pages of the Bible every day. Now, I have a pretty good education, went to college, and all that. But I must admit I do not understand most of what I read. The stories of Solomon and Esther and many others I found delightfully interesting. But who understands Isaiah and Jeremiah? Could the people of olden times have understood what they were reading, or isn't it necessary to understand? With so many changes in the Church, I wish they would copy the other churches and have Bible classes. I would be their first pupil.

The Bible is not always easy to understand. It wasn't easy for people two thousand years ago, and it is doubly difficult for us. There is a passage in Acts 8:26-36 that reflects your own experience to some extent. The officer of the queen of Ethiopa took it for granted that he could not penetrate the meaning of Isaiah's message unless there was someone to explain it to him.

We have two kinds of difficulty in understanding what we read in the Bible. First there is the difficulty that comes from the fact that we are reading the religious literature of a people separated from us by thousands of miles of space, thousands of years of time, and light years of cultural outlook. We must bridge these gaps and put ourselves in the shoes of these people, if we would catch the nuances of the words of these men. Secondly, there is the difficulty of perceiving the inner religious meaning of the words of God embodied in these words of men. The Christian conviction is that the Old Testament is religiously perceived only in the light of its fulfillment in Christ, who is the New Testament.

Even the writings of the New Testament pose problems for the reader. It was always so. An inspired author who wrote in the earliest days of the Church under the name of St. Peter remarks that St. Paul's writings are hard to understand in some points. "There are certain passages in them hard to understand. The ignorant and unstable distort them (just as they do the rest of Scripture) to their own ruin" (II Pet. 3:16).

Yet it is important that we should understand what we are reading. Unless there is some understanding, our reading is merely a mindless exercise, filling up time. Better you should knit!

In many places adult education classes are being conducted. And among the most popular courses offered are usually those on the Bible. I would suggest that you get in touch with your CCD office in your own diocese and find out what courses are available in your area.

In lieu of formal courses many people are discovering what they can do on their own if they have the proper books. Among the most recent is the *Jerusalem Bible* (New York: Doubleday, 1966). It has a very readable text, marvelous introduction to the books, and a veritable gold mine of helpful footnotes. For an even deeper study, the *Jerome Biblical Commentary* (Englewood Cliffs, N.J.: Prentice-Hall, 1968) would be very valuable. Both are rather expensive but worth the price. There are also pamphlet texts that are worth while: *The New Testament Reading Guide,* a series of twenty-six booklets, and *The Old Testament Reading Guide,* a series of fourteen (Collegeville, Minn.: Liturgical Press, 1960-1968).

There are also valuable footnotes in the New American Bible translation of the Sacred Scripture (Paterson, N.J.: St. Anthony Guild Press, 1970).

Just Stories?

I have just heard from a nun that Adam and Eve and Noah's ark are just stories. Father, can you discuss this. I'm a thirty-two-year-old mother of three, and suddenly I feel very stupid.

The first eleven chapters of Genesis have caused difficulty for centuries. There have been those who were convinced that since they are part of the Bible, everything in them is a divinely revealed account of *how* the world actually began. Working from this assumption, men have written volumes trying to harmonize the biblical six days of creation with the geological eras science has identified; they have framed laws, prohibiting the teaching of any form of human evolution in schools; they have spent fortunes trying to locate the resting place of Noah's ark and fruitless hours calculating the cosmic consequences of a world-wide flood extensive enough to destroy all life.

Underlying the assumption that these chapters describe how the world began was the further assumption that since they appear to us to be written in narrative style, they must be read as we would read any narrative description. But must they? Or even, can they? Biblical scholars are agreed that they cannot. And as early as 1948, the Pope's Commission for Biblical Studies declared: "The question of the literary forms of the first eleven chapters of Genesis is indeed very obscure and complex. These literary forms do not correspond to any of our classic categories and cannot be judged in the light of Greco-Roman or modern literary forms." (Pontifical Biblical Commission: Response to Cardinal Suhard, Jan. 16, 1948. Text is to be found in *Catholic Biblical Quarterly*, Vol. X, pp. 318-323.)

What this means is that if the account of human beginnings need not to be taken as a revealed description of how things happened, the alternative is not that it is to be put in a class with the story of the stork that brings babies. Adam and Eve and Noah's ark are not *just stories* like Grimm's fairy tales. Yet they are a kind of story; they are the divinely inspired creation of a vivid poetic imagination designed to teach God's own truth. They are a practically inexhaustible source for theological reflection. They speak of the total freedom of God in creating and of his almighty power and goodness. They show his intention from the beginning to bring man into personal relationship with him. They teach that man is a sinner from the beginning and in need of God's merciful grace. The goodness of the universe, the equality and complementarity of the sexes, and man's dominance over all creation — all this is here. God's eternal fidelity to his promise to save man in spite of all our willful rebellions is taught through the story of Adam and Eve, Cain and Abel, and the family of Noah. And so much more. Just stories? Hardly.

A book I think you'll find helpful — it's up-to-date and easy to read — is Father Bruce Vawter's *A Path through Genesis* (New York: Sheed and Ward, 1956). It is available in paperback.

Original Sin and Adam and Eve

I have been hearing a lot lately about the question of Adam and Eve and their apparently doubtful existence. If the Adam and Eve story is not entirely factual, then where does the doctrine of original sin come in? Is not the original sin the sin of our first parents, Adam and Eve?

The dogma of original sin teaches us more about Christ than it does about Adam and Eve. It speaks of our need of Christ's redemption. Why do we need redemption? Because every man enters the human race as a sinner, and he can be freed from his sinful condition only by the mercy of God in Christ Jesus. This is a fundamental truth of the Gospel. How does it happen that a sinful condition affects every man? It cannot be that God, who made everything and "saw how good it was" (Gen. 1:10), is the author of sin. The only explanation a religious man can provide — and it is the explanation of the Bible — is that sin entered the world through the rebellion of man. The book of Genesis gives flesh to this conviction by showing man's rebellion in the stories of Adam and Eve, Cain and Abel, Noah's contemporaries, and the Tower of Babel.

From one point of view, these imaginative, inspired stories are factual. They contain "historical" fact inasmuch as they tell of the supreme generosity of the Creator, who calls man to intimacy with himself, and the willful refusal of man to submit to God's design for his only true happiness. This refusal, this sin, *took place at the beginnings* of the human race, and it has a mysterious repercussion on all men.

One of the great problems in theology today is to fashion an explanation of the reality of original sin that will be richer than the old — enriched with the insights which our age has into the meaning of the Bible and the process of the formation of human life. This search is a risky business. Pope Paul VI reminded theologians that there are truths about original sin that have been revealed by God and that these serve as guardrails protecting any new thought from deviating from the faith. Among these guaranteed teachings, he mentioned the following: (1) Original sin is a fact, and it affects all men. (2) Original sin has the character of true sin, even in the descendants of Adam, depriving each man of the intimate relationship to God which he ought to have. (3) Original sin has unfortunate consequences on soul and body.

The first sin of man may be called "original sin," because it is at the origin of man's history. However, the name usually stands not for the first personal failure but rather for the sinful state or condition which is the lot of every man apart from Christ and which derives from man's primitive rebellion.

Our Savage Ancestors

How can we accept as inspired the slaughter of young and old, blind and crippled, which is described in the Old Testament? Did

**God truly inspire Joshua's brutal genocide at Jericho? How recon-
cile this apparent cruelty of God in the Old Testament with his
Fatherly concern revealed in Jesus Christ.**

Let's clarify one point first: the word "inspiration." It covers two
completely distinct realities. One is the inspiration of the books of the
Bible. A Catholic can have no doubts about this. It is a matter of
faith for him that the written accounts (even of this cruelty) were
composed and preserved for us by men who worked under a special
influence of the Holy Spirit. But it is entirely another thing to say
that God inspired the great warriors of Israel to this slaughter.

Religious opinion in the past (both Jewish and Christian, Catholic and Protestant) interpreted these instances of genocide as being
positively willed by God. His purpose was to keep pure the Jewish
religious experience and the Jews' worship of the one God. Since
their idolatrous neighbors were a threat, God removed that threat by
ordering their extermination.

At present, the explanation that is preferred is both simpler and
more satisfying. There is no effort to explain away the cruelty of the
slaughter. It is seen to be part and parcel of the savagery that was
a fact of life for the primitive peoples of the Near East. It is also
a fact that all of these people were convinced of the sacred character of their wars. God was on their side — and God willed the
most hideous carnage! Israel's patriarchs were primitives who shared
the attitudes and the undeveloped morality of their contemporaries.
(We should not expect people who lived 1,500 years before the birth
of Christ to act like Christians. Even 2,000 years after his coming,
Hiroshima was possible!)

The Bible accounts of these events were written centuries after
they happened. They are a religious interpretation of the events rather
than an eyewitness account. We may try to reconstruct the pattern this
way. The inspired authors were writing for the people of their own
time. They knew from their past history that every time the people
of God had become familiar with their pagan neighbors, the purity
of their religion had suffered. They wanted to persuade their people to
avoid those dealings with the Gentiles which would be apt to turn
them from fidelity to the covenant. How to do it effectively? Apparently they had records that told how the Israelites slaughtered the
peoples they dispossessed when they entered the Promised Land.
They reworked this material, making the slaughter seem to be something God demanded, and thus they communicated the religious les-

son which was the object of their writing: It is God's will that the people of Israel have nothing to do with the pagans.

There is no need for us to feel called upon to find reasons why God would have ordered the Hebrews to massacre their enemies. We have no clear evidence that he ever did. Rather, we should marvel at the power of the love of the one God who is merciful and gracious in all his ways. It is wondrous that he should have succeeded in drawing from such unlikely material Israel's glorious fidelity to himself. And the supreme mystery is that he should so temper all this violence and ferocity as to draw from this nation the flesh of the Son of God, the Prince of Peace, the Man for others.

True Authors

I just read in your monthly column your statement that "the authors of the Gospels do color what Jesus actually said and did." This is certainly contrary to what I learned in Catholic schools and colleges. To what extent and in what regard are the Gospels so colored, in your opinion? What is your evidence for this statement?

I think that you are misunderstanding what I wrote. Your objection seems to imply that if the sacred authors of the Gospels have colored what Jesus actually said and did, then the Gospels are false. It presumes that any coloring is a distorting.

If your premise is correct, then there can be no coloring in this sense. The Catholic Church is convinced that the Gospels give us the truth about Jesus and about our salvation. They are not the creation of fertile literary imaginations, nor are they part of a monumental fraud. She believes that the sacred pages as we have them were written under the grace of the inspiration of the Holy Spirit and that through them we really come into contact with the Jesus of history.

However, how were they actually written? Were the sacred authors merely passive tools in God's hand, and was the grace of inspiration something that gave each of them a superhuman gift of total recall so that he could write down the exact words Jesus spoke and describe the events surrounding his life with pinpoint historical accuracy? This is not part of Catholic faith or teaching. In the past, it is true, some Catholics have held to this type of literalness. The position of the Church today is far more nuanced.

The source that the inspired Gospel accounts depend upon is not a photographic remembering of what happened before the Resurrection of our Lord. It is the form of the life and message of Christ as it was preached in the early Church. As Vatican II reminds us in the *Dogmatic Constitution on Divine Revelation,* no. 19, this preaching was done "with the *fuller insight* which they enjoyed, once they had learned from Christ's glorious destiny and they were enlightened by the Spirit of truth." Armed now with faith's conviction that Jesus is the Son of God, a conviction they did not have when they walked with him, they told the literal truth about him. They used a preacher's embellishment to make sure that the truth would shine more clearly through the appearances than it had for them. This is a kind of "coloring," but not a falsification. They are communicating a message of faith in its historical roots; they are not merely reporting events the way a good newspaper reporter would be expected to do.

The inspired Gospels drew their material from this "preached account"' of what Jesus said and did. But they did not merely set it down verbatim. The Holy Spirit used human authors and editors. Part of their work was precisely to edit the material to suit their individual purposes and to meet the real needs of their people. The same paragraph of the document of Vatican II refers to this process when it says of the sacred authors: "Some (things) they brought together into a synthesis, or *they interpreted in keeping with the state of the Churches.*" This, too, is a "coloring."

At the risk of oversimplifying, the whole process might be understood in this way. Filled with the Holy Spirit, the apostles remembered the events of Jesus' life, the things he said and did. As is the case in every remembrance of the past, this was already selective: some things stood out as specially important. As they reflected on these things, it was like their coming to say: "This is what he meant!" "If this is in fact the truth of what he meant, why not say it more clearly than what it first sounded like to us when we tell the people about our Lord?" Later, when some of the disciples were moved by the Holy Spirit to write down the Gospels for readers who belonged to different local churches, the inspired authors sometimes interpreted the meaning of what Jesus said, in order to meet the particular problem and relate to the experiences of these churches. It has been suggested that this can help to explain the great variation we have in the different accounts of the Parable of the Sower, in the different versions of our Lord's words on divorce. A process something like this can also account for the long speeches St. John places in the mouth of our Lord and the clear statements concerning his equality with the Father (for example, John 5:17-47; 8:48-59).

If the Evangelists claimed to be writing a court stenographer's record of Jesus' words and life, their manner of writing would distort the facts. However, they don't claim this at all. They wrote true history, but from the viewpoint of faith in order to nourish faith. They wrote according to the accepted norms of their own time. "They wrote with the purpose that we might know the 'truth' of the words which we have been taught" (Vatican II, *On Divine Revelation,* no. 19).

Besides the Constitution I've cited, I think that you would find it interesting and helpful to study the 1964 "Instruction of the Biblical Commission," personally approved by Pope Paul VI. It is available from Paulist Press as a pamphlet entitled *The Historical Truth of the Gospels,* with a commentary by Father Joseph A. Fitzmyer, S. J.

Eyewitness? Yes. Eyewitness Report? No.

A statement of yours puzzles me: "The Gospels are not eyewitness reports. But they report the faith of those who either were eyewitnesses of Jesus' life or were in contact with eyewitnesses." (See p. 81.) I thought that John and Matthew were writing just what they had seen, while the other Evangelists were depending on those who had lived with Jesus.

An "eyewitness report" is an account that tries to tell things exactly the way they happened — just as the person who witnessed them remembers them. There is no room for embellishment or interpretation in an eyewitness account. This type of reporting figures in modern journalism. Historians use these recollections in their efforts to re-create a past event.

But an eyewitness does not have to write this kind of report. He may be moved to reflect on the meaning of the events or to fashion poetry out of the feelings stimulated by the event — all the while giving the truth of what he saw but not merely reporting facts.

The Gospels are in touch with the history of Jesus' life and death as it was seen and experienced by the Twelve — either the Evangelists are eyewitnesses, or they are connected with eyewitnesses in the Christian Church. But the Gospels are not a chronicle of that history — they are not eyewitness reports. Rather, they are theological interpretations of the events. They are written in the light of the clearer understanding of the meaning of Christ's life that the Apostles found in the events of Christ's risen life. They present the truth about Jesus, but it is a truth which they saw fully only by hindsight, and this hindsight and the particular needs of first-century Christianity affect the way they write the story.

Speaking of this special historical character of the Gospels, the Vatican Council's *Dogmatic Constitution on Divine Revelation* declares: "The sacred authors wrote the four Gospels, selecting some things from the many which had been handed on by word of mouth or in writing, reducing some of them to a synthesis, explicating some things in view of the situation of their churches, and preserving the form of proclamation but always in such a fashion that they told us the honest truth about Jesus" (no. 19).

Immortal Soul in the Bible

Where in the Bible does it say that the soul is immortal? I don't believe it does. In Genesis it states that the body and breath is a living soul. You take that breath away (as when one dies), and you have a dead soul. In James 2:26 it says, "When a man dies he ceases to be a soul." The Catholic belief is that the soul goes to heaven, hell, or purgatory. But if the soul is only living with the breath or spirit, when that is gone, the soul is dead.

The Bible is not easy reading. Don't misunderstand me. I don't want to discourage Bible reading. I wish everyone would read and study and profit by God's word written for our spiritual growth. Yet there are difficulties that can come up and cause confusion: difficulties of language and translation, difficulties of varying cultural and scientific perspective, and difficulties that come from our own tendency to find answers in the Bible to questions that the sacred authors never asked. To a certain extent, each of these difficulties contributes to the perplexity of our questioner.

There is, first of all, the matter of the accuracy of the quotation and the meaning of the verse you quote. The New American Bible translates the verse as, "Faith without works is as dead as a body without breath"; or the earlier Confraternity version reads, ". . . the body without the spirit is dead." The Revised Standard Version, used by both Catholics and non-Catholics, reads, ". . . the body apart from the spirit is dead."

Deeper than the matter of translation is the whole question of mentality. The Bible does not pose the problem of the immortality of the soul in the same way that your question does. Hebrew thought made hardly any distinction between body and soul. The Hebrews thought of man as a unity. When they used the word "soul," they thought of that by which the body lives — and man was considered to be a living body. Hence, it is almost unthinkable that the people of the Bible would ask: "Is the *soul* immortal?" The question they did ask was: "Is *man* to enjoy immortal life?"

The sacred authors of the Old Testament were men of their times. They did not reflect as the Greeks did on what elements come together to make up the being of man. But they do have a doctrine of Man: he is a special creature of God completely different from the animals, because he has received the breath of life (Gen. 2:7; cf. 2:19); he is master of the rest of creation and made in the image of God (Gen. 1:26-27). Man is something more than the soil from which he is fashioned. He is called to a community of life with God. And yet there is the enigma of death, which seems to be total annihilation. It isn't until around the year 100 B.C. that we find clear evidence of a Hebrew belief in personal immortality (II Macc. 7:9). It is significant that the hope is for bodily resurrection — there is no real awareness of the soul as something distinct from the body and able to survive bodily death.

The New Testament teaching on man is framed in the same Hebraic perspective. Its heart is the glorious resurrection of the body — this is the fullness of life in Christ that will come to all who believe in him. Implicit in this belief in the resurrection is the belief in the immortality of the soul — the conviction that there is an enduring life principle in each man which survives death and will reanimate the body on the last day. Otherwise there is no self, no "I," which makes the glorified "me" who will rise on the last day be one and the same person as the mortal "me" of the twentieth century. On the margin of the central biblical message are a number of texts that do affirm a real distinction between body and soul, such as Matthew 10:29: "Do not fear those who deprive the body of life but cannot destroy the soul. Rather, fear him who can destroy both body and soul in Gehenna" (Cf. also, James 1:21; 5:20; I Pet. 1:9; Rev. 6:9).

When the aged St. Paul writes that he "longs to be freed from this life and to be with Christ" (Phil. 1:23), he certainly does so with the conviction that he will enjoy an enriched form of personal existence after death while waiting for the great day of resurrection. Translate this conviction into the thought patterns that are our heritage in the West, and you have your answer again: Yes, the Bible does teach the immortality of the soul, though not in so many words.

Antifeminism in the Bible?

Would you please explain the meaning of Ecclesiasticus [Sirach] 25:17, "The wickedness of a woman is all evil"? Wickedness in any person, man or woman, is evil. Why single out women?

The author of this verse singles out women because he is writing about women. His point of view may be excessively masculine — something that is understandable enough in his time and culture. But he is not out to put down the girls or treat them with scorn or disdain. In fact, his language of reproach is so eloquent because he expects so much and loves women so well.

If you would see what the inspired author thinks of women, continue on and read the next chapter in praise of the good and perfect wife.

St. Paul on Women

I always thought we wore hats in church out of respect, but my Marian Bible says: "St. Paul insists on the wearing of a veil in church by women. He indicates that it is a sign of the subordination of the woman to her husband and to man in general but especially to the angels in worship." Did he consider women inferior?

Probably.

More of St. Paul on Women

You owe St. Paul an apology. He clearly proclaimed the equal dignity of all mankind: "There are no more distinctions between Jew and Greek, slave and free, male and female, but all of you are one in Christ Jesus" (Gal. 3:28). It is unfair to say that he "probably" considered women inferior.

My one-word answer was deliberately ambiguous. As I see it, St. Paul was of two minds in the matter.

On the one hand, he saw the perfect equality of everyone who had been baptized in Christ. This equality transcended every class distinction of social superiority or inferiority. It would even lead a husband to overturn all the prejudices of his society and treat his own wife as a "sister" in the Lord (I Cor. 9:5) or a master to receive his slave as "a brother . . . in the Lord" (Phil. 16).

On the other hand, St. Paul was a man of his own time. And it would be extremely hard to prove that he did not share the attitudes of his contemporaries on the inferior and secondary place of women in society. While his faith conviction enabled Paul to transcend the social patterns of class distinctions, it is not clear that they purged him of his era's mentality. Thus he thinks of wives as "submissive" to their husbands (Eph. 5:24) and searches to find theological arguments to support the existing social situation (see I Cor. 11:7-9). The author of the Pastoral Epistles, who at least reflects St. Paul's thought, permits no "woman to act as teacher" (I Tim. 2:12) because she is susceptible to heresies (I Tim. 4:7), nor is any woman to "have authority over a man" (I Tim. 2:12). In fact, there are other indications that the early Christians, like the men of their own times, consider woman as inferior, as the "weaker" sex (see I Pet. 3:7).

Paul the Apostle was certainly ahead of his time; in faith, he transcended his time, but he was not free from the social conditions of his time, and these certainly seem to have affected his ideas.

Another reader, a lady in Toronto, gets after me for the same wee response. Her letter is very interesting:

"Now to get back to good old Paul and your abrupt dismissal of him. You could have explained that the letter we call First Corinthians was written to a particular community at a particular time in history. Corinth was a notorious center of immortality in ancient Greece, and Paul was well aware of the situation. The prostitutes went around with their hairdo uncovered. Also it was a mark of disrespect to her husband for a married woman to appear in public without a veil. These were local customs, and Paul, with his great love and concern for his beloved converts, didn't want his Christian women to be contaminated or misunderstood in a corrupt milieu. He wanted them to realize that, as members of the new Christian community, they must conduct themselves with a decorum befitting their high calling. If you read the eleventh chapter of First Corinthians again with these facts in mind, you won't conclude that Paul 'probably' considered women inferior.

"The longest and weightiest of all his letters — the letter to the Romans — his spiritual legacy, his gospel, Paul entrusted to a woman. It was written in Corinth and taken to Rome by Phoebe. One does not entrust such a treasure and such an important mission to an inferior being. Of the twenty-eight people named by Paul for special greetings in the sixteenth chapter of Romans, eight are women. The tributes he pays to them show his great appreciation of the services of women. Phoebe, the deaconess of the church at Cenchrae, he commends to his readers and he requests that they receive her as befits the saints. It is interesting to note, too, that the first two people Paul names as active in the service of the Church are women, Phoebe and Prisca (Rom. 16:1 and 3). In verse 6, Paul uses the expression 'worked hard' to describe the work of (the church helper) Mary.

"On second thought, perhaps you have a better sense of humor than I have given you credit for. Perhaps you were throwing out bait to stir up fires, and now you have the laugh on me."

I'm not laughing. Thank you for your carefully worked letter.

Bible Anti-Black?

Is it true that there is a command in the Bible opposing Negro-white marriages? I cannot find it anywhere, but I have only an abridged version of the Bible.

The reason you can't find such a prohibition is that it isn't there.

St. Joseph

I often wondered what was the last time St. Joseph's name is mentioned in the Gospels.

The last time Joseph is mentioned as having an active part in the life of our Lord is when Jesus was found in the Temple (". . . his parents. . . ." "your father and I . . ." — see Luke 2:41-52). The last references to him in all four Gospels are placed in the mouths of those who wonder at Jesus' teaching or his claims: "Is not this Joseph's son?" (Luke 4:22; John 6:42; cf. Matt. 13:55; Mark 6:3).

When Did Christ Die?

I have read a theory that Christ was buried on Wednesday and rose on Saturday. What stand does the Church take on this?

From the Gospel accounts there can be no question that Christ died on Friday and rose from the dead on Sunday.

There is an apparent contradiction, however, between the Synoptic Gospels — Matthew, Mark, and Luke — and John. The first three place the Paschal meal on Thursday, and yet St. John (18:28) tells us that the Jewish leaders on Friday morning refused to enter the Praetorium of Pilate lest they be defiled and unable to eat the Passover.

This apparent contradiction has always been a difficulty for commentators on the Gospel. Some exegetes think that in the year in which Jesus died, when the Passover Feast fell on the Sabbath, some or all of the Passover lambs were sacrificed on Thursday afternoon, to prevent the possible violation of the Sabbath rest on Friday evening, the beginning of the Sabbath. In that case, many of the Jews, including Jesus and his disciples, would have used the sacrificed lambs on Thursday evening for the Passover supper, while others, such as those referred to in John 18:28, would have waited till the proper time, Friday evening, for eating the Passover meal.

Similar to this solution is the one proposed by other exegetes, who think that, when the Passover Feast coincided with the Sabbath, as in this year, the Pharisees celebrated the Passover meal (with or without Paschal lambs) on Thursday evening, for fear of violating the Sabbath rest: whereas the Sadducees followed the letter of the Mosaic Law and ate the Passover meal on Friday evening. Most of the Jews, who were influenced by the Pharisees, their popular leaders, would thus have celebrated the Passover on the thirteenth of Nisan in such a year — and Jesus and his disciples would also have followed this custom. The enemies of Jesus, who were mostly of the priestly party, the Sadducees, would have followed their own custom in this matter.

Recently, a new solution has been proposed by Mlle. A. Jaubert in *The Date of the Last Supper* (Staten Island, N.Y., 1965). She pointed out the fact that in the artificial solar calendar of the Qumran sects the Feast of the Passover always fell on a Wednesday. This calendar was also followed by other Jews at the time of Christ. Jesus and his disciples may then perhaps have held their Passover supper according to this calendar on *Tuesday* evening. This might explain the lack of any reference to the Paschal lamb at the Last Supper, since the Saducean priests, who followed the other calendar, would not have sacrificed the lambs till Friday afternoon. The trial of Jesus would then have lasted from Wednesday to Friday. This is not impossible, though it is not the obvious sense of the Gospels. There is even some evidence that the celebration of the Last Supper in the early Church took place on Tuesday.

3
Church
Law
and
Lore

Is the Catholic Church Christian?

Christ commanded that His followers teach what He taught. I understand that the Catholic Church teaches some things that Christ did not teach. Consequently, can the Catholic Church be considered a Christian Church?

I must confess that my first impulse was to set your question aside. (There is not enough room in these pages to handle every query that comes in, and I have to select those that seem to be of more general interest.) However, your question does reflect a serious religious problem that bothers a number of people, particularly those who are confused by the apparently plausible arguments of zealous people associated with fundamentalist groups or the Jehovah's Witnesses.

The trouble with a question like this is that it oversimplifies and falsifies logic and history and shows a misunderstanding of the mission of Christ.

I believe, with you, that it is correct to hold that a church which turns away from the teaching of Christ or that teaches the opposite of the truth he taught would lose any right to claim the title of "Christian Church." However, it is an abuse of logic to maintain that the Church has failed in its mandate because it *also* teaches about Christ himself, about the religious truths presumed in Christ's teaching, and about matters which apply the Christian truth to new situations and to the new questions which each generation asks.

Christ did indeed teach a message, and it is urgent that the Church faithfully hand that message on to all men through the ages. But his great service to mankind is not that of a teacher. Much more than that, he is the event of God's final loving entry into human history. By His life, death, and resurrection, he ushered men into a new and intimate relationship with God. His Church is his way of being present and living for us right now. In the Church, men are called to believe in him and to live of his life — this much more than to believe what he taught, although it includes that.

Even in the earliest years after our Lord's death and resurrection, the apostles and teachers in the Church found it necessary to do much more than repeat the words and teachings of Christ. The Acts of the Apostles and the many Epistles of the New Testament are filled with "new teachings" — all of which are in continuity with what Christ taught but go beyond what the Gospels record of his teaching. These new teachings draw out the implications of Christ's person, mission, and teaching. They apply the meaning of Christian faith to new circumstances as the Church struggled to understand its Jewish roots, to relate to the Greco-Roman world, and to develop the organization that would express and support the communion of all believers in one Spirit.

Christian faith sees this development, not as an apostasy from Christ, but as the work of the Spirit of Christ who was sent as the first gift of the Risen Lord to be with the Church and guide it *into* all truth. It is unfortunately true that the Catholic Church is always less than fully faithful to the guidance of the Spirit of Christ — the mystery of sin in the world affects all who share the human condition. But this stumbling fidelity continues to be, by the miracle of God's grace, a substantial fidelity to the person and teaching of Christ.

Is Law "for Real"?

I am a Catholic who has finally started to grow up spiritually. As a youngster, I was taught my religion by rote memory. Now twenty-four, I find that this memory course never gave me any roots in my religion. I have studied theology for three years, and I find deep and real meaning in the Scriptures. My problem is with the Church laws — are they "for real" in today's life? I don't understand her medieval laws and cannot in conscience live by them if I am to be Christian.

Law is "for real" in the Church, but some of the canon laws are not very realistic. This is why many men who are sincerely dedicated to the Gospel have worked tirelessly to recommend sweeping changes in the laws that govern the Church life of Catholics. Their recommendations have been submitted to a committee that is even now at work in Rome.

You manifest a feeling for the real interior of the Christian life. Our Lord died and rose, not merely to give us a securely ordered life under law, but to give us his Holy Spirit as a source of new life. This life brings us into union with God and is the basis of the ultimate unity of all mankind under the Fatherhood of God.

Characteristic of this life is the freedom of the sons of God. St. Paul preached eloquently about this freedom, especially in the Epistle to the Galatians, when some Jewish Christians were trying to impose the Mosaic Law on the young community. But St. Paul was not particularly tolerant of anarchy. He was conscious of his own authority as an apostle. Into the Church at Corinth, which was fragmenting under the influence of spiritual enthusiasts, Paul brought order and discipline. He regulated the worship service, gave guidelines for the relationships between the Christians and pagans, determined an excommunication, and even had something to say about the dress and public actions of women. In a word, the apostle of Christian freedom made laws.

If it is fundamental to the Christian religion that it is a community, then it must have some laws to give guidance and directions to the community. Law is necessary to protect the rights of persons in the community — even in the Spirit-filled community of the Church, as long as mankind has not reached that stage of full openness to the Spirit which it will have at the Second Coming of Christ.

The particular problem of the lawmaker in the Church is how to make his positive regulations be as sensitive an expression of the spirit of the Gospel as is humanly possible. Law in the Church must be in the service of the person, helping him to achieve his dignity in Christ. It should be the friendly voice of pastoral charity and should express the thought that the Church is for the service of men of every condition, in every weakness and need.

And while this flexibility and vision are being worked into the balanced language of new laws to help us to be more fully Christian, we have the possibility of following the present guidelines of the Christian community with loyal prudence or of becoming a law unto ourselves. I don't see where this leaves us much choice, if we are to be Christian.

Intelligible Laws

As Catholics, are we supposed to take the laws of the Church as absolute rules to be obeyed without question, whether or not they make sense to us in this modern age?

The laws that are enacted by the Church for the spiritual good of all its members and the smooth functioning of its organization are human things. They are intelligently worded and attempt to be sane directives. There is nothing about them of a magical nature.

Church laws, like civil laws, admit of exceptions. They are not absolute and inflexible. A human lawmaker takes into account the general good of all and the conditions that normally occur. He cannot be expected to foresee all the variables that can occur in individual cases. There will be cases where the rigid application of the letter of the law would go against the mind of the legislator. To break the letter of the law is not a violation of law in this case. The lawmaker is reasonable. He wants to serve the real good of his fellow citizens, not to sacrifice this in the name of law and order.

We should be careful to be self-critical when we call a particular law into question. Before we see our own case as an exception to the law we should be sure that we understand the meaning of the law, its purpose, and the impact that our own non-observance might have on others.

Territorial Laws

I know that holydays of obligation are not observed in the same way in all countries, nor do all countries celebrate the same days as days of obligation. When I visit another country, must I observe the American holydays?

No. When in Rome, do as the Romans do. The obligation of the Church laws on the religious observance of holydays is territorial, not personal. Whoever is present in the United States on our six holy days is obliged to observe them. A citizen of this country is not bound by these local laws once he steps across the border.

Thus, if you are in Canada on November 1, you are not subject to the law that declares it a holyday (All Saints) in the United States. But if you are in Ireland on March 17 (St. Patrick) you are subject to our sister Church's regulation that makes that feast an Irish holyday.

Sunday Observance

Is it wrong to sew, iron, garden or make plans on Sunday because it is the Sabbath, or doesn't it matter? I read in the Bible that God doesn't even want you to light a match under a pot on the Sabbath.

Unfortunately the Church has to make laws. They are made to preserve certain values. They remind us what is the minimum requirement of a wholehearted service of Christ. But often there are problems in the way we Catholics observe laws. We can separate them from the values they are meant to foster and elevate the law itself into a value in its own right. And I suppose it's the fault of us priests and teachers. We've been so precise in telling you what's right and what's wrong that we've conditioned a generation to stop thinking, to accept the letter of the law while forgetting the value it enshrines. As a result some become overanxious; many settle for a routine minimum.

The Sunday rest is a purely Church law. It is not a Christian way of observing the Old Testament law of the Sabbath. The Church's most secure conviction is that Christ has freed us from the demands of the law in giving us the Holy Spirit. We should not look to the Old Testament for a model of how Christians ought to celebrate Sunday.

Sunday is to be a celebration. We have it as the weekly feast day of the Risen Lord, and we celebrate it chiefly through the Eucharistic banquet. The idea of keeping it as a day free from work grew out of the need to have enough leisure time to share in the Eucharistic. banquet. It also came to be seen as a day of relaxation that would allow the whole man, body and soul, to anticipate the joy and peace of our own resurrection. The day of worship and of rest was not intended to have any of the joyless harshness of Puritan "blue laws" that are connected with it. The bishops in the Second Vatican Council reminded us that Sunday should be "a day of joy and of freedom from work" (*Constitution on the Sacred Liturgy*, no. 106).

Now, is it wrong to do the things you mention? I'd ask you: Are they really work? Do they interfere with worship, joy, and peace? Or do they perhaps help to foster these attitudes? It hardly seems possible that puttering in a flower garden on Sunday is a sin for a man who needs to relax from a week's work on an assembly line or a woman who has been taking dictation all week. And, by all means, light the stove for Sunday dinner.

Servile Work

How can you determine exactly what kind of work is forbidden on Sundays and holydays? If work is enjoyed — like gardening, woodworking, et cetera — is this considered servile? If you relax and

take pleasure in doing this, can it be considered as work?

Your question indicates the problems connected with the idea of "servile work" in our time. Even the word "servile" is a problem. It was introduced into the Christian vocabulary through a faulty translation St. Jerome made of the Hebrew expression for the work forbidden on the Sabbath. Yet, as we have indicated, the Christian custom and law of Sunday rest is not an offshoot of the Jewish traditions on the ways of observing the Sabbath rest, although there has been a tendency to interpret it in this way since the eighth century.

Years ago, when class distinction was the rule and everyone had his own place and work, we could more easily distinguish between the kind of work done by slaves and servants and that belonging to free men and the gentry. At that time, the law forbidding servile work (the work of slaves) gave the slaves and servants a weekly holiday from all but the most essential work to permit them to give the day to worship and the joyful anticipation of the Resurrection.

Today, the goal of the Church law on Sunday observance is basically the same, but the conditions of life are radically changed. The intention of the law is to provide people with leisure to celebrate the Eucharist, to hear the word of God, and to enjoy the change by which they can re-create themselves spiritually and physically. The Church law forbidding servile work on Sunday should be interpreted with these goals in mind. The way it ought to be applied in one area will differ from the way it should be applied in another.

Your rules of thumb are close to the way most American theologians see things today. The majority of people in urban America are caught up in daily work that has about it a large component of monotony or tension or anxious rush. For such persons, hard physical work on a weekend in a garden or in a basement tool shop is more apt to be a source of mental and physical recreation than it is to be a violation of the Sunday law.

At the same time, one should be sensitive to the feelings of his neighbors in all this. If the kind of Sunday recreation you choose is apt to break down your community's sense of the special character that belongs to the Lord's day, it would be better to forgo it for the greater good until all the members of the Church in your area can agree on what is the best way to renew the meaning of Sunday.

Cremation

Why doesn't the Catholic Church approve of cremation? After four

deaths in our family within two years, I certainly do. I was taught from childhood that when we die, if we are in the state of grace, we will go to heaven. So what's this nonsense about a thousand dollars for the undertaker? Is the Church in back of this deal? If I request to be cremated, and I hope with God's help to be in the state of grace, will I go to heaven?

The Church is not unalterably opposed to cremation as a way of disposing of the bodies of the dead. She is concerned not with methods and techniques for their own sake but with the meaning that these methods communicate or the meaning that men put upon them. Although cremation was in vogue in imperial Rome, the Christians shunned the practice completely. Remember the stories of the reverent care with which Christians gathered the remains of the martyrs and placed them in their special burial grounds. They saw the burial of the dead as a *profession of faith* in the resurrection of the body and the immortality of the soul. The burial rite was both a comfort for the bereaved and a prayer for the soul of the departed.

In Christian countries there was no serious challenge to this long tradition until the nineteenth century. It was then that cremation societies were formed in Europe. The Church reacted very strongly. The reason for her reaction was this: Although the societies urged cremation for reasons of public health and land conservation, it was apparent that they were part of a totally materialistic philosophy of life. They saw cremation as *a profession of disbelief* in the resurrection of the body and the immortality of the soul. The Church passed judgment not on the burning of the human body but on the irreligious mentality that rejected the most fundamental dogmas of Christian belief and that expressed itself in the gesture of cremation.

Times change, and mentalities change. It is more than possible that, in some places, the American way of death and burial has ceased to be a Christian profession of faith in the meaning of life and death and of hope in the resurrection of the body. We have made a fine art out of concealing the fact of death. How often we hear at wakes, "He looks wonderful." A corpse is decked in eyeglasses and cosmetics and covered in a "slumber robe." Lights and flowers and soft music conspire to create an illusion. Some illusion is desirable and merciful for the bereaved family. But too much of it can display just as much an anti-Christian materialist point of view as did nineteenth-century cremation. Things have come full circle, and now some non-Catholic Christians are working to reintroduce cremation. Their purpose is to foster a more Christian attitude toward death, to stress its spiritual significance. Clearly, in this context, cremation has a different *meaning* than it did a century ago.

What is the Church's present stand on cremation? She opposes it. Where there is a problem of extravagance or an anti- or un-Christian attitude toward death, she would urge reform, that is, more sober, sane, and less expensive forms of funerals. The Church does not want to set aside her two-thousand-year tradition of the burial of the dead and the prayers of the funeral.

However, the attitude of the Church is far more flexible today. On July 5, 1968, the Sacred Congregation of the Holy Office issued an instruction concerning cremation. The instruction reaffirmed the Catholic opposition to cremation, but it mitigated the penalties that had previously attached to the practice. These severe penalties apply only when the motive of a person's choice of cremation is to deny Christian dogma or to express a free-thinking, sectarian spirit or hatred of the Christian religion and Church. Unless these bad motives are present, the Church does not deny the sacraments or the sharing in her funeral prayers to those who have chosen to be cremated.

What does all this mean? It means that the Church no longer sees all cremation as a sin of scandal or as equivalent to the sin of apostasy. She recognizes that some people may choose cremation without being guilty of serious sin.

I can understand your being upset by the high cost of dying. But no, the Church is not in back of this "deal." The Church doesn't get any specially great amount of money out of it that I know of. Catholic diocesan cemeteries do try to maintain themselves in a business-like way and stay in the black. But I doubt that there are any considerable profits. Even if, in a particular instance, the operation of a cemetery is scandalously excessive, it is not at all to keep such scandal alive that the Church maintains her attitude toward the reverent burial of the bodies of her deceased children.

If you request cremation, will you go to heaven? I hope so. The motive you would have in choosing to be cremated is not sinful. And it is only sin that will separate a person from life with God. But isn't there another alternative? The priests and Brothers in our Passionist community are buried in a cloth-covered, wooden coffin (not a "casket"). It is not too stark, it is not offensive, and it is not terribly expensive either. It would be well to plan for burial while in clear mind and sound body. The shocking moment of loss can becloud a person's thinking and lead him, through a feeling of guilty devotion or an unrealistic sense of "what others will think," into ostentatious and extravagant expense.

Funeral Arrangements

Will the Catholic Church allow a member to be buried after death without any funeral ceremonies and then permit a memorial Mass at the church later? With few relatives, this might be a convenient arrangement.

There is no reason why not. The ceremonies in the Roman Missal have always provided for these alternatives: "when the body is present" and "when the body is absent."

The funeral practices are not meant to be an obligatory burden. They provide a setting to help the bereaved work through the shock of grief in the presence of God and to stimulate the community of relatives and friends to prayer for the deceased. If, in consultation with your relatives, another procedure is desired, I'm sure it could be worked out with the help of a funeral director or your local priests.

Fish on Friday

Some time ago, it was announced in my church that the obligation of abstinence from meat on all Fridays of the year except Good Friday was discontinued by the Catholic Church. Now I discover that in some Catholic countries the obligation is still in force. Would you please let me know where we stand?

Sunday announcements are rarely the best way to impart exact information. This is why most wise pastors use printed bulletins. Either you heard wrong or the announcement was made wrong. Here is how things are at present:

1. By general law of the Church, every Friday is a day of abstinence.

2. It is left to the decision of the regional conferences of bishops to substitute some other works of penance for that of abstinence, if they judge it opportune.

3. Effective November 27, 1966, the United States National Conference of Catholic Bishops determined that abstinence would be part of our obligatory Friday penance in this country only on the Fridays of Lent.

The Pastoral Statement of our bishops that announced this change is a beautiful statement on Christian penance. It makes it clear that the purpose of changing the penitential laws of the Church is not to make life easier nor to compromise with our national softness. Rather, it is to remind us of our own personal responsibility for penance and self-renunciation. This responsibility is not satisfied by the sheer tokenism of substituting a nice fish dinner for a meat meal.

It's several years since the change took place. It might be well for us to examine whether we have simply dropped an old custom or whether we have responded to the bishops' trust "by freely making of every Friday a day of self-denial and mortification in prayerful remembrance of the Passion of Jesus Christ."

More Fish on Friday

Our diocesan paper gives a different version of the obligation to Friday abstinence. It states: "In answer to numerous inquiries, 'Do we have to fast and abstain from meat on the Fridays of Lent?' we repeat that the law of fast and abstinence is in effect only on Ash Wednesday and Good Friday. The regulation was made by the National Conference of Catholic Bishops of the United States in November, 1966. In view of the above, one is not obliged to abstain from meat on Friday, but the practice of abstinence is highly recommended."

Please resolve this confusion.

Several people have been in something of a quandry about the conflict between my previous remarks and the directives published in their diocesan papers. By all means, follow your local regulations.

However, for the record, the bishops made two statements concerning the customary penitential practices of our people. One concerned the obligation both to *fast and abstain,* declaring that this applied only to the two days mentioned. The other reads thus: "We preserve for our dioceses the tradition of abstinence from meat on each of the Fridays of Lent, confident that no Catholic will lightly hold himself excused from this penitential practice." This passage does not use the word "obligation," though it is undoubtedly stronger in intent than the next reference to the bishops' recommendation of "participation in daily Mass and a self-imposed observance of fasting."

As a result of this difference in language, different bishops have interpreted things differently in their own diocese. In the Archdiocese of Newark, for example, the Lenten Regulations for 1969 declare,

"Abstinence is to be observed on all Fridays of Lent." And the Archbishop's pastoral letter adapts the wording of the American Bishops' statement in this way: "No Catholic will lightly hold himself excused from so hallowed *an obligation.*"

In spite of the differences from diocese to diocese, the bishops of the country are in accord on these points: (1) the obligations are diminished in order to keep them from becoming fetishes to the compulsive or tortures to the anxious; (2) the need for a genuine interior spirit of penance is to be more forcefully presented to their people; (3) all are recommended to continue the traditional penitential practices and to go beyond mere tokenism. And in some dioceses, the Fridays of Lent are obligatory abstinence days.

The Cruelty of the Church

I can name at least ten Church-made laws that, if broken by Catholics, carry with them the penalty of condemnation to hell. We know, of course, that the Church can no longer burn people on earth (as they used to do). But isn't the penalty above a method of doing it in the hereafter? It seems very cruel and vicious, hardly worthy of a loving Father.

Put it that way, and it surely does seem cruel. It sounds as if Church officials are trying to twist the good news of salvation into a horrible slavery. However, that's not the way it is.

The Church neither wants to condemn anyone to hell nor does she have the power. Only God can deprive a person of eternal life with him — and he does it only if he can't do anything else, only if a human will has so turned in upon its own selfishness that it refuses to accept his love and mercy.

Church law is not an instrument of condemnation but of instruction. By making laws, the Church teaches us how we are to express our love and service of God in community. When she tells us that a particular law binds under pain of serious sin, she is telling us that a very important Christian value is at stake: the need to do penance or to worship God as a community, for instance. Acting on the commission Christ gave her to be mother and teacher of all men and vested with his authority to bind and to loose, she expresses in a law the minimum response any son of God must make to the call of his Father. To fail here is to turn away from God. This is serious sin. And it is serious sin that leads to hell.

Hats in Church

Do you see, in the foreseeable future, women being released from the Church law of wearing a hat or head covering in church?

Oh, Oh! Fashions again. Others ventured onto this ice many times and found it thin indeed.

I looked it up and discovered that it is a law of the Church that women are to have their heads covered in church. Canon 1262 says so quite simply and categorically — well, almost. Actually it says you're always to be coifed, *especially* when you go to Holy Communion. Though how you can especially observe the recommendation *at one time* if you are observing it *at all times* eludes me.

The law certainly goes back to the labored passage of I Corinthians 11:2-16, in which St. Paul insists that the contentious ladies of Corinth be silent in church and veil their hair. "If a woman will not wear a veil, she ought to cut off her hair." And for those who do not agree with his reasons, he invokes his authority: "Neither we nor the churches of God recognize any other usage." The origin of the custom is extremely hard to discover. In the time of St. Paul, wearing a veil had a religious and social value. It expressed the modesty of women before God, and it was the social symbol of woman's subordination to man. It would seem that St. Paul was reinforcing a social custom of his day with religious reasons and his authority. His reasons for fighting to preserve the practice were appropriate in his own situation. But does this precedent bind the Church forever? Hardly.

The practice and feeling of women of good taste will probably be the arbiter of the future of this least important of Church laws. Is wearing a hat in church something that you think is still a worthwhile sign of reverence and respect? I take my hat off in church because it seems appropriate to do so in our culture. I had forgotten that there is a Church law telling me to do so. If women of good taste wear a hat to church only because they feel compelled to do so by Church law, then I think we can predict that the law soon will die, if it has not already.

In any event, I look forward to the day when the law will be observed with such free flexibility that no woman will feel compelled to resort to Kleenex and a bobby pin in order to make a visit to the Blessed Sacrament.

Buying Spiritual Bouquets

Please explain wherein buying and selling spiritual bouquets is any different from the buying and selling of indulgences, which occasioned the split in Christendom.

There really is quite a bit of similarity between the two practices. At their best, both are invitations to the generosity of the faithful. At their worst, both are subject to the same kind of abuse and misunderstanding.

Indulgences and spiritual bouquets are both based on the New Testament doctrine of the solidarity of all the members of the Mystical Body. Because all the members of the Church are bound to one another by charity, the good of all can contribute to the well-being of an ailing member. By granting an indulgence, the Church expresses her intention to come to the assistance of a person who performs a special work of charity or prayer. By giving a spiritual bouquet, a person or a group expresses its intention to pray especially for the one named in the gift.

During the period between the eleventh century and the year 1567, one of the works of charity to which indulgences were connected was almsgiving. In itself, I don't find it any more difficult to understand the Church's willingness to grant an indulgence to a person who contributes to a school, hospital, or project than her willingness so to favor a pilgrim or one who says the rosary. Theoretically, and ideally, nothing was bought or sold — alms were freely given. However, in practice the custom did tend to become rather shabby, and Pope Pius V put an end to every indulgence which was given on the occasion of a donation or collection.

Today, the Society for the Propagation of the Faith and most religious orders, including my own, make available spiritual bouquets. What they are really doing is asking the faithful to make a donation to help their groups to continue their work for God and men. In gratitude, they promise to offer special prayers and Masses for their benefactors or for the person they designate. From my experience of this present practice, there is little or none of the shabbiness, dunning, or superstition that brought the expression of "trafficking" into the indulgence picture four centuries ago.

A number of religious communities speak of these spiritual bouquets as enrollments in the Benefactors' Society. One becomes recognized as a benefactor by making a benefaction. It couldn't be plainer and is not a buying or selling of anything.

Stipends and Simony

As related to the Church, would you please define the words (a) "stipend" and (b) "simony." I have heard of some parishes and dioceses where there are fixed fees for priestly services. I have deep feelings about this sort of thing, and I cannot be at ease with such a system.

Literally, a stipend is a tax or a wage. In Church usage it refers to remuneration given to a priest for his daily sustenance. It is prompted by the devotion of the faithful on the occasion of priestly ministration, especially the offering of the Holy Sacrifice. It may be a matter of strict justice on the part of the priest and on the part of the donor, if given and accepted precisely for a particular service, such as offering Mass for a particular intention.

Simony, a sin against the virtue of religion, takes its name from Simon the magician, who tried to buy from St. Peter the power of conferring the Holy Spirit (Acts 8:18-24). It is the buying or selling of a spiritual gift or power or benefice. It is a sin to which there is sometimes attached an ecclesiastical penalty.

Regulations about stipends are not a form of simony. They are made to avoid a note of commercialism, not to promote it. There are monetary expenditures associated with priestly services, such as the cost of wine, altar breads, laundering of altar linens, purchase of candles, payment of an organist or choir director, et cetera. But more basic still is the priest's own right to a livelihood.

Most priests have few worries about committing sins of simony. Many people still give Mass stipends which were the conventional offering before World War I. Priestly counsel is given gratis to anyone knocking on the door of a rectory or monastery. Sometimes we need a sense of humor when the telephone rings at 1:00 A.M. and a voice with slightly slurred speech says, "Hey, Father, we'd like you to settle an argument we're having!" Someone who has made a retreat in the monastery sometimes thinks of us when he and his chums are enjoying a euphoric mood and a dialectical exchange in some tavern where men wrestle with problems like: Why does God create somebody when he knows that person is going to hell?

Most of us are glad that people come to us when we are needed. Simony is not a common sin.

Sunday Obligation or Worship

Could we please explore disposing with Sunday Mass "obligation" and consider Sunday worship instead? I don't mean for a minute not to have Mass scheduled as usual and daily when possible. But worship signifies true, loving freedom, and I feel that the threat, implicit in the stern admonition, is at odds with the connotation of Christ's loving sacrifice for us. I feel it is most important that the next generation of children be freed from the necessity of rushing breathlessly around while a harried mother scolds and pushes "to get to Mass on time." Without the penalty of mortal sin ominously overshadowing the presence of Christ in our midst as we prepare to serve him, we could all approach his altar in a more charitable frame of soul.

There is no one who would dispute with you as regards your objective. Everyone will agree that our emphasis should be on Sunday worship in a spirit of loving, joyful presence in Christ to our heavenly Father rather than on fulfilling the requirements of a law that hangs like a threat over our heads. To disagree would be to empty Christianity of the meaning St. Paul gave it in his powerful oppositions between letter and spirit, law and gospel, slavery and freedom.

The question, however, is about the prudent means to stimulate our people to gather in this spirit of worship. Would the abolition of the Church directive on Sunday Mass attendance help create this free spirit of worship, or would it tend to diminish still more the sense of awareness of God? I fear that the latter would be the more likely.

Law has an educative value. It is a reminder that helps us to stretch our will power to live up to what we really want to do and be. The response of our people to the changes in the regulations concerning the Lenten fast and Friday abstinence is not a very encouraging sign that we are ready to respond generously to exhortations. It worries me to think of the people who might drift away from the Eucharistic center of their faith, in spite of their genuine good will and good intentions, if they did not have the reminder of a "sense of duty" to spur them on.

The obligation of Sunday Mass shouldn't be experienced as a threat, any more than the obligation of daily school is. I think of it as being in the same category as the civil law that obliges a husband to support his wife and family. Most men do this out of a genuine loving concern and never give a thought to the law. Its presence on the books is only meant to push those who would be apt to neglect their duty — to give them an additional reason for performing it. Now there is a far greater probability that men will neglect the worship of God, whom they do not see, than that they will neglect the care of their families, whom they do see and whose living presence they feel. I think we still need the reminder of a Sunday Mass obligation. God forbid that it be a hated and resented obligation. But responsible people live with obligations that are gratefully received and personally accepted.

Catholic Schools and Sunday Mass

I find that many young people going to Catholic schools these days are losing their religion. I know at least three occasions, and one of these in a Catholic college, where the students were told that if they didn't feel they wanted to go to Mass, it was not necessary to do so. Is it no longer a mortal sin to miss Mass on Sundays and holy days of obligation without good cause?

There is an obligation for Catholics to participate in the Holy Eucharist on Sundays and holydays of obligation. It is formulated into law in Canon 1248. The common teaching of canonists and moralists is that the obligation is a serious one; that is, anyone who is knowingly and inexcusably absent from the entire Mass or from a notable part of it commits a grave sin. The obligation to participate in holy Mass is not merely a matter of Church law. It is more than an obligation of natural law, which requires every man to set apart some time for worship. It flows from the very meaning of the Christian life as a life of union with Jesus Christ and with the holy community which is his Church. It is when she celebrates the Eucharist that the Church is most perfectly herself and finds the ability to work for the salvation of the world. This celebration must engage the whole community and be solemnly proclaimed to the world by public action. The person who absents himself from this community action without a decent reason is failing to take seriously his belief in Christ and his Church.

I know that some are maintaining that the freedom of the children of God has emptied all ecclesiastical laws of any binding force. Poor St. Paul, who set up a number of directive laws himself for the guidance of his young communities, would choke to hear his great principle of freedom distorted this way.

There are others who look to the purpose of the law of Sunday Mass attendance. It is to get the Christian people to be and pray as Christians. They recognize that the Eucharist should be the central act of the Christian community. They realize that it should be an event that is characterized by the joy of a people who know that they share the fellowship of the Body of Christ through the breaking of bread. It is to be part of all this that the law invites them. Yet they experience Sunday Mass as a boring hour in which they find little that speaks to them. They feel that the priest and congregation do not welcome them, nor are they interested in them. They carry away the impression that no one in the whole assembly did any more than fulfill a functionary's task or a social duty. This is not an excuse for ignoring the law. But it does help us to understand the indifference of a generation which has a burning passion for "authenticity" and "meaningful" action. The refusal of priests to work at making the Mass an action that is humanly alive and living by faith may be partly the scandal that is turning off and turning away so many of our younger generation. This can be far more influential than faulty instruction.

I don't know just what the young people you refer to were actually told. When we hear stories like this, we ought to remember that the distance between the lecture hall and the bull session is often the longest mile in the world. And things that were carefully explained in the first place have a way of getting frightfully distorted by the time they get reported. On the other hand, there are those who confuse the reasonable rules of the community with the sham of externalism and legalism, and they fire buckshot at both. There are those educators who have become so extremely sensitive to the reactions of students that they tend to reduce their teaching to just what the students will swallow, rather than struggling to enrich them by showing them what there is to eat! But it would be excessively pessimistic to indict an entire educational system which is working most earnestly to renew itself as a genuine apostolate — a place where young people will discover for themselves the Christ in whom they were baptized as infants.

Genuine Religion

I'm a thirteen-year-old girl with a problem. Is there something wrong with me? I believe in God and bring him into my daily doings, such as "God, please help me on this test." However, I don't believe in formal worship such as Mass. It is fine, but I don't think anyone gets anything out of it. Many adults attend Mass on Sunday and act reverently; then all week don't do a single Christian deed. I believe you should worship privately and to yourself a few minutes each day. Confession is also OK, but many people go with the feeling "they have to." After they get out, they turn around and do the same wrong things all over again. Again, I believe you can think about your bad deeds and confess to God in private. Do you agree? Please give me your opinion.

No, young lady, there's nothing wrong with you. You're just becoming an adult, and you're asking real questions about the most important things in your life. And that's wonderful!

When you were a child, you did what you were told and you went where you were led — though there may have been some short-lived pouting or rebellion. Then whatever mother and dad and priest and teacher said was usually taken as wisdom and truth. When you asked the child's question "Why?" you expected to get *the* answer. So often a child's questioning is part of information-gathering rather than part of the process of judgment. Like many children, you may have approached religion as a series of practices — performed with sincerity, but not reaching much below the surface.

Now the child's "Why?" has given way to much more reflective questioning. As a person who is growing up, you examine things more critically. You are setting up the values you will live by. You want to know what is real and important and what is sham and excess baggage. You are coming to see that real religion is an affair of the heart. It is a person-to-person relationship with God, who has first loved us. Its most special moments are the intimate moments of prayer that let you experience that you are loved and that lead you to bury selfishness and to be kind and patient and strong and helpful to others. You recognize that a routine attendance at Mass or a "quick-rinse" approach to the sacrament of penance is, at best, empty, and, at worst, hypocrisy. You are right to want to avoid falling into that trap. This is what is so wonderful about being thirteen and a half and asking probing questions.

At the same time, a person's questioning should be a reverent search for the whole truth. This is something most of us find very difficult. We see one aspect of the truth so clearly that we become blind to the complementary aspects that make up the whole picture. Do you think you might be doing something like this?

Is it really enough to say: Religion should be personal and interior; yet many people seem to go to Mass out of loveless routine, and they seem to get nothing out of it; therefore the Mass is worthless? Is this the whole truth? Isn't it possible for me to make my participation in the Mass the high point of my own personal and interior worship of God? In my experience, I find that this is just what it is for many good and sincere Catholics. By their faith, they know that our Lord comes to them in a special way through the celebration of the Mass to raise their individual offering of themselves into oneness with his and with those of the whole Church. They find strength in receiving Christ's body and blood and in sharing their worship with others who are struggling with them toward the same goal. They believe that God is not calling them to worship him only in solitary privacy but that he invites them to come to him with one another in the Eucharist he has given to the Church. It is formal worship, but it is not a formalism for them.

The whole truth about religion is that it is God's gift to us and our sincere and personal response at one and the same time. We aren't really responding to him the way we should, if we set aside his gift and his guidance in order just to do our own thing.

Faith Alone

After a year spent at a Catholic university, my daughter returned home with the announcement that she no longer believes in the Catholic Church and never will. Among other things, she objects to the Church precepts of obligatory attendance at Sunday Mass under pain of mortal sin. I tried to convince her that this kind of thinking was part of Martin Luther's heresy: that is, that faith is sufficient for salvation, that good behavior is not necessary. In this case, I mean that loving God and believing in him is not enough and that the Church has every right to impose obligatory participation at Sunday Mass. Could you please explain why faith alone cannot gain a person's salvation?

The conviction of the Catholic Church is that faith alone is of no use for salvation if faith is divorced from a life conformed to faith. This, we believe, is the clear teaching of the Sacred Scriptures — even in St. Paul's Epistle to the Romans. This, too, is the basic understanding Martin Luther seems to have had — although, in the heat of controversy, he did say some things that are far different.

Faith, in the usage of the Scriptures, is not merely the mental assent to a revealed truth. Nor is it merely a trusting attitude in the presence of God. Much more than this, the New Testament sees faith as the total loving and loyal submission of a person to God, who has revealed himself in Jesus Christ. This faith does suffice for salvation. But it is never alone. It necessarily includes everything that Catholic theology has designated as hope and love and the moral virtues. The true believer is one whose life is ruled by his belief or who is at least struggling for this goal. The person who sets out deliberately to live and act on a level at odds with his belief is a hypocrite.

Can one truly say that a person is trying to give himself to our Lord (and this is what it means to live by faith) if he picks and chooses which of our Lord's words he will accept? Can there be a saving faith that neglects to "pray always" (Luke 18:1) or refuses to "take up [the] cross each day" and follow Christ (Luke 9:23)? Can a man be a believing disciple who refuses to hear Christ in his Church (Luke 10:16) or who does not "proclaim the death of the Lord until he comes" (I Cor. 11:26) by "eating the flesh of the Son of Man and drinking his blood" (John 6:53) in the Holy Eucharist?

These are all "works." Joined to genuine faith, they give it its body and express it. Divorced from genuine faith, they are an empty shell and useless. Among the problems of the sixteenth century was the fact that some popular defenders of the Catholic cause failed to say this clearly and seemed to make man's effort equally as important as God's graciousness in the process of salvation. On the other hand, Luther's emphatic "faith alone" degenerated into a popular slogan whose deep meaning was ignored.

The matter is far more complex than this sketch has indicated, but there is not enough room here to pursue the subject further.

Unfortunately, I don't think that this kind of answer will be of much help to your daughter. She is caught in the crisis of faith that is epidemic among so many of our young people. The reasons she gives for her present decision may be the best she can articulate, but I would imagine that they are not the underlying ones.

I don't think that you can argue a person back into faith. You can inspire him. You can provide him with the climate that will make him see the profound meaning that the love of Christ brings to the lives of those he admires. But you just can't reduce the problem to an intellectual exercise of proof and counterproof.

One thing that the anguish of our young people is telling us is that there is a great credibility gap in our lives. They know what we claim to believe, and they don't see evidence of it in the way we conduct our business, in the way we vote, in the way we approach problems of open housing, education, welfare, et cetera. Our Church is said to be in the throes of a great renewal, but they don't see our parishes, universities, clergy, or religious caught up in a revival of spirituality. There is no felt sense of a powerful movement opening the hearts of men to the action of God's grace. We change the surface. There is no great evidence that men's hearts are changing on any grand scale. Unless the Church becomes credible as the place where God's special love becomes visible, our young people are going to find it very hard to hang on.

I believe that, even in a barely credible Church, a man's ultimate responsibility is to hold on to God, who communicates himself in and through the weak thing that the Church is. But we who are the Church have a most serious responsibility to support the little ones in faith, not to be a scandal to them.

Proper Parish

Traditionally, we have been taught that parish boundaries must be respected; however, something more is now at stake. We have distinct trends in the Church — the liberal group is unhappy with the conservative, and the conservatives are very disturbed by the liberals.

Here is the problem. Is it just a person's misfortune if he is living in a parish which doesn't meet his personal spiritual needs? Is it justified by any arbitrary ruling to demand that someone "needing" the true renewal spirit of the liberals be forced to attend his own parish church merely because it is in his neighborhood?

I would hope that we find our Christian community with those whose spiritual needs run along the same path. When you find yourself up against a conservative pastor who does not take kindly to either suggestion or liberality, is it not reasonable to join the community which provides these things? It is very discouraging to understand and crave this type of worship and find that it is not a reality in the church you are "commanded" to attend.

One answer has been to attend Mass wherever you wish but to support your own pastor. This would offend justice in the respect that the spiritual community which is meeting your needs doesn't get the full measure of your support.

If there is an answer, please enlighten me. But please note that the change is prescribed not by whim but by spiritual needs and fulfillments.

Genuine spiritual needs take precedence over regulations that are made primarily for good order's sake. Certainly there is no cogent reason why a Catholic who is anguished by the lethargy of his local parish may not seek to share the vitality of another parish community — be that vitality of a liberal or a conservative bent.

However, simply to do it by parish-hopping has built-in difficulties that will show up when there is a question of baptisms that are to be registered in your own parish or the enrolling of children in a parochial school.

One possible remedy would be for those who find a parish that genuinely corresponds to their spiritual needs to ask its pastor if they may be enrolled as members of his parish. In the past, when such a request has been accompanied with very good reasons, it has been granted with chancery authorization in particular cases. If granted, then the person would belong as a full-fledged member of that parish. It would be his own parish, entitled to his full loyalty and support. I don't know how realistic this remedy would be in your case, but it might be worth a try.

If the fact of the matter is that the spiritual needs of very few in a particular parish are really being met and the ordinary channels of suggestion, cooperation, and gradual change are not working, some form of pressure could be applied. In the past, when the desires of the parishioners have not been considered in the question of things like religious education, I think that the Christian people have used the ballot box of the diminished collection to voice their disapproval. The obligation to support your pastor is a two-way street.

The Seamy Side of the Church

Recent movies and television programs have presented the Church of the past in a bad light. I'm thinking of programs about Galileo, Luther, Becket, Michelangelo, and Thomas More. I have been aware of the past evils of the Church for a long time, and this has not weakened my faith. But many people who discover for the first time how corrupt some of the clergy were in the past are very

much shocked by this. What can one say in defense of the Church in this matter? Please recommend books dealing with the question of evil in the Church.

It's good that people are shocked. Many of these affairs and many of these people were shocking. I don't think that we should try to defend the shabby actions of churchmen, whether past or present. Your own faith has not been shaken by the recital of the chicanery, greed, lust, and pride that have defaced the image of God in his Church. I think we have to hope that the power of the grace of God will be as effective in supporting the faith of others as they confront the same seamy side of the Church.

There has been a thread of sin running through the fabric of Church history from the beginning. It sets in relief the twin mysteries of man's perversity and the patient mercy of God. The Church will always be beautiful with the radiance of the wonderful things God does for man in her. It will always be the place where man is invited to enter into union with God. But the eloquence of the invitation will never change the fact that God does not compel. Each man must personally respond to the invitation in freedom. Each man! Even those who have positions of great trust and responsibility in the Church. And the free response of a wounded liberty can be tragic.

Writings on the Church are the hottest item in the Catholic publishing business. There are two books that might be especially helpful for you: Paul Simon, *The Human Element in the Church of Christ* (Westminster, Md.: Newman, 1954); John Powell, *The Mystery of the Church* (Milwaukee: Bruce, 1967).

Secrecy in the Church

What is a "secret consistory"? Actually, the why of it bothers me more. I can't understand why there should be any secrecy if the whole Church is the People of God and the hierarchy exists only to minister to it and serve it. Isn't the time past when it was acceptable to leave the little people in the dark and have everything come from the top down?

A consistory is a solemn assembly of all the cardinals present in Rome. It is presided over by the pope and is convened to consider the most important matters concerning the government of the whole Church. The ordinary consistory is "secret"; that is, no one but pope and cardinals may be present. There are also ceremonial gatherings called "public consistories," which others can attend.

It seems to me that you are reacting to a certain excess of secrecy that has existed in the Church. It is certainly hard to see why the Christian people have to be kept in the dark about Church finances, or why we can't be informed about on-going reform of canon law whose norms will affect our lives. Formerly some disciplinary procedures in the Church were enshrouded with a kind of secrecy that prevented the accused from making a reasonable self-defense. At present, there is a genuine interest in the Church for setting up the machinery that will facilitate a two-way flow of information and permit genuine representative participation in the decision-making processes in the Church. The senates and pastoral councils that are springing up everywhere are part of this, and their very existence will mean that the amount of secrecy in the Church will be limited.

However, don't you think that you may be reacting too much when you suggest that Church business should be conducted totally in the limelight? Every man has a right to seek confidential advice. And by its very nature, a confidence obliges the adviser to secrecy. A person's need and right to consult confidentially escalates as his responsibility and the sensitiveness of his position increase.

For all our national complaints about a "credibility gap" in recent years, I don't think that any serious American would require that every deliberation of the first servant of the people, the President, be a matter of public record. It serves the best interests of the people that he be able to confer secretly with his Cabinet, congressional leaders, the National Security Council, and his own personal advisers.

The pope is in a somewhat similar position. Though servant of the servants of God, his special grace of service is one that puts him in the position of being the one who is ultimately responsible for staggering decisions. The constitution of the Church is not so equalitarian that its every member has a divine right to know exactly what problems the pope is wrestling with at all times. It serves the best interests of the People of God that our leader have the freedom to confer confidentially with his cabinet officers and advisers, be they the Roman Curia, the College of Cardinals, or the Synod of Bishops. Whatever oath of secrecy there is serves only to protect this freedom.

Monasticism and Contemplative Life

What exactly is meant by monasticism, and what is meant by the

contemplative life as embraced by religious? Are they one and the same thing, or can one exist without the other? Could monks not add to their apostolate of prayer and penance one of contact with people — particularly people who are seeking spiritual values and who cannot easily find help for that in their ordinary contacts?

Monasticism is the form of Christian religious life that is lived by a community of monks. The word "monk" comes from the Greek for "one who lives alone." Technically speaking, a monk is a member of one of the great monastic orders like those that belong to the Benedictine family in the West or those who follow the rule of St. Basil in the East. They "live alone" in the sense of "living apart" from the ordinary affairs of their brother Christians whose vocations involve them in secular society.

Traditionally, monasticism is a contemplative form of religious life. The contemplative form of religious life is one which positively excludes a direct apostolate of teaching, preaching, charitable work, or missions which would take the members outside their religious community. The real aim of contemplative religious life is to follow the example of Christ in prayer — to help its members experience the reality of their relationship with God himself.

In actual fact, these definitions are a bit too abstract. Both monasticism and the forms of contemplative life are living things which have had a long and varied history. Members of monastic orders are deeply involved in education and in the apostolate of parochial life and overseas missions. The Benedictines are presently struggling with the problem of what form monasticism should take today. And the strictly contemplative orders of men and women are pondering the best ways of fostering the growth of their members as persons who will live in a deeper contact with the reality of God.

Contemplative communities have always been deeply concerned with the needs of mankind, even though their way of life deliberately precluded any direct involvement in providing for these needs. Today, a number of contemplative communities are asking if their almost total separation from the people is what the Lord still wants of them. Your rhetorical question is a good one, and many would answer it in the affirmative.

My own opinion is that the cloisters of contemplative communities should be opened somewhat to those who want to share the life experience of the men and women totally given to God. However, I think it would be a tragic mistake to try to involve contemplatives in the direct apostolate of the Church. What they are doing is the most important thing any person can do. It will be a sad day in the Church when the only service that is prized is that which has a measurable result in alleviating poverty or ignorance. At the very heart of the life of the Church is the person-to-person relationship with God which the contemplative consciously seeks through a life of prayer and worship. But there are many whose lives could be enriched by living for a time in the company of these contemplatives and sharing their life of search for God. And the experience of the contemplatives would stand to benefit from a contact with those who are searching for God in less privileged situations.

The Roman Church

In 1938 Fathers Rumble and Carty, of "Radio Replies" fame, said that they never use the term "Roman Catholic" in referring to our Church. "Catholic Church" is a sufficient and correct description of our Church. By that title it is sufficiently identified as distinct from all other religions, they affirmed. Furthermore, they stated that it insinuates a false idea that there are other kinds of Catholics. Therefore, shouldn't we all refuse to use the term "Roman Catholic" in referring to our Church?

No. I don't think there is anything to make a big fuss about. The double name seems to have been coined by the Reformers in England to support their claim to an equally valid Anglo-Catholicism. Hence there is some feeling against the term "Roman Catholic" among our British brethren. At the same time, it can be a useful identification. Some years ago, I was visiting Westminster Abbey when a lady with a strong Irish brogue stopped me. The conversation went something like this. "Excuse me, are you Roman?" "Yes, I am." With a sigh of relief, she said: "Oh, thank God, Father. This used to be ours, didn't it?"

4
The
Other
Churches

True Ecumenism

It is encouraging to see that the different religions are becoming united. Perhaps someday a traveler unable to locate a Catholic church will be able to attend a church of another faith. The important thing is that Mass be celebrated.

There are some points of confusion here, I think. True, there are profound changes in the relations of Catholics and the other Christian Churches. Formerly, the relations between us were mostly negative. They ranged all the way from aloof politeness to downright hostility. These attitudes colored our policies, and our policies reinforced the attitudes. Now, under the guidance of the Holy Spirit, the climate is changing. And policies are changing.

It really is not a question of uniting different religions and different faiths, though. The unity we seek is that all men be one in "one Lord, one faith, one baptism, and one God and Father of all" (Eph. 4:4-6). And where there is a faith in Christ and a true baptism, there is not a faith different from ours — though there is what we Catholics consider a less full expression of the true faith in Christ.

You are right in saying that the important thing is that the Mass be celebrated. For our unity is most complete when we share the Lord's gift in the Eucharistic Sacrifice. And it is also very important that the celebration of Mass together be a climax that says in effect: we all agree in the profession of our religious belief, we all are gathered as one people under the guidance of the same Shepherd. When the day comes that we are sure that the Holy Orders of the celebrant assures the full reality of the One Eucharist and that one and the same faith is professed and that all are joined as one body in communion with the full college of bishops presided over by Peter — then we will be free to worship in any of the churches. It may be a church of a different tradition. It will not be a church of another faith.

Salvation in the Catholic Church

A few years ago, one of your predecessors writing in the "Signpost" dismissed the case of a Catholic who had become a Lutheran with the comment: "Unless she repents, she won't go to heaven." I have recently been considering becoming a Protestant. Like most Catholics, I was baptized as a baby before I was even old enough to know it was happening. Since it was obviously solely my parents' decision that I should be baptized and raised a Catholic, is there any logical reason why I should consider it binding on me?

Your question is a serious one, and I want to take it very seriously. It is also a very complex one. I cannot solve it with a simple brief answer. Nor am I ready to say that everyone who was baptized as a Catholic is guilty of a serious failure if he should embrace another religious tradition. However, I think that for most Catholics, a choice like this would be such a failure and would seriously jeopardize their chance of salvation.

Let me go gradually into the complexities. There is, of course, no logical reason why a person should consider himself bound by every decision his parents made for him when he was a baby. Certainly, if your parents had decided that the girl in the next crib was to be your wife, there would be no reason why you should feel bound to marry her. They might arrange things so that you would choose her yourself, and then you would be bound by your own decision and would be responsible to live up to its consequences.

However, there are some decisions that a person's parents make which shape their child's life even though his wishes were not consulted. One of these is their loving decision to give him life. No sane society maintains that a person is free to commit suicide simply because he did not choose to be born.

The Catholic believes that the parents' decision to have their child baptized is one of these decisions. This is based on the conviction that human life itself exists only as openness to a fuller divine life that is offered to every man through Christ. Catholics believe that for no man is there any other ultimate meaning or fulfillment than that of a life of communion with God that is offered only through his Incarnate Son.

This fulfillment does not come automatically by birth. It comes to each person only by the generous act of God by which he takes a man to himself. The condition of this divine act is either a person's entrusting himself to God by faith or being grasped by God through baptism, which we call "the sacrament of faith." The normal place of this mysterious interaction of God and the human person is the Church of Christ.

Consequently, when Catholic parents have their child baptized, they are not merely imposing their own views. They believe that God acts through the sacrament to take their child as his own. They believe that they are giving their child a life as real as his biological and personal life — an enrichment of everlasting significance. The child is not bound merely to the arbitrary prejudices of his parents; he is freed by being given a head start in the only real world there is. He is empowered to reach the only real destiny he has as man.

It is only a start and a power. As the child matures, he must, of course, make decisions for himself. In some areas of his life, he is entirely free to set the course of his life. He can choose what career he will pursue, whether to marry or not, and whom he will marry. He may be influenced by his parents' wishes, but he is not obligated by their choice.

In other areas — those where the ultimate conditions of his existence are at stake — he still must decide. But the choices he makes are no longer matters that are completely open. He is bound to choose to live rather than to die. If he is a male, he is not free to choose a woman's life and sex role for himself. And similarly, if he is baptized and raised as a member of Christ's Church and thus consciously on the path that leads to the goal of human striving, he does not have the option of rejecting this situation.

However, there is another aspect that must be taken into consideration. The realities of faith do not force themselves on a person like the evident realities of human life, experience, and sex differences. A person must freely consent to believe, and it is possible to disbelieve. As a child grows, he must ratify the fact of his being part of the community of believers in a way that is not exactly the same as accepting the fact of one's human life and masculinity.

Sometimes there are tremendous obstacles that prevent a baptized Catholic from accepting the Church, her teachings, and her claim to be the only religious group in the world that is blessed with the fullness of the means of human fulfillment that Christ wants his Church to have. These obstacles may be intellectual, emotional, cultural, or any of a number of things. For example, one's indoctrination in the faith may have been so much a matter of learning oppressive rules that he can no longer accept such a negative view of life. The things that seem important to the people whom he identifies with the Church may be so foreign to a person's own values that he finds himself emotionally incapable of accepting their Church as his own.

When a person who is handicapped in this way decides against the Church of his baptism, does he cut himself off from God and the possibility of salvation? Only God knows. Perhaps the faith that was given him as a power at baptism was never able to grow at all. Perhaps his first real act of faith is one that he makes within another denomination. If this is the case, then what appears to be apostasy may in fact be conversion.

However, the unfortunate kind of situation we have been considering is not the normal state of affairs. Normally, one grows from a child's faith to an adult's. And growth is often a struggle at the awesome task of being a pilgrim toward God in a world where God seems to be silent. The silence of God and the shabbiness of men put faith to the test, a test that is a veritable crucifixion. Yet the difficulty of the test does not free a man from his obligations. He is still bound to hold fast to his commitment within the Church. And only by holding on under pressure will his faith grow and develop.

It is this normal situation that the Church has in mind when it teaches: "Whosoever, therefore, knowing that the Catholic Church was made necessary by God through Jesus Christ, would refuse to enter her or to remain in her could not be saved" (Vatican II, *Dogmatic Constitution on the Church,* no. 14).

The severe but constructive logic of this position binds the vast majority of the Catholic community to remain in the Church of their baptism. Does it bind you? I can't say for sure. But the fact that you are asking a Catholic priest about this problem strikes me as significant. It inclines me to think that you have been so much a part of the Catholic tradition that the move you have been considering would be a real abandonment of the faith.

Should I Join the Catholic Church?

In one of your columns you mention that the issue of the validity of Anglican Orders is not dead. This raises a new aspect of a question that has been on my mind constantly for years. You see, I am an Anglo-Catholic. I have been drawn to the Roman Catholic Church. Crucial for me was my lingering doubt about the validity of holy orders in my church. It seems to me that if Anglican Orders are invalid, and consequently the Sacrifice of the Mass also, I should leave the Episcopal Church. However, if these are valid, then I feel

that this is not necessary. I am confused. What do you think God wants me to do?

Your letter is very beautiful. I hated to trim it down to this size. It is also one that is very difficult to answer. I just don't have the wisdom to tell you what God wants you to do.

Let me tell you, rather, what I believe. I believe firmly in the Roman Catholic Church. (It is not God's greatest gift to us. His greatest gift is the gift of himself.) And I believe that he gives himself to all who search for him with that honest submission to his truth and love which the language of the Church and the Bible calls genuine faith and charity. Genuine faith and charity are not confined to the visible limits of the Christian Church.

However, I also believe that it is God's will in Christ to gather all who believe in him into a Church which is a visible reality with a history that includes days of glorious fidelity and days of shabby compromise. I believe that the Church of Christ has varying degrees of visibility in the churches that profess his name — but that the fullness of the means of salvation he wanted his Church to have is found only where the Eucharist is really celebrated and where the bishops teach and shepherd their flocks in union with the successor of Peter.

Because of this belief, I could not adhere in peace to a church body not united to Rome, even though it might have valid orders and a valid Eucharist and even though it might even have a richer spiritual life than I find at the moment in my own. I pray that I will always maintain this conviction.

Whether you share this conviction or not, I cannot be sure. If you share it, I think you will see what you have to do. If you don't as yet, it would be premature for you to take a step which would be so wrenching for you.

The question of the validity of Anglican Orders and its corollary, the validity of the Sacrifice of the Mass in the Episcopal Church, is an important one. But it does not seem to me to be the most important one. For example, there is no room for doubting the validity of orders in the Orthodox Churches. Yet, as a Roman Catholic, I do not believe that these institutions have the fullness Christ wants them to have *as churches* so long as the rift with Rome remains.

There have been several studies on the question of Anglican Orders in recent years. One of them was written by a convert Episcopalian priest who was himself ordained *conditionally* in the Roman Catholic Church. The fact that Rome would countenance a conditional ordination indicates some lack of certitude that his previous ordination as an Anglican priest was null and void! (John J. Hughes, *Absolutely Null and Void: The Papal Condemnation of Anglican Orders 1896,* Washington, D.C., Corpus, 1968).

For the present, then, I think that God wants you to continue to search and to pray for light. While you are seeking the proper step which you should take, continue to hold fast to our Lord, who has blessed you with a real gift of closeness to himself.

The light you can hope for will probably not take the form of an absolutely compelling argument. I believe that there are arguments for my position — that it is quite reasonable. But I do not claim that the reasons and arguments are so clear that any intelligent and open-minded person would have to assent to them. It may be that the light is already leading you, not by unshakeable intellectual reasons, but by the nagging persistence of your question. I pray that you will see what you should do.

Should I Leave the Catholic Church?

I'm a thirteen-year-old girl, and I have been wondering about our religion. Is it right for a Catholic to leave the Church if he really believes some other religion is better?

A person must always follow the path that his conscience indicates is right for him. This is true even if teachers, parents, Church, and the judgment of other good men consider that what you are doing is wrong. If a person has considered all the facts available to him and sincerely concludes that the disapproved course of action is what God is asking of him, then he is obliged to take this step.

Note, however, that conscience is not a matter of feeling. It is a judgment based on facts and principles about what is right or wrong here and now.

I think it is a very rare thing for a mature person to have such absolute clarity that he can appeal to conscience against the basic convictions of the Church. Do you really think that, at thirteen, a young person is apt to have considered all the facts necessary in order to come to such a decision?

Other religions may indeed seem to be better. That is, one may find better people living a deeper spiritual life in another church community than he might find in his own Catholic parish community. But this does not mean that he is bound in conscience to join this group. Rather, I think that he should see this group as a prod to his conscience to live Christianity in his own Church more generously.

The central issue is not whether Christian life seems more generous and vital in the other church. It is rather a question of which church possesses the fullness of the means of salvation that Christ wanted his Church to have.

Catholics believe that this fullness is found in the Catholic Church alone. We do not look down our noses at the others in whom the Spirit of Christ is at work. We wish we could share our wealth with them. And we regret that we use this wealth so poorly.

Even when the sin and weakness of the members of the Church makes her seem a frail and shabby thing, the Catholic holds fast in the sentiment of the apostles: "To whom should we go? You have the words of eternal life."

Ecumenical Services

In our parish we have many ecumenical services to which the members of other churches in the area are invited. The other churches reciprocate. What puzzles me is this: when we have an ecumenical service in our church, we don't have our main service; we don't have the Mass. But when we go to their church, they have their own main form of worship. Why the difference? None of our guests will ever know our service.

Possibly you have two different things in mind here. It is one thing to attend the worship service of another Christian community in order to observe the shape of its service and to come to see the religious experience of its people. It is another thing to bring the adherents of different Christian traditions together in a united prayer and worship of our common Father pleading for real Christian unity.

Ecumenical services are gatherings of separated Christians who come together to pray for the unity of the Church. These services are always made up of those things we have in common — the Scriptures, the preached word, and common prayer. The idea in providing this kind of service is to make it possible for everyone present to participate fully in the united prayer.

I think you will find that "ecumenical services" in the other churches never include their celebration of the Lord's Supper, even though in some of them this is their most special form of worship.

The reason why ecumenical services are never Eucharistic, whether they be conducted under Catholic or Protestant auspices, is doctrinal. The way is not yet clear for Catholics and Protestants to participate fully in the Eucharist as it is celebrated in one another's churches. We cannot comfortably allow the ministers of the other churches to concelebrate at our Mass, nor the members of other congregations to receive Holy Communion. Nor are Catholic priests and people free to join to this extent in the Lord's Supper in the other churches. Rome is quite clear in its directions that the way to this kind of united worship is not yet open.

However, besides "ecumenical services," there is no reason why the members of the other churches cannot be invited to observe our main form of worship and the devotion of our people. Nor is there any reason why Catholics may not occasionally go as observers to the regular Sunday services of the other denominations. This sort of thing can foster an ecumenical spirit as we come to know each other's life and faith and devotion.

Ecumenism is much more than ecumenical services. It is also served by everything that contributes to mutual understanding, openness, and generosity to all.

Truth—Plain or Distorted?

A friend of mine has been giving me literature by Herbert W. Armstrong. This person, although a good Catholic, seems to think that Mr. Armstrong's organization has some kind of inside track on what is the truth — based on the Bible. Since my objections don't seem to carry any weight with this friend, I am asking for your opinion on Mr. Armstrong, his Bible organization, and his magazine, "The Plain Truth."

The Plain Truth is, in the words of its founder and chief architect, "a magazine *not* for church members but for the general public — the unconverted and unchurched — an evangelistic-type publication to bring to the world God's TRUTH — making it PLAIN!" It began modestly in 1934. Today it is a slick-paper magazine, published internationally in three editions, with a circulation of over one million.

The underlying religious view of the magazine is Mr. Armstrong's own. His autobiography shows him to be a strong individualist, vigorous and enthusiastic. Theologically, he is a biblical fundamentalist — one who finds the meaning of life and the solution of all human problems in the literal words of the Bible, understood in a rather simplistic way. For example, in his own personal search, which took him from a career in advertising to religion, Mr. Armstrong accepted ordination in a small group called the Church of God. What impelled him to associate with this group was the fact that it was a Christian church that observed the biblical seventh day and not Sunday (which has no explicit warrant in the Bible). While not questioning the sincerity of the man's action, one can hardly maintain that such a naive approach to the Bible is the way to discover God's truth.

The Plain Truth is strong for morality, decency, purity, and marriage and equally strong against crime, communism, liberalism, and evolution. It's hard to fight someone who is against sin! Yet there are insidious things in *The Plain Truth's* approach to life and religion. It is aimed at the gullible and the fearful. It is adept at discovering plots, like that of an alleged neo-Nazi United States of Europe dominated by a "bad" Germany that will devastate a Britain and America that have fallen from God's favor. And the truth of these frightening forecasts is found guaranteed in the editor's personal and strange way of interpreting the prophetic books of the Bible. I'm sure the prophets who wrote the inspired texts would not find this truth plain!

I think that this whole complex of founder-organization-magazine is a menace. For those who accept this vision of life, the end result of continuing exposure is likely to be a narrowness that ties them to a political chauvinism and a fearful superstition. For all, the linking of a crusade for an upright life to a biblical interpretation that is so easily discredited puts in jeopardy the struggle of all men who are working to renew the face of the earth in the image of Christ.

Faith Healing

What is the Church's view on Pentecostal faith healers and their campaigns? Are they "fixed"? While I believe it is possible for God to heal through men, I can't believe he would do so through ministers of a church opposed to his true Church.

The Catholic Church firmly believes in the reality of the ministry of healing. It is part of the messianic work our Lord entrusted to the Church. The Church exercises this ministry through the dedicated services of Christian doctors and nurses and, in a most special way, through the sacrament of the sacred anointing of the sick.

Concerning the ministry of healing exercised by the men you call "Pentecostal faith healers," the Catholic Church has no single position. It really isn't the place of our Church to investigate the practices of another religious body and take a definite stand one way or another. Personally, I find it hard to imagine that men who lead a congregation in the name of Christ would resort to fraud to maintain that following.

Are the cures, then, truly a miraculous sign of the finger of God at work? It's possible. God does not reject the united prayer of sincere believers simply because they lack all the benefits he wants his Church to have. However, it is difficult to know whether the cures are supernatural. The ailments of the people who are healed may be psychogenic — that is, they may be the result of some emotional condition rather than a truly organic disorder. Medical science is familiar with the process by which psychically induced sufferings can be alleviated by strong emotional suggestion. Certainly the climate of a faith healer's campaign has powerful overtones of suggestion and emotionality. Probably the only way we could prudently conclude that the healing is a divine work would be with the assistance of a medical investigating team — like the Medical Bureau that functions at Lourdes. I am not familiar with any study of this sort that has verified the reality of cures reported in faith-healing meetings.

At the same time, we Catholics should not begin with the assumption that God acts to heal and save only in the Roman Catholic Church. This simply is not true. Nor should we fear that admitting this is equivalent to affirming that God is placing his seal of approval on a religious body other than our own. This simply does not follow.

Religious communities that preach Christ help people come to faith, even though that faith may be incomplete in its expression. And where God's gracious intervention takes place, it can be seen as a seal upon the substance of that faith, not on its defective element.

Men who oppose the Catholic Church may be genuinely dedicated to Christ. And it is possible that even men who are less than dedicated to Christ may preach him effectively enough. St. Paul noted this apparent contradiction nineteen hundred years ago. From his prison, he heard of some who were preaching Christ "from motives of envy and rivalry." What does it matter, he calmly stated, so long as Christ is proclaimed (see Phil. 1:14-18). Wherever we find genuine faith and the power of the risen Lord at work to heal the tortured bodies and souls of our separated brethren, we should thank God for his mercy and avoid needless contention.

The Pentecostal Movement

Please tell us about the pentecostal movement. What is the Church's stand on this movement? Are there any books published by Catholics by Catholics giving accounts of their experience in this sect?

There is a pentecostal movement in Protestantism and one in Catholic circles. The Protestant Pentecostal Churches emerged from a movement that began at the turn of the century. Currently, they are reputed to be the fastest growing denomination in the religious world.

The Catholic pentecostal movement, however is not a church or a sect. It is just a movement — small groups of Catholics have begun to gather together in the past few years to sing and pray and form a community. The gatherings are loosely structured. They do not replace the sacraments and the liturgy. Rather, they provide an atmosphere of people who are "accepting" and who are open to one another, a climate that is often charged with emotion. Through meditation and shared reflections and experiences, they strive to enter into a direct and personal contact with the Holy Spirit. They have a profound conviction that the Holy Spirit dwells within his people (John 14:16-17), and they expect that he should let himself be *experienced* by those who seek him.

Those who have participated in these prayer meetings claim that the presence of the Spirit has been shown by the phenomenon of "speaking in tongues" in praise of God, by apparent liberation from moral or psychological problems, by a new eagerness for and penetrating understanding of the Scriptures, and by a new fervor in prayer and life and fidelity to the Church.

What is the Church's "stand" on the pentecostal movement? Among our separated brethren, she regards with respect the genuine religious aspirations of the genuinely good people who belong to these rather informal assemblies. This is her basic ecumenical stance toward men of every religious affiliation. I know of no "official stand" of the Church on the pentecostals among us. The movement has arisen as a somewhat spontaneous lay initiative. If it bears good fruit, all Catholics will rejoice in its spiritual vitality. If it gives rise to the questionable fruit of excessive emotionalism, illusion, delusion, or the separatism of an "in" group, then I expect that the leaders of the Church will exercise their God-given responsibility to help these people to channel their enthusiasm more appropriately (cf. I Thess. 5:12, 19-21; Vatican II *Constitution on the Church*, no. 12).

A paperback book is available that gives a good account of the pentecostal movement in the Church: K. and D. Ranaghan, *Catholic Pentecostals* (New York, Deus Books, 1969). Also, *The Pentecostal Movement in the Catholic Church*, by E. D. O'Connor C.S.C. (Notre Dame, Ave Maria, 1971).

To the extent that the movement is healthy, it seems to me to be a reaction against approaches to religion that so emphasize the group that they leave little room for the person and so insist on the truth that we find God in human encounter with our brethren as to seem to forget the truth that God also calls us to an intimate person-to-person relationship with himself. The Spirit always reminds the Church that Christ would not only have us be his servants and agents in the world; he calls us to be with him as friends (see John 15:15).

Worship in Another Church

I have always understood that a Catholic who, without obtaining permission from the proper authority and on his own volition, participates in a non-Catholic church service is guilty of serious sin. Is the Catholic partner of a valid mixed marriage exempt from such a law?

The general law of the Church concerning a Catholic's attending services in a non-Catholic church is not as strict today as it was when we were growing up. Today, the law is content to describe certain situations in which reasons of public office, blood relationship, friendship, a desire to be better informed, et cetera, can suffice to permit a Catholic's occasional participation in our separated brethren's worship.

There are two considerations that we must keep in mind in these situations. The first is that I must be sure that my action does not endanger my faith, that it does not implicitly say "one church is as good as another." If going to another church should begin to mean this for a particular person, then it would be a serious sin to continue to place his faith in jeopardy. The second consideration is that a Catholic should be careful that his action is not the occasion of weakening the faith of one not as strong as himself.

Is the fact of a valid mixed marriage something which exempts a Catholic from these considerations? By no means. It might mean that the occasions on which it is appropriate for the Catholic to attend his non-Catholic partner's church might be more frequent than they would otherwise. But even here, if this would involve a danger of real scandal to children, partner, or neighbor — then it would be necessary to take a very restrictive stance.

Rather than lay down a law that seems to cover every case, the Church is content to offer guidelines and urge us to apply them wisely. And where there is a sticky local situation, the bishops may give their directives. If the local bishop hasn't said anything then there doesn't seem to be any permission needed to follow these broad guidelines.

Teaching Authority Limited

I understand that the Roman Catholic hierarchy has interpreted as applying to themselves the words of Christ granting authority to bind and loose on earth. They see this as an authority to teach (not merely an authority to declare what is or is not sinful). Are there no restrictions on their authority? Could they abolish the Ten Commandments or teach the opposite of what Christ taught?

You are right. The Roman Catholic Church does interpret the "binding and loosing" texts in chapters 16 and 18 of Matthew as authorizing the successors of Saint Peter and the apostolic college to teach and rule in the Church.

But it does not understand this mission as a declaration of independence freeing the hierarchy from obedience to the word of God. Their authority is a service. They are to serve the Church by holding fast to the faith confided to them and by exercising the appropriate leadership that will strengthen men in this biblical faith. They are not answerable to a board of directors — in this sense, there is no restriction on their authority. But they are responsible to teach in accordance with the Sacred Scriptures and the Christian faith.

There is a passage in one of the documents that the hierarchy approved during the Vatican Council that expresses its understanding of how the teaching authority is limited. "The task of authentically interpreting the word of God, whether written or handed on, has been entrusted exclusively to the living teaching office of the Church, whose authority is exercised in the name of Jesus Christ. *This teaching office is not above the word of God,* but serves it, teaching only what has been handed on, listening to it devoutly, guarding it scrupulously, and explaining it faithfully by divine commission and with the help of the Holy Spirit; it draws from this one deposit of faith everything which it presents for belief as divinely revealed.

"It is clear, therefore, that sacred tradition, Sacred Scripture, and the teaching authority of the Church, in accord with God's most wise design, are so linked and joined together that one cannot stand without the others and that all together and each in its own way under the action of the one Holy Spirit contribute effectively to the salvation of souls" (*Dogmatic Constitution on Divine Revelation*, no. 10).

5
Questions
of
Belief

For Whom Can We Pray?

Could you explain why announced Masses for non-Catholics are not permitted? If priests may say a Mass in private for non-Catholics, why not priest and people, too?

It is hard to understand why there should ever have been any fuss about praying for our non-Catholic friends and neighbors. The policy forbidding this seems to have been punitive in intent. It presumed that those who belonged to the other churches had been guilty of the sin of heresy and had cut themselves off from the community of believers. Consequently, they were excluded from the public prayers of the Church. Their freely chosen separation was made visible. Anyone who might be tempted to follow would be induced, it was hoped, to think again when he saw such a total exclusion. But really, did people like Abraham Lincoln and Herbert Hoover qualify as personally guilty of the sin of heresy because they did not belong to the Catholic Church? Did it make sense to refuse to gather a parish together to celebrate the Eucharist for the repose of their great souls when they died?

The only basis in Church law that I can find for the practice of "no announced Masses" is Canon 2262, which forbids publicizing a Mass that is offered for an excommunicated person. And Canon 2314 proclaims an excommunication for those who commit the sin of heresy. However, as the recent Council declared in its *Decree on Ecumenism*: "One cannot charge with the sin of separation those who at present are born into these communities and in them are brought up in the faith of Christ" (no. 3). Those who are converts may remember the solemn ceremony of the abjuration of heresy and the absolution from censures that accompanied their entrance into the Church. This implied that their former allegiance was a sin of heresy — and this simply was not true. Just as the Church has now abandoned the general requirement of the abjuration and absolution, so, and on the same grounds, announced Masses are being celebrated for non-Catholics in many places already. I'm sure that the policy will soon come abreast of the principle everywhere.

How Many Dogmas?

Since there are so many changes in practices and beliefs in the Catholic Church lately and since only the dogmas have to be be-

lieved, could you please tell me how many dogmas of the Church there are and what they state? Are there too many to list in your column and, if so, where can I find a list?

This looks like a simple enough question that ought to get a straight-forward answer. We know what a dogma is: a truth revealed by God and proclaimed by the Church as something that every Catholic must believe. The proclamation of a dogma must be absolutely clear. It may be either a formal definition by pope or council or the universal teaching of all the bishops of the Church in union with the pope. So, how many are there? Honestly, I don't know. Nor is there any list of dogmas available that I know of.

The task of identifying which official teaching of the Church is a dogma and which is just an authorized explanation of the content of the faith is not as simple as we once presumed it was. Clearly the Immaculate Conception and the Assumption are dogmas. So are the infallibility of the pope, the divinity of Christ, the divine maternity, the consubstantiality of God the Son with God the Father, and the unique real presence of Christ in the Eucharist. But is it a dogma that angels exist, that women may not be ordained priests, that artificial birth control is always wrong, that all men are physically descended from Adam? Several years ago, I thought so. Now I no longer do. This does not mean that I am now certain that these are in no way revealed by God. Rather, it means that I now see that it is not perfectly clear that the Church has ever made a once and for all judgment that states these things are contained in God's revelation and must be believed by all the faithful.

Does this make our faith a shaky thing? It shouldn't. What we believe most of all is not dogmas but a Person. By faith we hand ourselves over to God in Jesus Christ, whom we find in the Catholic Church. Belief is a loving, trusting relationship to God. Because we trust him, we are ready to accept whatever is guaranteed by his word. And we have the assurance that it is his word when we receive it in and through the Church.

In these times, it becomes increasing apparent that God's truth is found in a middle-of-the-road position between two extremes. There are some who are minimizing, who are attempting to explain everything away. This is hardly the way to that purity of faith by which we will be wholly open to the word of God. Pope Paul was thinking of this when he lamented that some "are trying to attribute to the council every type of novelty, especially in the way of understanding the faith and presenting it to the contemporary world, even going so far as to question fundamental doctrines of Catholicism, declaring that truths defined by the Church are matters of opinion, demanding freedom of conscience and attributing to the inspiration of the Holy Spirit arbitrary and personal judgments regarding important and often constitutional principles of ecclesiastical thought and discipline" (August 9, 1967).

On the other hand, there are those who would see dogma in every practice of the Church up to now. Consequently, any change appears to them as an abandonment of the truth of God. Both are extremes, and both are false.

The core of our faith endures through every change. We believe that the Church is the community of salvation. They belong to it who accept in faith the Good News that God our Father has gathered us together. We are a worshiping community in the only Son, Jesus Christ, through the gift of the Holy Spirit. The truth of this gospel we all profess in the Apostles' Creed. The practice we share is the service of love and worship which comes to fullest expression in the liturgy of the seven sacraments — especially in the Eucharist.

The Church has a message and a teaching, but one need not be especially learned or even well informed to be a Catholic. In this time of change, our ground of security rests with the Church. Not every theologian's suggestion or proposal will be found by the Church to reflect the truth of the Gospel. But we can be sure that when the Church — above all, the pope and bishops — accepts a new view and institutes changes in the way we express or practice our faith, it will be the Spirit of Christ who is leading us into new riches in the selfsame faith.

Jesus—A Historical Personage

I have read your writings at the request of a friend who is trying to get a feather in his hat by bringing me back into the fold of the "Mother Church" which I left in disgust many years ago. I have had debates with him on the historicity of Jesus and the Gospels, and I have promised him to write to you. I do this knowing full well the futility of this letter, but at least you shall know not all your readers are illiterate, if you know what I mean. . . . It can be shown that the Gospels cannot have been written by eyewitnesses, nor even by Jews or Romans. Rather, they were written from one to two hundred years after the alleged death of Jesus. Jesus simply was **NOT** a historical figure. I challenge you or anyone to produce

genuine historical evidence of the existence of Jesus. I offer to forfeit one thousand dollars to anyone who will provide such evidence.

I'm sorry you are so angry. It makes it far more difficult to discuss things rationally.

The life of Jesus does indeed present a problem for the modern historian, but not the fact that he lived. Throughout the ages there have been many men who have challenged the Christian faith. They reject our conviction that Jesus is the Son of God, in a unique and proper sense, that he was born of a virgin, and that he rose from the dead. Some claim that the disciples of Jesus conspired in a Passover plot and that the faith of Christians grew out of a hoax. Others maintain that the exalted religious experience of the first Christians caused them to embellish the story of his life with fictional details of their own contriving. But none of these denies that a man named Jesus lived in Palestine during the reigns of the Roman Emperors Augustus and Tiberius and that he died on a cross as many other Jews of his time did.

The modern historian has a problem with the life of Jesus because the Gospels, our sole source of information about his life, are not written with a modern biographer's concern for time and place and sequence of events. There are interpretative elements. From the vantage point of a full faith in the risen Lord, the authors of the Gospels do color what Jesus actually said and did, in order to make it express more fully the truth of his Person and mission. Before his resurrection, this truth was not fully manifest. The Evangelists are writing for believers to help them in Christian living. They are not writing a chronicle. It is not a distortion for them to present the portrait of Jesus enriched by the light of their faith. Today, while modern scholars agree that this makes it impossible to compose a "Life of Jesus," in the modern sense of a biography, they also increasingly agree with the Catholic conviction that there is a great deal of real historical detail to be found in the faith-portrait of the Gospels.

You ask for genuine historical evidence that Jesus lived. It exists and is accepted, as far as I can ascertain, by all serious historians. However, it isn't the same kind of evidence we can offer to show that Franklin Roosevelt existed. We can't produce a birth certificate, tax receipts, police records, order of execution, et cetera. We have no documents signed in his own hand. Outside of Christian writings, we have only two undisputed first-century references to him in

Latin authors (Tacitus, *Annals*, 15:44, and Pliny the Younger, *Epist.*, 10:69), and one in Flavius Josephus, the Jewish author (*Jewish Antiquities*, 20:9-1). The evidence for the existence of Jesus of Nazareth rests primarily on the fact of Christianity. Before the year seventy, we find communities of Christians all over the Middle East and in Rome and Spain. This means that a great many men and women, separated by only a generation from the "alleged death" of Jesus, have given credit to a story of the resurrection of Jesus. It is beyond probability that so many could have committed so much of themselves to the service of a man who never was. For this was at a time when the facts of his life or nonexistence were still available to them through those who had lived with him. People just aren't that gullible.

You say that the Gospels were written very late. This was a view held in some circles, but it was conclusively discredited early in this century. All agree that the Gospel according to John is the latest of the four canonical Gospels. Papyrus fragments containing small sections of this Gospel, just as we have it today, were discovered in Egypt during the 1930's. These remnants of a perished volume can be dated no later than the year 150. What this means is that early in the second century, the last of the four Gospels was already known in Egypt. Clearly, then, the date of its composition must be set no later than the year 100. Otherwise, there would hardly be time for it to have circulated and been copied in Egypt. There is, then, no basis for attacking the conviction that there is a personal link between the written Gospels and the events of the life and death of Jesus. The Gospels are not eyewitness reports. But they report the faith of those who either were eyewitnesses of Jesus' life or were in contact with eyewitnesses.

Granting your present state of disbelief in Christianity, I couldn't expect you to agree with our faith that Jesus of Nazareth is true God. We hold this, not on the basis of historical evidence, but solely on the authoritative word of God. But forgive me for feeling that a man must be very angry or very unreasonable to maintain that the Son of Mary existed only as the product of a deranged and fertile collective imagination. That Jesus lived and died almost two thousand years ago is a fact. It is supported by the same kind of genuine historical evidence that leads men to affirm the existence of Moses and David and Cleopatra and Alexander and Charlemagne.

Did Jesus Know He Was God?

We have been hearing some religious teachers say that Jesus did not know that he was God until after his resurrection. When we cite passages from the Scriptures which indicate that he did know, we are told we can't be sure he said those things in just those words. What does the Church teach on this?

The Church has no official teaching on this matter. It is a matter of theological interpretation and conclusion. The Church confesses the faith, to which all Christians must subscribe, that the man Jesus who was born of the Virgin Mary, died on the cross, and rose glorious and immortal is the Son of God. The Church teaches that he is, and always was from the first moment of his human existence, true God and true man.

It is a matter of faith that he lived a span of mortal existence, a man like us in all things, sin alone excepted. What was his mind like? How did he think of himself? Unfortunately, we don't have any direct way of knowing. We have no written records nor personal reminiscences that would unlock for us the secrets of the inner workings of the human consciousness of the Man who was personally One of the Trinity.

It might seem, at first, that the Scriptures would help us. They do indeed assure us that Jesus identified himself by some extraordinary titles derived from the religious experience of Israel that indicate his awareness that he was uniquely related to God and that his mission was of decisive importance for the salvation of his people. But they do not tell us, in words that we can be sure he himself spoke, of the nature of his unique closeness to the Father. (To repeat what we have written elsewhere, the words ascribed to our Lord that point most explicitly to his divinity are not verbatim quotations. They are the divinely inspired words of the sacred authors, who are underscoring the reality they have come to know by faith. They tell the truth about Jesus. And they are written in order to lead men to the same faith. But they are not necessarily a transcript of what he said.)

How about the disciples of Christ? If they lived with him through the years of his public life, must it not have occurred to them to ask this kind of question? Not if they did not come to an awareness of the mystery of his divine Person until after the Resurrection — and most students of the Bible would maintain this.

The only data that we have, then, with which to approach this question is the Easter faith of the Church as it came to be reflected upon and clarified during the early centuries of the Church's life. The central conviction is this — Jesus is true man and true God. He is not two beings. And yet the single person that he is exists as man and as God.

Jesus was a man whose contemporaries knew him to be one of them. He grew up in a family. He knew hunger and pain and fatigue. He was a man of genuine human feeling. He had a brilliant flair for getting to the heart of things and a most magnetic and persuasive personality. But like other men, the evidence available to us indicates that he worked by trial and error, changing his style and plans when obstacles arose. It is hard to see that this manhood, this assuming of the human condition, this sharing of pain and anguish could have been real if he were constantly aware of the mystery of his divine person in such a way that if someone had asked him who he was, he could have responded, "I am the eternal Word of God made flesh."

On the other hand, the reality of his divine Personhood would seem to be reduced to nothing if one were to maintain that it made no impact on his human mind. You are rightly repelled by the suggestion that the Resurrection brought him into contact with his true self in a way that he would practically be meeting a stranger.

So here we are at the heart of the mystery that theologians have been wrestling with, more or less unsatisfactorily, for centuries. I know of no reputable theologians who will say that Jesus did not know that he was God until after the Resurrection and leave it there. Yet a number of modern theologians will distinguish, in the human knowledge of Christ, between a self-consciousness that is intuitive and inexpressible and the ordinary form of knowledge that is conceived through experience and expressed in words. They will suggest that Jesus' human knowledge of himself as God took the first form. It was a genuine union between his human mind and the divine Self — and therefore it was knowledge. Yet it did not come to him in a way that had anything in common with the world of images, ideas, and speech. It was a knowledge that was made possible by a divine light like that which makes beatific vision possible for the saints. But since it was illumining a mind still bound by the conditions of this life, the content of this knowledge was something that was literally inexpressible. From the beginning of his human existence, Jesus would have this intuition of who he is. But it would be only gradually that he could acquire the ability to articulate it in human thought and word, even to himself.

In this view, the man Jesus was present to himself, and that Self was divine. Yet, since it was a presence that was incapable of being brought to the level where the affairs of human life are lived and reflected upon, it did not make Jesus' experience of being a man essentially different from ours. He had to grow and learn. And when his life climaxed in the awful days of the Passion, he died as men die: with all of a man's anguish and the need to entrust himself into the hands of his Father.

All of this is merely a theory — and my reporting of it is but the barest sketch of a tendency that has been worked out by fine and loyal Catholic theologians. Granted that it is not entirely satisfying, nevertheless it skirts the pitfalls of those theological views that describe the psychology of Jesus in ways that make him seem to be God masquerading as a man or merely a good man who "becomes" God in the Resurrection. In the last analysis, we must admit that we cannot imagine what the self-awareness was like of him who is God in a human way and man in a genuinely divine way.

Risen—Raised?

Formerly the Resurrection was emphatically described by phrase "He is risen." In the new Missals, it has become "He has been raised." This is not nearly as strong, and I want to know why this change?

The mystery of the Resurrection can be considered from two points of view, one passive and the other active. In the first, the emphasis is on the truth that the Resurrection is the heavenly Father's acceptance of Jesus' sacrifice — an acceptance that is expressed by God the Father raising the dead body of Jesus to new and glorious life. This point of view predominates in the theologies of St. Paul's Epistles and the Acts of the Apostles. The characteristic phrase of this view is, "He has been raised."

In the second point of view, the emphasis is on the truth that the Resurrection is the supreme victory of the God-Man, who has power to lay down his life and to take it up again. This is expressed by "He rose again."

Both points of view are correct, and the expressions are complementary. I think that if you examine it closely, you will see that the expression "He is risen" expresses the state in which the Lord is and remains rather neutral as regards these two points of view. I also think that it used to be used to translate a passive tense of the Greek verb which is far more accurately rendered by, "He has been raised." In any event, the passive point of view, which emphasizes the role of God the Father in the economy of salvation, does not in any way diminish the conviction of faith that Jesus, as the Incarnate consubstantial Son of the Father, "of his own power rose the third day" (Pope Paul VI, *The Credo of the People of God,* June 30, 1968).

Why Sacrifice?

Why is sacrifice supposed to be pleasing to God? Is God pleased with man's suffering, or does he want the death or destruction of any living thing?

Your instincts are good. If the whole idea behind sacrifice is to make men miserable, then there's something unhealthy about it. Some people tend to think of sacrifice after the model of horribly depraved ritual murder. To say that this sort of thing "pleases" God is to make God out to be some sort of sadistic monster who is pleased when he "gets even" with sinful men. It is even to imagine God to be a bit stupid — one who can be conned into being on our side because we offer him a ritual gift, however insincerely.

Obviously these notions are out of kilter with everything God has revealed about himself. God is not one who pouts about our misdeeds and waits for us to take a first and costly step toward him. He is always like the father of the Prodigal, anticipating our return. We can give him nothing that enriches him in any way. He is not greedy or grasping. Consequently, our sacrifices and gifts either enrich the people who offer sacrifice or are worthless.

How does sacrifice enrich man? By providing him with the means of expressing his profound need of God and his desire to enter into communion with him. In every true sacrifice, there are always two elements. One is external. It is a symbolic, religious action which may take the form of offering a gift to God or sharing a meal offered to God. The other element is interior. It consists in the inner religious sentiments of humble adoration, gratitude, contrition for sin, and dependence on his mercy.

If ever we have the external symbolic action without the inner spirit of adoration, we have the kind of hideous fraud that God abhors. Against this hypocrisy the prophets of Israel cried out with fierce indignation (see Amos 4:4; Isaiah 1:11-16). On the other hand, where there is such a spiritualization that it never finds any external expression, we can begin to wonder if there's anything really there in the first place. It begins to look like the case of the husband who professes a profound love for his wife and family but who always manages to stay away from them.

The one sacrifice of the New Testament is that of our Lord, in whose reality we share through the sacramental sacrifice of the Mass. Christ's sacrifice was an offering in blood. It involved horrible suffering. Yet is was not suffering and death that had the special force of "pleasing" God. Rather, it was Jesus' personal act of submission and love in laying down his life for his friends, in handing himself over into the care of his heavenly Father.

God is not pleased with man's suffering. But the suffering that is an inevitable part of man's life can now be a way of his sharing in the redemptive death of Christ that issued in the glory of his Resurrection.

Predestination

St. Augustine's writings about divine predestination have been very troublesome for me. According to St. Augustine, the only souls that reach heaven are the ones God has prechosen. God arranges the circumstances of life that will lead a soul to him. He provides a special grace which a soul must have to reach heaven. It seems to me that the lot of the non-elect is hell, no matter how good they are. Does this not seem to contradict Christ's purpose for coming into the world? Augustine's philosophy, as I see it, is one of despair?

St. Augustine was a genius and a man profoundly attuned to God's own thoughts about himself, as only a saintly theologian can be. But he was also a man. And every human expression of the mystery of God is always partial and stammering. There are aspects which he does not take into consideration. There are elements insufficiently emphasized for our tastes. But in no way does St. Augustine make God into the master of a cosmic puppet show who manipulates us in a way that makes a mockery of our freedom.

Augustine was led to consider the mystery of predestination because of a struggle that embroiled the Western Church in his day. His antagonist was a Celtic monk named Pelagius, who preached a doctrine that made salvation a merely human work.

In the process of human self-betterment, Christ's role was reduced to that of a useful example; an interior gift of grace was unnecessary; in fact, it is hard to see where a real, personal God fitted into his scheme of things at all. A good part of St. Augustine's writing was directed against this perversion of Christian asceticism and moral life. Augustine wrote most eloquently on the radical impossibility of any man's coming to eternal life apart from an absolutely gratuitous gift from God, the gift of grace.

Beginning with a consideration of man's need of grace and underscoring the fact that grace is a totally unmerited and free gift, Augustine did not stop with his reflections on the effects of grace in man. He looked at the mystery of grace and human destiny from God's point of view. He saw that in speaking about God's plan, we cannot say anything that implies that he has to wait for a man's co-operation before determining to grant the grace that will enable him to come to eternal happiness. If it were otherwise, God would be dependent on his free creature. God's gifts have no other motive than his mercy, and his mercy is from all eternity. In God, then, there is not merely a foresight of what man might do or will do; there is an absolutely certain knowledge of those who will be saved and an arrangement of the gifts of grace that will bring man to this goal. There is predestination.

This does, of course, raise the problem of those who are not predestined. But St. Augustine would never raise it in the same way you do — nor would any knowledgeable Catholic theologian. He would not say that the non-elect, "no matter how good," go to hell. There is no despairing fatalism in St. Augustine or in Catholic theology. The only way to hell is by a person's own free hardening in sin. No one is damned "no matter how good" he is or how hard he tries. His goodness and his effort are the result of the free gift of grace that God is giving him, and Christian hope expects that God, who has begun a good work in him, will see it through to its heavenly completion (Phil. 1:6).

St. Augustine's theology of predestination was not a total picture, nor is it totally satisfying. Its substance has become an integral part of Catholic doctrine. Many theologians have attempted to harmonize the various aspects of this mystery that baffles our minds. They have struggled to correlate the eternal with the temporal, God's definitive certainty with man's responsibility for his unknown future, God's changeless omnipotence with man's genuine freedom. None of them answers all our questions, but all of them hold fast to these conviction:

1. God calls all men to salvation in Christ.

2. God, in his mercy, has predestined to grace and glory those who will be saved.

3. God does not predestine any man to evil, nor does he refuse the grace of conversion to those who have freely turned away from him.

4. "Those who have done good shall go into life eternal, but those who have done evil into eternal fire" (Athanasian Creed).

For my part, I don't find Augustine's thought to be one of despair. I feel more secure leaving my eternal destiny in the hands of a merciful Father than I would if I trusted only in the unpredictable stability of my own free will. As St. Paul reminds us, "Is it possible that he who did not spare his own Son but handed him over for the sake of us all will not grant us all things besides?" (Rom. 8:32).

Providence and Luck

I have read the following in a prayer book concerning the will of God: "Nothing happens in the material or the moral world which God has not foreseen from all eternity and which he has not willed or at least permitted." On the other hand St. Thomas Aquinas says, in his "Summa contra Gentiles" that divine providence does not exclude fortune or chance. Will you please explain this seeming contradiction.

Hold onto your prayer book but by all means read St. Thomas. He is becoming a forgotten author today. Yet his doctrine deserves the praise Pope Paul showered upon it on September 10, 1965: "Among the Doctors of the Church, St. Thomas Aquinas holds the first place. He had such a brilliant intellect, such a sincere love of truth, such wisdom in penetrating, presenting, and synthesizing the most profound truths that his doctrine is a most efficacious instrument, not only to shore up the foundations of the faith, but also to reap the fruits of healthy progress effectively and safely."

You quote St. Thomas accurately. The citation is from *Summa contra Gentiles,* III, 74. The double negative (*not ex*cluded) does not mean that some things happen that God did not foresee. The whole burden of the chapter is to affirm that even those things which *we* cannot predict (what the ancients called fortune or chance) are *included* in God's master plan of the universe. The certainty of God's providence does not prevent some things happening to us that are humanly unpredictable. Our best calculations cannot provide for every contingency. A bolt in a steering assembly might be defective, and the most careful driver in the world may have an accident. For the driver, it is chance, bad luck if you will. Has this escaped God's providence? No. God's providence includes what we consider luck or chance.

Why does God's plan make room for these chance happenings that often bring such tragedy? No man can give a perfectly satisfying answer. Speaking of the mystery of Israel's apparent rejection, St. Paul writes: "How deep are the riches and the wisdom and the knowledge of God! How inscrutable his judgments, how unsearchable his ways" (Rom. 11:33). On the other hand, if God's providence excluded what we call chance or fortune, many wonderful friends would never have met, the medical and technical marvels we take for granted would never have been discovered, and life would be rather drab. God's providence is such that he "makes all things work together for the good of those who have been called according to his decree" (Rom. 8:28) — all things! including those which happen by chance or fortune.

Reincarnation

I have become convinced of reincarnation. It explains many of the unanswered questions of life, such as the inequality of birth. Also, it is a more Christlike doctrine than that of an everlasting hell with no hope of salvation. I cannot believe that God ever completely withdraws from us in this life or the next. I hope I'm not a heretic, but I believe everyone will return to God through the spiritual evolution of reincarnation. I understand that some of the early Fathers of the Church taught this same thing.

Belief in reincarnation is incompatible with the Gospel of Jesus Christ as it is taught in the Catholic Church.

The word "reincarnation" refers to the belief that the human soul passes from one human body to another, in which it is born to a new earthly existence. It is narrower than the term "metempsychosis," which refers to the passing of the soul at death into another body — human, animal, or vegetable.

The idea that the soul passes at death into another body is part of the common patrimony of primitive peoples. In India, the primitive idea was caught up with a religious philosophy; first, that of Brahmanism, and then that of Buddhism. In both of these views, the goal of the cycle of reincarnations is an interior, personal purification that will be complete when the identity of the self and the world is attained or when the soul reaches that state of annihilating all desire and individual consciousness, which are seen as the source of suffering. The idea of reincarnation also appears in ancient Greece in the mystery religions and in some currents of Platonism and Pythagoreanism.

In recent times, the idea of reincarnation has been propagated in the religious thought of Theosophy. In some Theosophical and Spiritist reflections, reincarnation seems almost to be a substitute for the Christian dogma of purgatory. Through his separate bodily existences, which are pleasant or miserable, depending on his having lived well or badly before, a person expiates the sins of his prior life. Unlike the doctrine of purgatory, there is no room in all this for genuine personal love or responsibility or for any ultimately relevant choice that fixes one's relationship to God. Eventually and inevitably, every person will complete the purifying process, whether he wants to or not.

It is interesting to note what are the bases of these doctrines of reincarnation. They are not based either on any compelling evidence or on a special revelation. They come either from a primitive intuition of the special deathlessness of the human spirit or from a point of view that permeates a vision of the nature and goal of the universe. As Christians, aware that we are called to live forever in a glorious resurrection, we have the reality which the primitive intuition pointed to without having the primitive's need to have recourse to a questionable theory of reincarnation. As contemporary men of the West, we cannot share the real meaning of the Hindu and Buddhist teaching, unless we share their vision of the nature of human existence and of material reality. While reincarnation might perhaps be an acceptable *symbolic* way of thinking in the East, in Theosophy and the popular cults it tends to be a mishmash that cannot be accepted by a believing Catholic and that is hard for anyone to justify rationally.

The early Fathers of the Church did not teach reincarnation. There was a theory that Origen (who died around 254) put forward which has been called "Apocatastasis" (the final restoration of all things). This was part of the package called "Origenism" that was rejected by the Church in the sixth century. According to this view, every evil that a man endures has a directly medicinal purpose. There is no room in this doctrine for ultimate alienation from God as the penalty for sin. In the end, the victory of the Redeeming Christ will restore all things to the order originally intended by God — every rational creature, including the damned and the demons, will surrender to the love of Christ and be saved.

The roots of the theory are found more in Platonic philosophy than in the Gospel. In common with reincarnation theories, Origenism maintained the preexistence of human souls and the view that after death there is still time for conversion. The Church rejects this possibility by her definitive teaching that a person's eternal lot is fixed immediately upon dying.

Your conviction about reincarnation seems to derive from the fact that it makes some problems of human existence easier to live with. However, a theory that comforts a person for the time being is of little value unless it is correct.

It is certainly easy to understand the unequal and disadvantaged situation into which some men are born, if one has a theory that explains all this as the result of sins they committed in an earlier existence. Then we can be comfortable knowing that their miserable way of life is a purifying opportunity for them to have a better existence the next time around. It may be easy to understand, but I think it's hideous.

If man is not endowed with the capacity for full freedom and personhood, then the poor, spineless victim deserves an unlimited series of second chances forever. However, the Christian view of human life proclaims that man is made in the image of God, gifted with everything that is necessary for him to accept Christ's invitation to turn to his heavenly Father. This vision of human dignity also involves a tremendous risk. For the mystery of the person who has the capacity to love is that he also has the option to shut himself off from love. God never withdraws from men in this life or the next. But man can choose to be eternally closed to him.

I suggest that you talk over your spiritual problems with a competent adviser. I believe that a balanced Catholic theology can give you far more help with the problems of injustice, suffering, and eternity than you will find in any questionable theory of reincarnation.

Body and Soul

In a recent issue of a daily paper, I read these words attributed to a member of an experimental form of religious life. The Brother

said: "Under the old Platonic idea, man had a body and a soul. The body belonged to this world and was bad automatically. The only thing important was that the soul ascend to God. But modern ideas have changed. With modern science, there is a new view of the world. The body and soul are one thing. They cannot be divided." Have things changed so much?

Let's take the statement as it stands. We have no way of knowing if the young religious is being quoted accurately — exact quotation is becoming a disappearing art, and the poor man's observation may be misrepresented. Now, then, a few remarks. It is true that the Platonic view of man was flawed by a dualism that saw the body and the soul as two things joined in an alliance that was unfortunate for the soul. The goal of authentic human striving was to free the soul from all the material conditions that imprisoned and limited it. It is also true that this Platonic view infected some Christians and gave rise to an excessively pessimistic view of the human body, of the world, of secular reality, et cetera. But it is not true that Platonic dualism belongs to the Christian vision or that it has been in official possession in Catholic teaching and Catholic theology.

The Church does not teach that man *has* a body and soul. She teaches that man is composed of a body and a soul — that is, man *is* his body and soul. He is an incarnate spirit or an animated body, whichever you prefer. He must reverence his bodiliness, while not losing sight of the fact that he is "superior to bodily concerns." There is "in him a spiritual and immortal soul," which is destined to enjoy a happy life with God after death while awaiting reunion with its body. (Cf. *Constitution on the Church in the Modern World*, nos. 14, 18.) Body and soul are one thing — that is, they are the perfect unity of a single human person. But they are not of one and the same material stuff, and they can be divided, or rather, separated — as they are, in fact, at the awful moment of death. The remarks of the young man are, then, at least intemperate, and the concluding sentence is wrong.

My own immediate reaction to remarks like these is hostile, I must confess. I find it difficult to abide the arrogance with which angry young men caricature the venerable convictions of the Christian people in order to devastate them. Yet this reaction is itself intemperate. Far better, we should try to understand what the Brother is trying to say. Can't we read here a rebellion against a distortion of Catholic truth and life? A distortion which makes the quest of spiritual perfection into a neurosis of fear: fear of being soiled by accepting the simple human joys of life and love and art and friendship. This fear has been cultivated in some religious living and in some of the writing that is professedly spiritual.

Don't we perhaps have here a rejection of that ersatz religiosity that prays in selfish and solitary indifference to whether the hungry, naked, and sick are fed, clothed, or visited? The Christian mystery is replete with paradoxes. The Church is a harmony of apparent irreconcilables. Vatican II describes it this way: "It is of the essence of the Church that she be both human and divine, visible and yet invisibly endowed, eager to act and yet devoted to contemplation, present in this world and yet not at home in it. She is all these things in such a way that in her the human is directed and subordinated to the divine, the visible likewise to the invisible, action to contemplation, and this present world to that city yet to come, which we seek" (*Constitution on the Sacred Liturgy, no. 2*). When we find distortion and exaggeration swinging out in one direction, it might indeed be salutary to see if our own narrowness in the opposite direction has not perhaps provoked the reaction.

What Happened to the Angels?

What's this about the new theology on angels? I asked one young priest to recommend something to read on the subject. He told me there could be nothing written about the angels, since angels do not exist. Has the Church taken the position that angels absolutely do not exist or that they may possibly exist? I understand that the Church can change its opinion or its explanation, but I do resent being told told "angels do not exist" and, with no explanation, being asked to accept that.

As far as I can make out, the rumor about the demise of the angels is a bit premature. Let's look at the facts.

In favor of the existence of God's ministering spirits we have the following evidence. Angels are frequently mentioned in both Old and New Testaments. Angels are referred to in the solemn statements of the Church's faith: the Creed confesses God as creator of all things, visible and invisible. Angels are celebrated in the feasts of the Church's liturgical year.

Where's the problem? Well, the fact that the Bible mentions angels proves that the Jews, like all peoples of the Near East, believed in their existence, but it does not necessarily prove that their belief in this unseen world is based on a word of God. It could be simply a common and unchallenged assumption of their culture — as when our Lord mentions the "sign of Jonah" who was three days in the belly of the whale. He does not teach that a person named Jonah had such an experience, He uses the central character of this beautiful parable (which his contemporaries probably assumed was history) to make another point entirely. Similarly with the references to the angelic world in the creeds and definitions of the councils. The point that they are teach is that God created *all* things: nothing comes into being independently of his creative power, be it visible or invisible. These statements are not directly concerned with the question: Has God told us that there is a world of invisible beings? Remarks made along the way by councils (sometimes called *obiter dicta*) are not the object of their authoritative teaching. What about the liturgy? The liturgy celebrates the feasts that express the faith and religious feeling of the Christian people. It does not provide an independent guarantee of the content of that faith that is more solid than its sources. Hence it *is thinkable* that we can reexamine the question of the existence of angels.

However, what reexamination has occurred has not resulted in any conclusive evidence that permits us to set aside the warning of Pope Pius XII against those who "question whether angels are personal beings" (*Humani Generis,* 1950, no. 42). As a salty theology professor remarked, "Don't throw out the whole of Catholic theology just because some Bible student discovers a Hittite gerundive."

At the same time, it is an exaggeration to say that the existence of angels is a defined dogma of our faith which cannot be denied without one's being guilty of heresy. It may well be revealed that we share God's life with a host of unseen companions — but it does not seem that the Church has ever looked squarely at this question and given a binding, definitive answer.

Meanwhile, the Church still celebrates in her liturgy the feasts of the great archangels and of the angels guardian. She finds no reason to stop the faithful from thinking that God's individual care of each of his children is mediated in part through a created spirit whom we call a guardian angel. And personally I find no difficulty in believing that our universe is peopled by fellow creatures who reflect God's glory so much better than I and with whose unceasing chant of praise I can daily join my voice saying, "Holy, Holy, Holy."

More about Dogma

I find it difficult to understand your insistence that you no longer feel obliged to believe in the existence of angels. Your implication that a future pope or general council might declare angels nonexistent seems somewhat "outre." They would have to tear out whole pages of Sacred Scripture, eviscerate the liturgies of the Jews and the Eastern and Western Catholic Churches, and unsay the dogmatic declaration of the Fourth Lateran Council that God "by his almighty power, from the very beginning of time has created both orders of creatures out of nothing, the spiritual or angelic world and the corporeal or visible universe." And this last declaration was incorporated in a dogmatic decree of Vatican I.

The texts that you cite are the reason why I formerly thought that the existence of angels was a dogma of the Church. It seemed that the Church, in solemn council, was proclaiming its faith, and henceforth the matter was to be considered settled. But the question I raise is this: did the Church *intend* to proclaim its faith in the existence of angels? The only question that a council settles or defines is what it intends to define. And it is only its definitions that are absolutely guaranteed by God's gift of infallibility.

There is no doubt that the Councils mentioned take for granted the common belief that a world of angels exists. But do they set out designedly to affirm this as a truth of faith? Do they fix this common belief as a dogma expressing for all time something revealed by God that must be accepted by all the faithful? Most recent theologians agree that they do not.

Lateran IV is reacting to the Albigensian problems. It is solemnly proclaiming the faith of Christians in the unity of the Triune God, the Creator of everything that exists. It is concerned with excluding the idea that God has an eternal rival who, independently of him, made material and evil things. The bishops, in 1215, *assumed* that "everything" included the angelic world, the material world, man, and the demons — so they mention them all. Their purpose seems to be to make it clear that nothing escapes the creative power of the one God and that all things were created good.

More than 650 years later, the bishops at Vatican I faced new problems about God the Creator. They especially intended to express the faith that creation is an act of sovereign love and liberty, that the created universe is totally other than God who made it, and that there is more to the created universe than matter. This is what they defined. They did not address themselves to the question "Do angels exist?" Hence, their use of the words of Lateran IV does not give these words any more meaning or authority than they had in the first place.

I'm not writing all this to eliminate the angels from our faith and devotion. I have no difficulty accepting the affirmation of Pope Paul VI: "We believe in one only God, Father, Son and Holy Spirit, Creator of things visible . . . of things invisible such as the pure spirits which are also called angels, . . ." (*Credo of the People of God*). The reasons inclining the Church to a belief in the existence of angels are stronger than those that have been alleged against that conviction. However, there is a question of methodology at stake: How are we to read and interpret a decree of a council and how are we to determine which teaching of the Church is a dogma and which not? I cannot agree that this question has been so definitively settled that those who question it are to be considered guilty of heresy.

Theology and Religion

All the distinctions you make concerning what is or is not dogma seem to me like playing with semantics. Our faith is not a question of methodology or of semantics. Too many Catholics are talking to death the basic love and the teachings of Christ. Christ's concern, was never based on methodology, et cetera. Don't encourage people to cut the heart out of our holy faith.

Your point is an excellent one. Theological niceties and true religion are two different things. Theology is concerned with the exact expression of our ideas about God. Religion is concerned with the life of man with God. A person can even become so involved with the problems of theology that he can avoid ever entering the presence of God. That would be a hideous distortion.

Many of the questions I receive are requests for information. It is natural that this would be so at this time when so many of our ways of thinking and speaking about God are undergoing such a profound change. People want to know why a new interpretation of the Scriptures has arisen, how this new thing harmonizes with what they have learned to believe. They want to know what the Church has affirmed as a dogma, what she has taught with lesser certainty, and what is merely a pious, educated guess. They are concerned about the changes in the Church and the thread of continuity in the Church.

The only way to answer these questions honestly involves going into questions of methodology and separating the absolutely certain from the merely probable. It may seem to be hair-splitting. It may seem to be turning aside from the simple and warm statements of our belief that the Gospels give us. It may seem to be playing with words. However, even a surface acquaintance with the history of the Church shows that this apparently sterile approach is absolutely necessary. In the fourth century, over the objections of rigid traditionalists who wanted no new expression of the faith, the Church's theologians coined the word "homo-ousion" to describe the way the Son is like the Father. At that time, it was *the* way to guarantee the orthodox faith of Christians in the redeeming Incarnation and preserve the unity of the Church that was already so badly shattered. It was the theologian's special service to the Church — a service that requires him to pay close attention to the meaning of words and the consequences of ideas.

However, the richer thing by far is what is at the heart of Christianity. More than methodology and words, it is the inner life of a person who is at home with the God who has opened himself to men. It is uniquely personal, while being a life lived in the community of the Church. It is not the preserve of the learned and the brilliant. It is accessible to everyone who can gaze on the crucified Christ and see there how much God loves the world. Even more than theological information, we desperately need men and women who have learned how to pray, those for whom to live is Christ. Even more than the updating of outmoded structures, we need the renewal of men's hearts, which can only come as they learn to abide in God's presence. We need active, involved, and concerned laymen to bring the riches of Christ into every corner of our world. But their deeds and words will ring true only if they are men who live in constant closeness to Christ himself, whom they meet in the Eucharist and in the familiar conversation that is the prayer of faith.

Will I Be Damned?

I am having a terrible time. I cannot force myself to go to confession. I just don't believe in it any more. Also, I think the Pope is wrong about some things, such as the celibacy of priests and the pill — although I am not personally concerned with these matters. Am I going to be damned?

Stop being afraid. No one is ever damned unless he deliberately chooses to separate himself from God and holds fast to that terrible choice at the moment of his death.

As you say, you're having a terrible time — one filled with anxiety. But are you really abandoning our Lord?

It certainly feels to you as if you must be. After all, aren't you giving up convictions that are central to the Catholic faith: the sacramental forgiveness of sins, the belief in the teaching authority of the pope?

However, I am not so sure. Loyal obedience to the Vicar of Christ does not require us to think that he is right when he makes a decision to uphold the rule of celibacy for priests in the Roman Rite of the Church. Good men may hold contrary opinions about important matters of Church policy. One need not be a "yes man" to be a good Catholic.

Again, very good Catholics have defended ideas at variance with the pope's encyclical on birth control. In fact, the bishops of your country, in their pastoral letter applying the pope's teaching to the Canadian scene, took into account the problem of those who could not accept the pope's reasons nor his conclusion. They did not exclude these sincere people from the Church. Far less did they tell them that they were obliged to think that the pope was right in this matter under pain of damnation.

The question of belief in the sacrament of penance is a more serious matter. If your statement were to mean that you no longer believe that God takes sin seriously enough to forgive it or that through his Son he confided the ministry of its forgiveness to the Church, then we would be dealing with something that strikes right at the heart of the Christian faith. If there is no sin nor need of forgiveness, then "redemption" is an empty word, the Church is little more than an amateur social agency we'd be just as well off without, and there would be no point in hoping for salvation or worrying about damnation.

The fact that you are worried about damnation inclines me to think that you are not questioning either sin or its forgiveness. I suspect that you are questioning the value of your own experience of that forgiveness — and that's an entirely different matter. Perhaps you have experienced the sacrament of pardon and peace as a source of anxiety or boredom. Perhaps you expected to feel a sense of wholeness and acceptance through the sacrament, and instead you feel yourself still wounded and unsure after all these years. Perhaps the confessors you have encountered have not really listened to hear the hurt hidden behind the recital of the month's failings. Perhaps the lack of Christlikeness in us priests who are charged with the responsibility of forgiving sin in his name has become too great a hurdle to surmount.

If I'm reading things at all accurately, I see pain and anxiety and frustration and disappointment here. I do not see a rejection of the faith nor an abandonment of our Lord. People are not eternally cut off from God (and that's what damnation is) because they are troubled or anxious but only because they refuse to remain joined to him.

When a person is having as terrible a time as you are, it usually helps very much to talk things through with an understanding counselor. I'm not asking you to force yourself to go to confession. I would urge you, though, to sit down with an understanding priest to try to break through the difficulties that are causing you so much concern.

Fear of Death

How can I overcome my terrible fear of death? Many times my mind is preoccupied with thoughts of some terrible disease I might get. I am married, am in my mid-thirtties, and am the mother of four children. I try to have calm, sensible answers when I talk to my children about death — but I feel terrible panic at the thought of death happening to me or anyone close to me.

Your letter implies that you are in good health with no more than average reason to fear being afflicted with a serious disease. It speaks of a great deal of anxiety, but you are not writing for amateur psychological counseling. You address a priest in a religious magazine, and I want to try to help you cope with this anxiety in the context of your faith.

First of all, don't be afraid of fear. It is natural for any person to be afraid when he faces something that threatens him. Two things can make fear intense. One is the proximity of the threatening evil. Fortunately, there seems to be no special reason for you to presume that death is on the doorstep — although we can never be certain. The other is the enormity of the threatening evil. And there is nothing in human experience that is as total a threat as death. That's why everyone fears death to a greater or lesser degree.

Even our Lord feared and hated death. He did not want to be

parted from his friends through death. This is why he wept at the loss of his friend Lazarus, even though he was to restore him to life. The thought of his own death was overwhelming. He told his apostles, "My soul is sorrowful even to the point of death." In the Garden of Gethsemani, he prayed that this hour of pain and death might pass him by (Mark 14: 34-35). His agony and bloody sweat were the awful struggle within himself to bring under control his intense fear of the death that was so imminent. Death is always a wrenching plunge into the unknown. It tears a person away from his family, his friends, and everything that has been familiar and comfortable. Every leave-taking is sad, but none is like this one, which feels like the pointless end of life and being.

However, the fearful mystery of death became a new thing when Christ died. His Resurrection made clear to us that dying is not only a move away from all that we cling to; it is also a move toward a new and eternal life.

There are some things concerning this move that we know about. When a person is uprooted and moves to a new city, the prospect is less alarming if he knows that a friend is living in the new area and has promised to be on hand to welcome and help the new arrival. Through death, a person moves to a new city, the city of God. Who is there to welcome him? He will find his parents, relatives, and friends. For the first time, he will see the friends he knew only as the saints to whom he prayed and the souls for whom he prayed. And, at long last, he will recognize his best friend, the one who has loved him all his life, who has given him the gifts he most needed, and who has brought him into his own home — God himself. He will understand the mutual love of the Persons of the Holy Trinity and their love for him. And he will revel in the love of the Incarnate Son of God, who shared human life and the fear of death in order to help him travel safely to heaven. He, above all, is the friend who has moved to the new city before us.

When we say our Lord is our friend, we imply that we are his friends. Are we? Friends trust each other. They are mutually respectful and generous. They are careful, even eager, to do everything that pleases the other and to avoid causing hurt feelings and real injury. True friends listen to each other, treasuring each confidence, genuinely striving to understand.

Friendship with our Lord is similar to ordinary human friendship. If we let friendship bear its fruits, then we trust him and cherish a respectful intimacy with him. We are generous in helping his other friends who are in need of physical necessities and spiritual help.

We are eager to please him by lovingly keeping his commandments and following his example. Most of all, we enjoy his company, being with him in prayer and inner quiet as well as in the service of his body which is the Church.

Friendship with God in Christ is not an accident, neither is it automatic. It can begin to grow at any point in a person's life, but it is meant to continue to grow toward the great happiness of being together forever. It is our physical death after a lifetime of fidelity which enables us to be always with him.

As we move toward that day in fear and hope, the Lord, our friend, is one who reaches out to us. He understands our fear and suffering, for he experienced it himself. It is he who can replace our panic and terror with strength, trust, and confidence in himself.

And when someone close to us dies, it is not the end. We give him back to God, but we do not lose him by his return. Those who belong to God belong also to us, when we belong to God.

Apparent Death and the Sacraments

My husband recently passed away in his sleep. It was at least one and a half hours before the priest arrived, at which time he anointed him. Would this be the same as conditional absolution? What if the hour of death were far earlier than we thought? Although he had not been to confession or Communion in about a year, he had a firm intention of going the following day, which was Christmas eve. Would that have the same effect as if he had lived to go? He had a heart condition but rarely missed Mass.

Death is a great mystery to us. What is the actual moment of a man's passing over into the new kind of existence that makes heaven possible? Certainly, when decomposition sets in, a man is dead. Almost certainly, when an electroencephalograph ceases to register brain-wave activity. But is a person dead when his breathing stops? Or his heart? We don't know for sure. And because we have a gray area of uncertainty, the Church treats a person who appears to have died recently as one to whom she can minister. She never gives the sacraments to the dead. But when we are not sure, she is willing to administer them conditionally in the hope of benefiting the person before the time of real death.

From what you tell me, I see no reason to be anxious for your husband. A man who is living in a way that shows that he is aware of God's love is one who is already responsive to it. We might wish that his good life were swept up into Christ's love more explicitly by a more frequent reception of the sacraments. But people have their own reasons — and why a person delays confession and Communion so long is often rooted in old customs that have nothing to do with his real state before God. The firm intention of a Catholic to celebrate the sacrament of penance and to go to Communion normally implies a real sorrow for sin and a desire to be more closely united with Christ. Our Lord already is meeting him and healing him through this faith and desire — meeting him in the sacramental sign would be a completion of what was already begun. It is not the same, though — in the sacrament there is a greater gift made present. But we can trust that when he came to your husband in death, he completed the gift in person rather than in sacred sign.

Asleep in the Lord

What do we know of the state of existence of those who have died? Might they not be asleep in some mysterious way until the general resurrection?

The question you raise has puzzled mankind from the beginning, and it caused a measure of confusion in the Church during the fourteenth century. When you read the Scriptures, it appears that the people of the Old Testament did not have any clear hope of a personal life beyond the grave until a couple of hundred years before Christ. Even in our Lord's day, the Sadducees and the Pharisees were split on the question of whether there would be a resurrection (cf. Acts 23:6-8).

In the New Testament, the whole emphasis is on the wonderful experience of the risen Lord. He is the center of the apostles' preaching and the source of faith. And for Christians, this puts the accent on the hope of glorious resurrection that would be the lot of all who had lived a life in union with Christ. As it became obvious that this event was not just around the corner, Christians became aware that the interim period, while shrouded in mystery, would somehow be a life with Christ. In other words, the Bible proclaims that the ultimate blessedness of those who die in the Lord will be resurrection. It teaches more subtly that the waiting period of those who have passed away will be life, not unconscious sleep.

During the late Middle Ages, the question again became a burning issue. Is the glory of heaven given to those already purged of sin immediately after death, or must they await the final resurrection? After study, debate, and a sounding of the faith of the Christian people, Pope Benedict XII solemnly defined that the blessed life with God which we call "beatific vision" was not deferred until a "Last Day." This is the faith of the Catholic Church today.

Just what is the condition of existence of those who have passed over into this new life? Do they exist as separated souls (most Catholic theologians hold this), or does each man's spirit somehow have another bodily existence immediately? (some theologians are toying with this idea) — we do not know. But all Catholics share the conviction of faith that just across the barrier of death is the fullness of conscious, loving life — a joyous life with the Father, Son, and Holy Spirit.

Faith and Theology

How can you say that the soul might have another bodily existence after death and that you don't know? What's right or wrong any more? Aren't you opening the door to reincarnation?

I do want to be an instrument of peace in these pages. It is very distressing to hear of your being upset by them. There's a lot of upset today, and one of the reasons for it is our failure to distinguish between faith and theology. Faith gives us a guaranteed view on certain ultimate questions that pertain to our salvation. It rests on God's word, and its truth is unfailingly certain and eternal. Theology, however, is but a human effort to understand this truth and its implications. It rests partially on the human genius of a believer. Its truth is often no more than the best possible approximation man can attain, given the facts that are at his disposal. The conclusions of theology are open to question, and one of the theologian's most important tasks is continually to question.

Religious teaching is a combination of what both faith and theology teach. Both enter into our catechisms, our sermons, and the statements of pope and council. Unfortunately, we have sometimes given the impression that believing in Christ and being a Catholic means accepting the teachings of both faith and theology with equal loyalty. This is not the case. Salvation hinges on believing the truth of God revealed in Jesus Christ and proclaimed to me by the Church. While the conclusions of theologians are very valuable for the faithful, they are not more solid than the facts and reasons that support them.

Faith assures us that a blessed life with the Triune God is given straightway after death to those who die in the grace of our Lord. It gives us no clear information about what the human life of the blessed will be like before the end of time.

Theology has wrestled with this interesting but secondary question, and theologians have answered it in terms of their understanding of the kind of creature man is. For centuries we have thought that those who have gone before us live like pure spirits, enjoying beatific vision, yet wholly disembodied until the resurrection at the end of history. This theory has been taken for granted in most of what the Church has taught about eternal life. However, for all that, it never became more than theology. If he thinks he has some better theory to offer, a theologian may question whether this is really the way man exists after death. This does not mean that he is calling any teaching of faith into question.

Does this open the way to reincarnation? By no means. Reincarnation theories all agree in imagining that man lives a succession of mortal lives — none of them decisive and each of them open to the possibility of personal success or failure. This is opposed to the conviction of faith that death ends our one mortal life on which depends our lot forever. The theologians who are suggesting the possibility of another bodily existence after death profess this faith. They are only speculating about how a man experiences this eternal destiny.

Communication With the Dead

Is it not against the Catholic faith to go to spiritualists' seances to discover if any of one's dreams are coming from deceased friends? Can people who have passed away communicate with the living through dreams?

The effort to communicate with the spirit world is probably as old as mankind. Ancient literature is filled with references to the use of the divining arts in its many forms. Some looked for glimpses into the future through the omens discerned in the entrails of an animal or in the configuration of the stars or in the interpretation of dreams. Others sought for contact with the deceased or insight into secret things through the same inept means.

Christianity struggled from the beginning against this sort of thing. It recognized it as at least a superstition which sinned by attributing to creatures something proper to God alone and as perhaps a horrible commerce with the devil. There is an incident in the Acts of the Apostles where St. Paul incurs the wrath of the masters of a slave girl who was possessed by a diabolical divining spirit. Paul's exorcism destroyed a lucrative fortune-telling practice (Acts 16:16-20).

The Catholic faith considers it seriously wrong to become involved in such superstitious practices, because they always involve a danger to faith and they may be a form of contact with the devil.

Could it be true, though, that the deceased can communicate with the living through dreams? Yes, it could be. The history of Christian experience does record instances where God appears to have used his saints in this way to communicate his intentions to men.

However, this is not the same thing as saying that the deceased are capable of communicating with us directly and are free to do so. We simply have no data on this. We know that the dead continue to have a personal existence and that their interest in us continues through the Communion of Saints. But beyond this, we know little or nothing.

Even apart from the very serious risk to faith that would be involved in attempting to communicate with the deceased, it is both foolish and risky to presume that the stuff of our dream life is made up of telepathic influences from beyond the grave. What standard can a person use to distinguish such an alleged communication from the dream that wells up from our memories and hopes or from the depths of our unconscious or even from our dietary indiscretions?

Would you place your trust in the special power and insight of a medium? On what grounds? Some famous mediums of the past have been shown to be not above using theatrical tricks to defraud their suggestible clients. The person who is looking for contact with the world beyond is psychologically apt to be quite credulous. Or again, if a diabolical preternatural power is at work, what significant truth can be expected from the Father of Lies?

A person would be foolish indeed who, on the basis of his dreams, would conclude that a loved one is urging him to dispose of his property, invest in a risky enterprise, or give up the profession and practice of his faith. In times of personal anxiety or when under the dominion of overpowering curiosity, we poor mortals are apt to deceive ourselves into taking what we would wish were so as if it were so in fact.

Bodies for Science

May Catholics leave their bodies to science, rather than have them buried immediately after death?

Yes. There is no point of Catholic teaching or Church law that forbids a Catholic from making such a request. It would be unusual, though, for a deeply felt religious sense and the strong recommendations of the Church authorities incline Catholics to bury their dead.

The underlying intentions of this age-old practice are many. It expresses our reverence for the body, which we believe was a member of Christ and the temple of the Holy Spirit. It affirms the dignity of human life. A normal wake and funeral provide the living with the opportunity to work through the shock of grief. Burial in consecrated ground helps us to localize our belief in our continuing relationship with the departed through the communion of saints.

Yet these values are not so intrinsically connected with our usual practices that any departure from the ordinary would be tantamount to a denial of the faith. It may be true that some people leave their bodies to science because they despair of the resurrection and any future life. But a person of great faith and genuine Christian love for his fellowman might well be inspired to leave his remains to help the living in the fight against disease.

I'm not recommending anyone to make this choice. But if a person does so out of a sense of genuine charity and a humanitarian concern for future generations, without offending the sensibilities of those he leaves behind, he does a good thing.

Evolution—the Church's "Stand"

I am going to take some summer courses in biology at a secular university. On the program there's a course on evolution. What is the Church's stand on evolution?

Many people have the mistaken idea that the Church has "a stand" on just about everything. This is not true. She does have a position on matters revealed by God for our salvation: the meaning of human life, the message of Jesus Christ, and other religious truths. She has a stand on certain philosophical truths which are the underpinning of religious sanity, such as the ability of the human mind to come to a sure knowledge of God's existence. But she does not have a definite stand on strictly political, economic, or scientific matters.

The teaching authority of the Church enters into the arena of the social order or science only to protect the integrity of the message of Christ and our faith. It proclaims the dignity of the person and the sacredness of human rights, but it does not decree a Catholic political system. It rejects attacks on the substance of the faith, but it does not predetermine what conclusions science is to draw from its evidence.

Modern science sees evolution as the only view of reality that is able to account for the evidence that has been uncovered by serious and objective investigators. The Church's "stand" is that of rejoicing in this development of human knowledge. She has no desire to press for a Scopes trial, for she knows that the Bible accounts of the six days of creation and the formation of the first human beings tell us nothing about the way the universe and life came into existence. She cautions us against an excessive enthusiasm which might trap us into using the method of modern science to find answers to strictly religious questions. And she warns against the bad science that would betray itself in an effort to destroy a belief in God or to reduce the phenomenon of man to the level of the beast.

Evolution does, of course, pose some problems for religious thought. The way we express our faith has always been closely linked to the view we took of the world. As an evolutionary world view is increasingly accepted, it is becoming necessary to reexamine our *expression* of our unchangeable belief in the unity of the human family, the spirituality of the human person, and especially the dogma of original sin. This must be done with discretion. Pope Paul showed this need for being careful in integrating the certainties of faith with the views of science when he spoke to a group of theologians on July 11, 1966: "With reference to the theory of evolutionism, it will not seem acceptable to you when it does not clearly harmonize with the immediate creation of each and every human soul and when it does not consider the disobedience of Adam, the universal first parent, to have been of decisive importance for the destiny of mankind."

Adam's Sin

What specifically, was the sin of our first parents, Adam and Eve?

It is always risky for a religious person to attempt to fill in the gaps that God has left in his record of the history of his dealings with us. I believe that we are certain that mankind in the beginning stood in rebellion against God. Beyond this we know nothing.

The account of the Fall that we read in Genesis is purely poetic in its details. The whole picture of the tree and the fruit of the tree and the tempting serpent derives from the culture and environment of a Hebrew poet who came on the scene very much later. It is not a recollection of an event, but a poetic retelling of a story that teaches the reality of man's sin without telling us anything about its specific nature.

Theologians have speculated whether it was primarily a disobedience (disobeying the Lord's command) or an act of pride ("you shall be like God . . ." — cf. Gen. 3:5 footnote, *New American Bible*) — and certainly they are not wrong, inasmuch as every serious sin indicates a setting up of oneself in preference to God (pride) and a refusal to submit to the designs and plans and commands of God (disobedience).

Some moderns, reflecting on the many sexual indications in the first chapters of Genesis, suggest that the first sin may have been a sexual sin. This hardly seems likely, in view of the gift of the woman to the man as helpmate and the divine command to increase and multiply.

To sum up, no one knows what specifically was the nature of the first rebellion of man against God that we call the sin of our First Parents.

Men of Many Colors

If all men come from Adam and Eve, how did mankind come to be divided into peoples of different color: black, yellow, red, and white?

Your question is a scientific one, and it requires a scientist's answer. Don't look for this kind of answer in the Bible account of Adam and Eve. The Bible gives us a religious certainty that mankind depends on God, that it is profoundly one people, and that evil is in the world because of man's rebellion. It does not speak of the historic beginnings of the human race. Nor do the certainties of our faith and the teachings of the Church prevent us from examining the evidences from the past and drawing probable conclusions.

I can't find anyone who has *the* answer that tells us how the various "racial" differences began. There are two main categories of opinion. One begins from the hypothesis that all mankind descends from a single couple who were the culmination of all the earlier evolutionary processes. These first parents came into being many tens of thousands of years ago. During the subsequent ages, environment (climate, radiation, diet, et cetera) brought about those minor genetic mutations that account for the differences of color and physique in their descendants.

The second kind of opinion begins with the conviction that the appearance of man did not just happen once and in one place through a single couple. It is the conviction of most scientists that a group emerged and then gradually and slowly attained the status of humanness. If this is the way things happened, it would leave considerable room for variations in the accidental characteristics of men — for they would descend from different family trees from the beginning.

Years ago, most Catholics thought that this second opinion was heresy. It seemed to undo our fundamental doctrine of original sin.

However, since 1950, when Pope Pius XII in his encyclical *Humani Generis* remarked on the "difficulty" of reconciling this theory with the dogma of original sin (he did not claim it was impossible to do so), theology has been far more open to this possibility. We are no longer certain that our faith obliges us to hold that in the beginning two people were created from whom all mankind descends. But as we have said before, we must believe that original sin is a fact and that it affects all men; that original sin is a true sin; and that it has unfortunate consequences for all human beings.

Whatever differences there are among the members of the human family, they are not nearly as significant as the similarities. There is no evidence that the differences make any one group more or less human or intelligent or cultured than any other. We are all brothers in the family of the Eternal Father, who calls us to be his adopted sons in his only Son.

An Infant's Heaven

Our physically deformed child died three hours after birth — but not before baptism. We believe that he has now achieved supernatural happiness for all eternity. Will he be infantile for all eternity or does he have the intelligence to understand his great gift? Would he know who his mother and father are? Could we pray for his intercession as part of the communion of saints?

Your baby enjoys the fullness of human maturity and lives a life of communion with God. This supernatural happiness is a fully conscious, personal life. In heaven, nothing is imperfect. There is no more sickness or pain. Neither is there any more the psycho-physical limitation that comes with infancy or senility or mental illness. The resurrection is anticipated, at least to the extent of restoring or bringing to full vigor the power of the human spirit to know and love.

The Church teaches that those who are with the Lord in heaven care for and intercede for us who are still on the way. She urges us to seek this intercession by praying to the saints. Certainly this implies that somehow the saints know of us and our prayers. And the word "saint" includes the numberless throng who have received the crown of human existence in personal union with God. Your baby is among them by God's mercy.

May you pray for his intercession? I did before beginning to write these lines.

Last Judgment

During a discussion on the Last Judgment, some of our group maintained that everyone's sins and faults will be made known to all before according them God's blessing to enter heaven; others, that being a loving, kind, and merciful — though also just — God, he could not shame or embarrass us in this way. They claim we wouldn't be mean enough to treat each other in this manner, and they don't believe our Lord will. Please give us the Catholic Church's teaching on this matter.

No matter how much or how little we may be able to say about the Last Judgment, we should begin with the conviction that God is not mean. The Last Judgment cannot be pictured as God's way of getting even. He cannot be cruel or catty. However thoroughly the world might see the hidden shabbiness of those who have been saved by his mercy, there will be no embarrassment, no censuring clucking of tongues. All will be peace and gratitude, unclouded by the kind of shame that the disclosure of a double life brings with it today.

The Catholic Church's teaching on the Last Judgment has all the clarities and obscurities the Lord left us in his teaching. Many times he affirms in the first three Gospels that he will come as man to judge humanity and the whole historical process. The long passage in St. Matthew's Gospel presents the scene of a judgment based on love and the refusal to love (Matt. 25:31-46). St. Paul describes the triumph of Christ: "Such as these will suffer the penalty of eternal ruin apart from the presence of the Lord and the glory of his might on the Day when he comes, to be glorified in his holy ones and adored by all who have believed" (II Thess. 1:9-10). And again: " . . . On the day when, in accordance with the Gospel I preach, God will pass judgment on the secrets of men through Christ Jesus" (Rom. 2:16).

The thing that is clear is that the Church believes that there will be a General Judgment, that Christ will be the Judge, and that his place as Lord of the Universe will be manifest in a universe entirely submissive to his royal power. Everything that was hidden will be laid bare, so that everyone can see the mystery of God's providence that was always at work in the redemption of the world. Here, too, the record of each individual with all his actions and motives will be made known as the reason of his condemnation or reward.

Just how this will take place is God's secret — the obscurity. Preachers and artists have used their imagination to make us vividly aware of the central truth of the judgment. It is not a bad thing. We need creative imagination to make the truths of faith live for us. But we should not make a theology out of creative imaginings.

The thought of the Last Judgment may be an added incentive for us now to remain faithful to God's will, because we think we would be so ashamed to have everyone know our weakness. But on the last day when the Lord appears in his glory, the only thing that anyone will see will be transformed in the vision of that glory. The hidden adulteries and selfishness we now appropriately conceal even as we repent of them will appear only as prisms that reflect the merciful love of God that brought good out of evil. There will be no more vanity or curiosity or suspicion — the blessed will have better things to do than to be shocked at our sins or to peek at our smirched records.

The closest parallel we have to the Last Judgment is not the seamy stories of gossip magazines but the personal revelation of the confessional. I know no priest who shies away in disgust from the penitents who come with their sad stories of failure. They are too struck by the goodness of God who has drawn these people to humble conversion to be shocked by what they have been or done. How much more will this be the case on the last day, when the blessed will see all things only in the light of Christ and with the vision of Christ their Judge.

On Purgatory

I am engaged in a dispute with an agnostic on the subject of purgatory, and I need help. He claims that purgatory is an invention of the Papists, that the only real states of man after death are in heaven and hell. He will not accept the argument from II Machabees 12:43-45, because he maintains that the Books of Machabees are not part of the inspired Scriptures. Can you point out a place in the New Testament where the word "purgatory" appears?

Your agnostic friend is not far from the Kingdom of God. I'm surprised that the question of inspiration and canonicity would make a real difference to him. It means that he recognizes the mysterious fact that a saving God has spoken to man and caused a record of his designs and interventions to be written down for our instruction. And I'm delighted that he acknowledges the reality of an irrevocable destiny for every man — either blessed union with God in heaven or total alienation from him in hell. Not everyone does so.

The Catholic doctrine of purgatory does not rest on any particular text of the New Testament that clearly and certainly teaches the existence of purgatory. It rests, rather, on the view that the Scriptures give us of God, of man, and of heaven.

The Bible supports the view that no man enters the presence of the all holy God in heaven unless he is totally free from the wounds of his sins. It also reveals to us that God is entirely merciful. We also know that human liberty is such a mixed-up thing that some men who are basically turned toward God are not fully integrated in their love of God when they pass from this life. Consequently, one of these two things must take place: either God ignores man's situation and purifies him immediately, or he provides an intermediate situation, a time of supreme personal trial, in which this purification can take place. From the beginning, the belief of Christians has gravitated to this second choice. This belief was expressed in the tradition of praying for the dead, which dates back to the earliest centuries of the Church's existence — at a time when there was no difference between the Protestants and the "Papists."

The word "purgatory" was coined by the Latin Church of the Middle Ages. It was unknown in the Christian East. However, there is no doubt that the Oriental Churches believed in the reality of an intermediate state of purification, for they too prayed for their dead. During the thirteenth and the fifteenth centuries, when the East and West were struggling to come to doctrinal agreement and put an end to the division between them, the question of purgatory came out into the open. There were no great debates. The Churches of the East found no great difficulty in professing their faith in the reality which the West called purgatory.

It seems to me that when a person argues strongly against purgatory, oftentimes he is really objecting to a notion of purgatory that sees it as a place where a vindictive God gets even with a person who was a bit too free with him. But this is not at all the Catholic understanding of purgatory. We do not see it as a place of punishment. It is a place where the shriveled human spirit can rid itself of the last vestiges of selfishness that cripple it. It is a place where man is prepared to be truly great enough and open enough to receive the fullness of love that God is ready to lavish upon him. Its flames are the intensity of God's love that inflames the soul with yearning for the richness it will soon receive. Purgatory is not a punishment; it is a mercy.

Mass for the Dead

One of our priests, ordained less than a year, has told us at Mass that a Mass may be offered in memory of a deceased person but not for the repose of his soul. Has not this priest implied that purgatory does not exist?

If the priest said just what you report he said, he is wrong. The Catholic Church believes in the existence of purgatory. Her teaching on the communion of saints includes the conviction that we can help those whom Vatican II says "are still being purified after death" (*Dogmatic Constitution on the Church,* no. 51). This help is not just the remembering of a person who used to be but is no more. It is some real kind of assistance in the process of purification which will be completed by his entry into the happiness of heaven — the repose of his soul.

This teaching has not changed. Vatican II explicitly reconfirms the decree of the Council of Trent which declares: "There is a purgatory, and the souls detained there are helped by the suffrages of the faithful and especially by the acceptable sacrifice of the altar" (Denzinger, *Enchiridion Symbolorum,* 1820 [983]). I'm sure that Father was taught nothing at variance with this in the seminary.

Why, then, is he preaching such a thing in the pulpit? Since I didn't hear him in context, I can only hazard a guess. It might be that we have here another instance of the problem every theology teacher faces: how to give one's students a conviction of what is the essential heart of a doctrine while conveying, at the same time, an awareness of the unanswered questions associated with the mystery and a feeling for the search for ever new insights into its hidden aspects.

The core of the Church's teaching on the help we can give to our brothers in purgatory is contained in the few lines quoted from the Council of Trent. But there are many things that are uncertain and matter of dispute. For instance, what does a long or short purgatory mean? How does our assistance really "work"? Precisely how do the Masses and prayers of the Church help in the personal purification of the deceased? Does the special intention of the priest who receives a Mass stipend make a significant difference in the benefit a soul in purgatory receives from the Mass offered for the repose of his soul? Et cetera.

Good students succeed in keeping straight the distinctions between what is the certain and sure teaching of the Church and what is merely probable or tentative. It is the fond hope of seminary professors that all their students will be this "good" by the time they are ready for ordination. Unfortunately, we sometimes are disappointed.

This disappointed hope is not a new thing in the Church. Forty years ago, the authentic teaching of the Church was also sometimes distorted in our pulpits. Then the distortions were more likely to be along the lines of an excessively rigid and legalistic moralism. Nowadays, we hear more about the excesses that whittle away at the content of the faith and that move toward a vague humanism. Both distortions are ugly and wrong.

But I think it is unnecessary to panic. The Holy Spirit dwells in the Church to lead it into all truth. He is with all the faithful, laity as well as clergy. And the day is past when our people lapse into the quiet assent that it must be so "because Father said so." If you think that your priest is preaching another gospel than that which we have received, you will do him a kindness to talk with him about it. Perhaps he did not realize he was giving the impression you took from his words and will want to set things right. Perhaps your reminder will bring him back to a more humble approach to the teaching of the Church, if he is in fact out of line. Or perhaps you will find, after presenting your hesitations to him, that some recourse to the priest's superiors might be needed. This is not to advocate a witch hunt, but coresponsibility for the truth.

A View of Hell

All that the Church has defined concerning hell seems to me to be summed up in these two propositions: (1) the punishment of hell is of varying degree according to the person's guilt; (2) the punishment is eternal. In your opinion, does the following proposition accord with the Church's dogma? Souls who die in "mortal sin" are punished for a length of time depending on their guilt and then suffer the eternal punishment of annihilation. This view seems orthodox to me and preserves the concept of God's mercy. Extinction of life is a punishment.

I don't think your view squares with the Church's understanding of eternal punishment. The Catholic view of eternal destiny rests on a view of the kind of being man is. The Church sees man as a creature who will never cease to possess a personal existence. While it is hard to deny that the One who calls man to personal existence and sustains him in it could conceivably cease to preserve him, we have no indication that any person is ever annihilated.

I wonder about your presuppositions when you use the word "punishment." In your example, it almost seems equivalent to "getting even." And it seems to me that this is where you have a problem preserving the concept of God's mercy.

The orthodox view of hell does not picture God ready to pounce on a poor unfortunate who breaks his law nor as a vindictive judge looking for his pound of flesh. Hell is more like the punishment a man brings on himself when he deliberately pushes aside all who would love and support him and ends up finding himself empty and frustrated. No one is ever trapped into hell; it is the fruit of quite free choices.

In the Catholic view of life, every man is made in such a way that he can find real happiness and fulfillment only in a life of intimate communion with God. Whatever he does in life, in every free and personal act, he is either opening his life to this goal or shutting it out of his life. However much he can hide his ultimate destiny, even from himself, he can never fashion another for himself. The ultimate "mortal sin" is to go to death clinging to one's own distorted vision of happiness, refusing to accept as a gift the full life of a personal relationship with God.

The Catholic Church teaches that the quality of each person's unending personal existence is fixed forever in this final free choice. Heaven will be the condition of the man who accepts the mercy of God. Hell will be the condition of the man who freely refuses to accept the mercy of God. By his own choice, he remains forever shut in upon himself, empty, cold. His whole being continues to have its built-in yearning for the fulfillment of being with God in love, but the whole of his free, personal choice is fixed in its refusal to let itself go in love of anyone but himself.

Hell is not a punishment to make up for guilt; hell is the logical consequence of a final free choice to refuse life and love.

Destroy the World by Fire

Could you tell me if and where the Bible teaches that God will destroy the world by fire?

The destruction of the physical universe by fire is not a teaching of the Bible nor of the Catholic Church.

The references to fire in the Bible must be seen in the context of the symbolic meaning the ancients attached to fire. Fire consumes, illumines, heats, destroys, purifies — and all these properties evoked the sense of the divine for the religious man. God showed his presence through fire. The holiness of God was represented by fire. The prophets describe the wrath of God as a fire: destroying the ungodly and purifying those who cleaved to God.

The poetry of fire is used by the early Christians to describe the end of time. Thus Paul speaks of the coming of the Lord "with flaming power [to] inflict punishment on those who do not acknowledge God nor heed the good news" (II Thess. 1:8). Then "the heavens will vanish with a roar; the elements will be destroyed by fire, and the earth and all its deeds will be made manifest" (3:10).

Whatever these descriptions mean, they must be understood in harmony with the constant teaching of the New Testament that the destiny of the universe is not destruction but transformation and renewal. What is promised is "new heavens and a new earth where, according to his promise, the justice of heaven will reside" (II. Pet. 3:13). "All creation groans and is in agony even until now" (Rom. 8:23). It is in the act of giving birth to that state of glorification where "everything . . . , both on earth and in the heavens" (Col. 1:20) will share the full fruits of Redemption.

The Church has most recently professed her belief in this transformation of the world, rather than its destruction, in Vatican II, *Constitution on the Church in the World Today,* no. 39: "We do not know the time for the consummation of the earth and of humanity. Nor do we know how all things will be transformed. As deformed by sin, the shape of this world will pass away. But we are taught that God is preparing a new dwelling place and a new earth where justice will abide and whose blessedness will answer and surpass all the longings for peace which spring up in the human heart. Then, with death overcome, the sons of God will be raised up in Christ. What was sown in weakness and corruption will be clothed with incorruptibility. While charity and its fruits endure, all that creation which God made on man's account will be unchained from the bondage of vanity."

6
Sacraments and Liturgy

Baptism

Eucharist

Penance

Marriage

Holy Orders

Sacraments
and
Liturgy

The Effects of the Sacraments

I am puzzled about the value of receiving the sacraments frequently. I believe that the sacraments give a person the grace of real control over his passions. However, I notice that some of my acquaintances who receive the sacraments only twice a year are always gay and smiling — in other words, apparently happy. I have yet to achieve this disposition, even though I have been receiving every Sunday for the past several years. I still fail to be in control of my passions. Would you venture an explanation why this is so, as I am inclined to lose faith in the sacraments.

What the sacraments do is to place us in person-to-person contact with our Lord Jesus Christ. And as this personal union of love grows between us, we normally tend to recognize the hidden tendrils of selfishness and to have the courage to cut them away. This seems to be what we mean when we say that the sacraments provide a grace that helps us to gain control of our passions.

However, the way this takes place is different for different people. Don't expect that the sacraments are going to change our basic temperaments and patterns of reaction, so that we will all become charming and smiling and apparently happy.

If you go through a list of the saints, you will find there is no such thing as a "typical" saint. Every type of person is represented. Some of them were buoyant, lighthearted people; some of them were very severe and demanding people. Some of the saints found a rather easy and calm control of passion. Others found that, even as they were practically on the threshold of heaven, they were still struggling to maintain control of their rebellious inner drives. I believe that all the saints had that measure of happiness that comes from a realization that they are loved by God and that they are trying to respond to it. However, not all their acquaintances recognized them as particularly affable or happy people.

What does all this mean? Just this. The effect of the sacraments should be to make us saints by putting us in touch with the person of our Blessed Lord. But it is a "being-in-touch" which is not always felt. And since it is not felt, it does not noticeably affect our tendency to be joyous or depressed. This depends more on the bodily constitution, the emotional makeup, and the life experiences that shape our personalities.

Do we ever know whether the person who is apparently happy is really sharing in that profound contentment that comes from being at peace with God? This is true happiness. And this is what is increased by our repeated contacts with our Blessed Lord in faith through the sacraments.

Sacraments and Talismans

Terence Cardinal Cooke, upon his elevation, was presented with a mezuzah by one of his Jewish friends. Cardinal Cooke does not need a mezuzah. As Archbishop of New York, he is afforded every security possible. What of the small homeowner and apartment dweller? Does the Catholic Church have anything equivalent to the mezuzah? There are so many sacramentals and talismans connected with the Catholic Church, but to my knowledge nothing as simple as a mezuzah at the door to bless the visitor as well as the family within.

I want to be gracious. But I have printed your letter because it exemplifies the persistence of an approach to God and the use of religion which I would desperately like to uproot. An example of it appeared in the remarks of a prominent layman recently. He spoke with a reporter when the legendary St. Christopher was dropped from the Church calendar. He said, "I'll continue to carry my medal for the same reason I always have — it's a tradition of luck, like a rabbit's foot, or maybe like the black lace garter a friend of mine carries."

A talisman is defined as "an object bearing a sign or character engraved under astrological influences and thought to act as a charm to avert evil and bring good fortune; or something producing apparently magical or miraculous effects." The whole idea of talismans and good luck charms strikes at the very foundations of genuine religion. It represents a throwback to a superstitious fear. It makes God into a power we can use and manipulate in a vain hope for a magical security. Men may be led to religion through the path of the occult and the superstitious. But religion cannot peacefully coexist with superstition. Its perennial task is to smash the idols — even those which seem to breed in a religious atmosphere.

A mezuzah is not a talisman. It is a small parchment scroll inscribed with the name of God and these verses from the Bible: Deuteronomy 6:4-9 and 11:13-21. These passages, too long to quote in full, contain what Jesus called the "great commandment" of the Law (Matthew 22:37-39) and God's promise to be the eternally faithful partner of the true Israelite who will live in the spirit of the Covenant. The Jew is to be always conscious of God's love for him and his religious commitment to an all-embracing love for God. The inspired author enjoins his reader to keep these words in his heart and, as a reminder, to write them on his doorposts. The mezuzah on the apartment doorway is meant to remind the family of its special relationship with God. It is not a magical guarantee to remind God of anything. One hopes it will bring devotion. It has nothing to do with good luck.

The Cardinal's mezuzah is not a substitute for police protection and fire insurance on Madison Avenue. It is a reminder of the gracious esteem of the friends who gave it. And it is also a religious reminder that our life as Catholics is to be lived in a conscious awareness of the same God of the Covenant who chose Israel for his people.

The holy water font inside the entrance of a Catholic home is in the same tradition as the Jewish mezuzah. Making the sign of the cross with it, the Christian is reminded of the mystery of the New Covenant relationship with God he entered through the waters of baptism. In the prayer for the blessing of holy water, the Church of the New Covenant prays: "O Lord, shine on this water and salt with the light of your kindness. Sanctify it by the dew of your love, so that, through the invocation of your holy name, wherever this water and salt is sprinkled it may turn aside every attack of the unclean spirit and dispel the terror of the poisonous serpent. And wherever we may be, make the Holy Spirit present to us who now implore your mercy." No magic. No talisman. No security but that of a faith in the God who loves and cares for us.

Liturgical Dress

When was the first Mass celebrated in vestments as we see it today?

Originally, the liturgical dress of the clergy was the same as the ordinary clothes of well-dressed people. The change came gradually. As styles changed, the clergy kept to the old style, and it came to be the distinctive sign of their special role in sacred worship. This change to "vestments" began in the fifth century in the East. By the twelfth century, the vestments of the ministers of the altar were fixed by law and were just about what we have today.

Liturgical Dance

I have heard that some groups are introducing the dance into Catholic worship, even during the Mass. I can't understand this. Would you please comment on it?

You heard rightly, and I'm sure that most of our readers have seen pictures of talented and beautiful people dancing in or before the sanctuary on various occasions.

In many cultures, the dance has always been a privileged expression of man's religious sense. It involves a person totally, body and spirit, and is quite suited to express man's gift of his whole self to God and his joy in the Lord. There are examples of religious dancing in the Old Testament. The most famous is probably the whirling, leaping dance King David performed in the presence of the Lord before the Ark of the Covenant. Even then, the dance didn't meet with universal approval, and David and his wife practically broke up their marriage in the squabble that followed this episode (II Sam. 6:14-23).

In Western Christianity, the religious dance has survived more sedately in the form of the religious procession and also, until recently, in the rubrics for the priest celebrant of the Mass. All the gestures, bows, turns, kisses, and genuflections minutely prescribed for him were, in fact, a choreography of religious worship. They were stylized body movements designed to express religious thought and feeling. In some sense, then, a dance.

The dance is as truly an artistic expression of the human spirit as music is. In itself, then, there is no reason why it cannot be the handmaid of liturgy, just as music is. As the Vatican Council declared: "The Church indeed approves of all forms of true art and admits them into divine worship when they show appropriate qualities" (*Constitution on the Sacred Liturgy*, no. 112).

This citation, which might be considered the legal title for introducing dance and other art forms into the liturgy, also suggests the reservations with which the dance may be introduced. Among the appropriate qualities any religious art should have is that it "accord with the dignity of the temple and truly contribute to the edification of the faithful" (*ibid.*, no. 120). There is a cultural element that has to be taken into account here. We have to consider what associations a particular people have attached to dancing.

I think it is fair to say that for most people in Western Europe and America, the dance is associated with entertainment, the theater, and romantic emotions. To the extent that these associations prevail, it is hard to see that the dance is an entirely appropriate adjunct to liturgical worship. These associations can be transcended. In special gatherings, I have seen an interpretative dance done reverently and beautifully in a way that carries the mind and heart beyond the dancers to the source of all beauty. But for the time being, I doubt that the religious dance can be generally introduced in our culture without occasioning more upset and distraction than edification of the people.

Latin in the Mass

I am an organist and choir director in a typical Catholic parish. We hold five Masses each Sunday in our church: two guitar, two English sung Masses with the organ, and a Latin High Mass. Does the new Mass order forbid the use of Latin in the liturgy? Our Latin Mass is well attended, both by the adults and youth of the parish. The Vatican's ruling on Church music endorsed the use of Latin in the liturgy as a sister to the vernacular; yet I fear that Latin is dead within the Church.

You really aren't in a typical Catholic parish. As far as I can see, the typical Catholic parish uses no Latin. In fact, in a number of American dioceses the public celebration of the Mass in Latin is forbidden.

The reasons for making the prohibition were probably pastoral. It prevented priests from dragging their feet in a time of change. It guaranteed that the greatest number of people would experience firsthand the celebration in their own language. It was designed to help the people make those shifts in attitude that would enable them to be a community of active participants rather than a churchful of silent spectators.

The prohibition is purely local. It is not world-wide. The official language of our liturgy is still Latin. The revised ceremonies of the Mass were first made available in Latin. Certainly, a priest may celebrate in the Latin language when he celebrates the Mass in a private setting. Whether or not he may do so at a public parish Mass depends on the regulations in the diocese.

Regulations are meant to be reasonable directives, responsive to the needs of the people. If a substantial number of Catholics in a particular area really want the use of Latin restored or preserved, as it is in your parish, I would imagine that the authorities would try to oblige them.

For Non-Singers

I am in my senior years. I liked and got accustomed to the old Church rules. Now with the new rules in effect, singing seems to be the main objective. This kind of irks me. How can one get up and sing when he hasn't the voice to peddle fish?

I'm glad you said "Church rules." That's all they are. It is not a new faith but a new etiquette.

In some places, and to some people, it does sound as if singing is the main objective. Really, it isn't. The main objective is to have every member of the congregation take a full, active, and conscious part in the liturgical celebration. The Mass is designed to be everyone's — priest's and layman's — expression of worship. The layman does not merely attend the priest's expression of worship. We all should be actively involved — heart, mind, body, and voice. This is where singing comes in. It is a means, not an objective. It should help us by its beauty to pray better. It should show the harmony of our worshipping community by the harmony of our voices blending into a single chorus.

Sometimes the means is ineffective. If it is shoved down our throats, it is unlikely to have those qualities of joyfulness and beauty that carry the heart and mind aloft. If it is shoddy music, and so much of it is, it can only turn off anyone with normal taste. If the "fishmongers" among us are in full voice, the singing is more likely to fragment the community than to express its real and felt unity. Full, active, conscious participation of those who cannot sing could perhaps be best achieved by their standing and silently raising heart and mind in union with those who are endowed with good voice.

On the other hand, there are those who do very well at joining in the singing at family get-togethers but feel uncomfortable about singing in church. They should be encouraged to lose their inhibitions and learn to feel as much at home with their brothers and sisters in their Father's house as they do on their friends' patios.

Date of Easter

Is there anything in the documents of Vatican II concerning having a fixed day each year for Easter?

There are two explicit references to the date of Easter which I can find in the documents of the Council. One is in the appendix to the *Constitution on the Sacred Liturgy*; the other in the *Decree on Eastern Catholic Churches* (no. 20). At present, there are different rules used for computing the date of Easter in East and West. Some years, both celebrate the feast on the same Sunday; in other years, it may be as much as five weeks later in the East. The Council desires that we all get together — but it very carefully insists that agreement be worked out amicably. It would be tragic to have the Day of Resurrection become a renewed source of tension and conflict between Christians of the different Churches.

The possibilities to which the Church is open are these: (1) that East and West, Catholic and non-Catholic, work out a mutually acceptable formula for determining the date of Easter — even though it is not a fixed date like that of Christmas; (2) that all agree to a fixed date, either within the frame of our present calendar or in any other perpetual calendar the nations may adopt.

Baptism

Baptism in the Name of Jesus Christ

Matthew 28:19 speaks of Jesus' command that the Apostles baptize "in the name of the Father and of the Son and of the Holy Spirit." Yet Acts 2:38, 10:48, and 19:1-15 indicate that the Apostles baptized "in the name of Jesus Christ." Is there a discrepancy here? Does the Church recognize the baptisms of fundamentalist sects that do not use the formula that mentions the names of the Three Divine Persons?

There would be a discrepancy if it could be shown that the texts in the Acts of the Apostles intend to give us the liturgical formula the Apostles actually used when they baptized. Great theologians of the Middle Ages thought that this was the case. For instance, St. Thomas Aquinas suggested that the Apostles baptized this way by virtue of a special revelation of Christ, so that the despised name of Jesus Christ would be glorified during this primitive period by the signs of the coming of the Holy Spirit.

However, for centuries the view has been that these texts do not intend to express the *formula* used in the ceremony of baptism. Their exact significance has been interpreted in various ways. Perhaps baptism in the name of Jesus Christ expresses the realization that this is something other than John's baptism (cf. Acts 19:1-5). Again, it may indicate that by baptism a person begins to be "in Christ Jesus" (cf. Rom. 6:3-4) or that in baptism a person confesses his faith in Jesus. In fact, the Bible doesn't provide us with any clear evidence that the *minister* of baptism pronounced any baptismal formula in the earliest times. Baptism seems to have been a fully participated liturgical action in which the one being baptized confessed his faith in the mystery of Christ, while the minister of the Church performed the action of plunging the neophyte into the waters of baptism. The belief that Jesus is the Lord explicitly acknowledges the true divinity of the Son and hence is at least implicitly an expression of belief in the Trinity. Matthew 28:19 indicates that before the canon of the Scriptures was closed, the primitive Church explicitly invoked the names of the Trinity of Persons at its baptisms.

So much for the ambiguous data concerning the early Church practice. Even if it were clear, it would not settle the question of how baptism is to be conferred today. It is the conviction of the Catholic Church that the care of the sacraments has been confided to her. She determines what actions and what formulas of words express the intentions of Christ and her faith in his salvation. The only baptism that the Church recognizes as valid is one where the formula names the Three Divine Persons in a way that expresses their unity in the Godhead.

While not impugning in any way the sincerity of the fundamentalist sects, the Catholic Church does not consider that person baptized who received the bath of initiation with words like, "I baptize you in the name of Jesus Christ."

Valid Baptism?

A priest told me that my baptism in a non-Catholic church was valid, because I knew that there are three persons in the one God. Now I am beginning to wonder if my baptism was really valid, because I think that I may have considered God the Father as the "real God" and the Son and Spirit somehow less.

Your baptism was valid — but not because you knew of the mystery of the Blessed Trinity and understood (or did not understand) the meaning of the terms in which Christians express this truth.

The validity of the sacraments does not depend on a person's theological orthodoxy nor even on his belief. It depends on his true intention to receive the sacrament that Christ gave his Church. Certainly an adult who makes a decision to be baptized has this intention, even though he may not even believe in the Blessed Trinity or may be mistaken about the nature of the sacrament.

It is also the conviction of the Church that the validity of baptism does not hinge on what the minister of the sacrament thinks about its meaning or whether he is a holy man or whether he is even a believer. He may even declare that what he is doing is performing a mere ceremony which has no real effect. It is enough that he intends to do what the Church does. And this intention is presumed to be present if he performs the ceremony with water in the name of the Three Divine Persons. There is no need to inquire further.

In the rebirth of baptism, our Lord himself acts to bring us to a new life. He does not want us to waste time anxiously wondering if that life is "for real." He wants our energies to go into living it in the name of the Father and of the Son and of the Holy Spirit.

Infant Baptism

Would you discuss the history of infant baptism in the Church and whether you see prospects in the Church for returning to adult baptism exclusively, as in the days of the early Church?

It is extremely difficult to trace back to their origins the practices of the Church. Some things developed in practice as a normal consequence of the belief of the Church, without anyone thinking to leave a permanent record of what was being done. On the question of infant baptism, the New Testament gives us no certitude, no clarity, one way or the other. There is no passage that clearly affirms that the children of Christian parents were, in fact, baptized. Nor is there any indication that no one but adults were baptized. The Scriptures are addressed to those who can hear the word of God as a personal call to conversion and the full commitment to faith in Jesus Christ. They are not preoccupied with the problems of those who can neither read nor listen intelligently. They simply have nothing to say about the situation of infants in the Church.

There are, however, indications in the Scriptures that infants were baptized. St. Paul baptized whole households when his preaching brought the heads of these households to conversion (cf. I Cor. 1:14; 1:16; Acts 16:15 and 33). It is not unlikely that these families included infants, though of course we do not know for sure. For centuries, Scripture scholars have seen an allusion to the primitive practice of baptizing infants in the Gospel passage where our Lord sharply rebukes the Apostles for preventing infants from coming to him and receiving his tender care and blessing (Lk. 18:16). The passages in John 3:5 and Matthew 28:19 are phrased in such all-embracing language that it is hard to say that the inspired authors think that only adults need to be "begotten of water and the Spirit" (Jn. 3:5) or that only adults are among the "every creature" (Mk. 16:15) who is to be made a disciple of Jesus Christ.

Immediately after the New Testament period, we find references in Polycarp (d. circa 155), Justin (d. circa 165), and Irenaeus (d. circa 202) that seem to refer to the fact of a baptism of rebirth received in infancy. From the beginning of the third century, we have explicit references to the baptism of little children. It is presented as the custom of Mother Church, not as an innovation. St. Augustine in the West and Origen in the East see in the practice of baptizing infants a tradition that has been received from the apostles. The Fathers of the Church write to urge their people to have their boys baptized as babies, not to put it off until they have passed through the turbulent and oftentimes sinful period of adolescence. (It seems that some fourth- and fifth-century Christians would baptize their girls as babies, expecting that a sheltered life and early marriage would keep their baptism unspotted, but that they feared their young men would wander through a time of wild oats.)

From all of this it is quite clear that "adult baptism exclusively" was not the rule of the early Church. The universal practice of baptizing infants was fully accepted, even before the Church had clearly formulated her conviction concerning original sin. In fact, St. Augustine takes this practice as something that everyone agrees comes from the earliest times, and then he goes on to argue from the fact of infant baptism to the existence of a universal original sin. One thing that infant baptism means, he argues, is that all men are born into a sinful condition, all are in need of the Redemption of Jesus Christ, which is applied to them by baptism.

The tradition supporting the practice of infant baptism is so firm that Martin Luther found himself struggling fiercely with a revolutionary group of dissenters from Rome who would restrict the benefits of baptism and membership in the Christian community to adults. The debate within Protestant circles was renewed in recent years, with the great theologians Karl Barth, Joachim Jeremias, and Oscar Cullmann as the principal protagonists.

However, in Catholic circles I see absolutely no prospect of the Church's reversing its stand. And I think it would be a reversal, not a return to a primitive practice, if the Church stopped baptizing infants.

Infant Baptism—Commitment to the Church

At my infant daughter's baptism recently, the priest commented that baptism does not commit the child to the Catholic Church, but rather it is a sign of God's love for the child and, in a sense, commits the

parents to bring the child up with a knowledge of the Church so that when the child reaches consenting age, he or she will, it is hoped, choose the Church. This surprised me, as I had always been taught that the child is received into the Church as a new member at baptism — and this must be interpreted as a commitment made in the child's name.

There is a sense in which it is true to say that a baby's baptism is not a commitment to the Catholic Church. This simply means that a baby is incapable of making the free, personal decision that commits him to a way of life. But if we concentrate on this viewpoint, we can also say that your daughter's birth does not commit her to your family. You hope that, through the years of experiencing love and security from her mother and father, she will respond in a personal commitment when she becomes old enough to reflect on the meaning of love and commitment.

For the Catholic, the core of baptism does not consist in the person's act of faith and commitment — although it implies this or normally gives rise to it. Nor is baptism merely a sign that tells us that God loves the baby. Rather, it is a sign filled with the power of the Holy Spirit by which God's special love makes the baby be what he was not before: an adopted child of God; a person filled with the shared life of God; a temple of the Holy Spirit; a member of the community of believers, the Church of Christ, which subsists in the Roman Catholic Church. We believe that, more important than any free human act of commitment is the fact that God acts through the sacramental sign in an irrevocable way to take the child as his own in the Church community. By baptism, he belongs to God in and through the Church, just as truly as by birth he belongs to his parents and family.

There will come a day in each person's life when he must make a personal decision to live the life of Christ in the Church or to reject it. There is no advantage in approaching such a decision from a completely neutral viewpoint. It is the privilege of parents and their pledge made at baptism to share their personal conviction of faith with their children, in the hope that they will find life and its meaning in the Church.

To Be a Godparent

I would like to have my brother be godfather to our first child.

However, as he is married to a Lutheran girl in her church, does that mean he is no longer a Catholic? Can he still be godfather to our child?

First of all, your brother is still a Catholic. He has not abandoned his fundamental allegiance to his Church. Nor has he been excluded from the community of the visible Church by an excommunication. However, his status in the Church is an unfortunate one. The highest authorities in the Church have determined the ceremonies that are required for her members to enter a true marriage. Your brother has not observed these directives, and consequently his marriage is not recognized as a true marriage. In the eyes of his own Church, he is considered to be a single man living in a situation that is reckoned as a "state of sin."

Can he be the godfather of your child? This depends on a number of factors. The law of the Church does not automatically exclude persons who are invalidly married from sponsoring a child at baptism. But it does leave room for the local authorities to decide what to do in cases like this. In some areas, the sponsor must be one who is known to be a "practicing" Catholic, and most pastors would hesitate to call the Catholic living in an invalid marriage "practicing." I recommend that you present all the facts to the priest in the church where your child will be baptized to see what should be done.

The reason why the Church makes any regulations about who may or may not be a godparent is that she sees this as a very important role. The sponsor acts in the name of the Church and assumes a personal responsibility for fostering the faith of the newly baptized. Normally, we would expect that both of these offices should be filled by a Catholic in good standing with his Church. To do otherwise would tend to water down the meaning of godparent — to make it a mere ceremonial honoring of a friend or relative.

Yes and No

My brother-in-law, who is not a Catholic, says he was godfather for a Catholic child. When my first child was born, my parish told me that a non-Catholic could not be a sponsor for a Catholic child. Is there any way possible for a non-Catholic to be godparent for a Catholic child?

A godparent at baptism does two things. He assumes a serious obligation, and he performs a religious act. His obligation is to see to it that the newly baptized is raised as a Christian. But the more important thing he does is represent the Catholic community which is receiving a new member and expressing its faith.

It is possible for someone who doesn't share the fullness of our faith to act as representative of the Church. We have always recognized that, in an emergency, even someone who does not believe in Christ or in baptism can truly confer the sacrament. Yet there is something awkward about this situation which should be avoided whenever possible. This is the reason why our sacramental practice and law have excluded even relatives from being godparents if they are not Catholic.

There is a change of perspective now and an increased readiness to permit exceptions. On May 14, 1967, the Secretariat for Promoting Christian Unity — one of the pope's bureaus in the Vatican — issued a *Directory* which opens new possibilities. The pertinent points are these.

A member of an Orthodox Church may be permitted to be a godparent at the baptism of a Catholic. This is so because there is such a close unity in the confession of the faith and celebration of the sacraments between the Orthodox and the Catholic Churches.

A member of another Christian community, a Protestant, cannot be a godparent. Yet, where there are good personal reasons for it, he may stand with a Catholic godparent as a "Christian witness of the baptism." The Christian witness looks like a godparent in the ceremony, but he does not have the same religious role. This is something quite new. Previously, not even this was permitted. And even though a priest mistakenly allowed a Protestant relative to act as a godparent without some authorization from the Church authorities, the act was invalid — he really was not the godfather.

Refusal to Baptize

Please discuss what reasons a priest could have for refusing to baptize a baby.

The decision to baptize or not must be made on the basis of what faith tells us the sacrament is. Baptism is the beginning of a new life in Christ. It is the door through which men enter the Church to share its life and faith. There are two situation where a priest must decide not to baptize.

One is easy to see. It occurs when the parents are unbelievers.

Since the unbeliever does not belong to the Church and does not belong to the Church and does not intend to raise his child in the faith of the Church, no priest would baptize the child unless the baby were dying. To baptize the child against the parents' wishes would be a serious violation of their natural right. To do so at their request would be to reduce the sacred rite to some kind of superstition. What sense would it make to initiate a baby into the life of Christ when you are really sure that the child will never even hear of Christ when he grows up? The effects of baptism are indeed real and immediate. But the seed of the Christ life which it plants can mature only if the faith be presented in word and life.

The other situation is not so simple. It can occur when the parents are Catholics who are not practicing their faith. The underlying difficulty is this: Do they really want their baby to receive the sacrament Christ gave the Church? Does their request mean more than a willingness to conform to family custom and pressure? Do they really want their child to enter the larger family of the Christian faith? When parents decide to have their baby baptized, they commit themselves to help the child grow to a personal profession of faith within the community of believers gathered around the Eucharist.

If a priest thought that the child would be raised with scarcely any reference to the Christian faith and still went ahead and baptized him without any further consideration, he would be failing in his duty. A priest should refuse to perform a merely routine baptism. But I hope that no priest would simply turn down the request of a Catholic couple whose practice of their faith is defective. Their request is a pastoral opportunity for him to help them to grow in their faith, which may be barely alive like the biblical "smoldering wick" (Matt. 12:20). One needs a great deal of perceptiveness and charity to know whether delaying baptism would quench the spark or fan it to flame.

Emergency Baptism

Is a miscarriage or a baby born dead or one that dies very shortly after birth to be baptized? If so, how would I do this in the case of the miscarriage? Also what would be the proper way of burying the baby who miscarried?

The pastoral practice of the Church, codified in Canon 747, is to baptize the fetus which miscarries. This is done if the child is certainly or probably alive. And life is to be considered probable unless there is some decomposition. This applies, then, to the stillborn child and to the one who dies shortly after birth.

In the event of a miscarriage, baptism is usually performed by immersing the fetus in water while saying the words: "I baptize you in the name of the Father and of the Son and of the Holy Spirit." If it has not happened by itself, the membrane surrounding the fetus should be broken to allow the water of baptism to touch the body of the child.

Is all this necessary to ensure the eternal happiness of the tiny person born out of due time? Some theologians have been saying it is not. They base their judgment on their understanding of God's merciful will to save all men (John 12:32; Col. 1:17-20). Perhaps they are right, and their theories are a source of consolation to parents whose children die without having the opportunity to be baptized. However, these theories are not sure enough to warrant a deliberate choice to omit baptism. As recently as February 18, 1958, the Holy See warned that in this matter the theories concerning the eternal destiny of infants dying without baptism "lack a solid foundation" and should not be alleged in favor of delaying or neglecting baptism.

In the event of a miscarriage, the body of the newly baptized member of the Body of Christ should be handled reverently. Catholic undertakers usually provide for the burial of the body and will best be able to advise you.

Private Baptism by Grandmother

My son is married to a non-Catholic girl. Their first child was baptized in the Catholic Church. However, their second child has not been baptized. It seems that the child's mother is upset by some of her neighbors who do not (in her estimation) live their lives in a Catholic way. When I was taking care of the child, I performed lay baptism. I did not have the chance to take the child to a priest for baptism. Is the baptism I performed a satisfactory one as far as making the child a child of God is concerned?

Presuming that you used natural water, had the intention to baptize, and used the words prescribed by the Church, the child is baptized. However, this type of underground church ceremony should never be done unless there is clear danger the child is about to die.

The baptism of an infant is not only God's action taking the child into a new relationship with himself; it is also a religious ceremony in which the parents express their determination to nurture the seed of faith by raising their child to a full Christian life. No child should be baptized without his parents' consent. And no priest should baptize the child of consenting parents unless there is some basis for hoping that they will raise their child as a Catholic.

Obviously, the young couple have some problems to work out. The wife may have a prophetic insight into the shabby hypocrisy of the lives of some professional "good Catholics," she may be an unrealistic perfectionist, or she may be burying a deeper problem under this excuse. And your son doesn't seem to be very sure of what he believes or where he is going. In any event, the best thing would have been to give them time and opportunity to work out their problems — even if it meant letting the baby's baptism wait.

Meanwhile, you did what you thought was right. I hope that no well-meaning grandmother ever makes the same mistake again. Now, since the baby has in fact been baptized, you ought to let the priests of the parish know what you did, so that the baptism can be registered and so that the parish priests can be made aware of a problem in the young family. They may be able to find the right way to raise the question with them and help them to work it through.

Eucharist

The Greatest Prayer

I have seen it stated in prayer books that the Holy Sacrifice of the Mass is the greatest of all prayers. Is this true or false?

I could answer a simple yes, it is true. The Mass is the sacramental presence of our Lord's prayerful offering of himself, and how can it help but be best! The Mass is also the action of the whole Church, and how could our prayer not be enriched by being joined to that of all the holy people all over the world!

But is it my best prayer? That depends on a lot of variables. The best prayer of any person will be that which most fully expresses his faith and love and devotion. It will be the prayer that lifts his mind and heart out of their own narrowness and opens his whole self to receive God's love.

It's just too unreal to say that the Mass is this all the time. Sometimes the way the Mass is celebrated can get in the way — and instead of being a "best prayer," it becomes an occasion of endurance.

The thing which is objectively best does not always work out to be best in a particular case. For example, as a Catholic, I believe that our Church is objectively the best Church, because it is the authorized Church of Christ: in it alone can I find "the total fullness of the means of salvation" (Vatican II, *Decree on Ecumenism,* no. 3). Yet I would be blind if I did not recognize the fact that sometimes there is a better quality of Christian life and love and prayerfulness in another Christian community than there is in a particular Catholic parish or diocese or religious order. This does not warrant my leaving the divinely authorized Church. But it does show that we must work personally to raise the level of our life, that there is no room for a smug sense of superiority in our conviction that our Church is "best."

So, too, to make the Mass be our best prayer, we need adaptations in ourselves and in the Mass. We must want to pray. This means we must want to come to be on familiar terms with God. Otherwise, we aren't even praying when we attend the "best prayer." Also, the way Mass is celebrated must come to be something that can express our own inner yearnings and self. There is something a bit ludicrous about having an avant-garde type of liturgy which is designed for the hyperactive young presented to older people as the prayer form for them. And vice versa.

In the last analysis, the best prayer for me is the one in which I can most fully hand myself over to God in and with our Lord. There are times in a person's life (and, I believe, in each day) when this prayer should be in that silent communing with God which is the fruit of his liturgical enrichment. And this, in turn, will lead him to enter more fully into Christ's great act of prayer in the Mass.

Location of the Tabernacle

In one of our large churches, an open-work screen separates the table altar from the organ and choir. The tabernacle is behind the choir. Why is the tabernacle given a secondary place, here as in many churches?

In the book of official instructions for the celebration of Mass, the following recommendation is given: "It is highly recommended that the Holy Eucharist be reserved in a chapel suitable for private prayer. If this is impossible because of the structure of the church or local custom, it should be kept on an altar or other place in the church that is prominent and properly decorated" (*The Order of the Mass,* no. 276).

In the church building itself, which is designed primarily for the celebration of the sacred liturgy, the altar is to be given the most prominent place. And the arrangement the Church prefers is that the tabernacle should not be set on the main altar (Sacred Congregation of Rites, *Instruction on Eucharistic Worship,* May 25, 1967, no. 55).

The reason for this stems from the nature of the liturgical celebration. In the celebration, Christ becomes more marvelously present by gradual stages. First. He is present in the assembly gathered in his name. Then in the word of God through the Scripture readings, in the person of the minister; finally, through the Consecration, when bread and wine become the Blessed Sacrament. It is more in keeping with this celebration that the Eucharistic presence of Christ should not be on the altar from the beginning of Mass through the reservation of the sacred species in the tabernacle.

This is a change from the practice we grew up with. It does relegate the tabernacle and the reservation of the Blessed Sacrament to a secondary place. But it should not make the Blessed Sacrament secondary.

The place chosen for the tabernacle should make it clear that the Eucharist is not merely stored away for sick calls. It should remind the faithful of their belief in the real presence and invite them to come and rest in prayer.

It is difficult to balance out all these genuine concerns when an older church is adapted. I'm sure that the pastor and the diocesan officials believe they have made the best arrangement that was possible under the circumstances.

Communion in the Hospital

I wonder about the way Communion is given at our hospital. The chaplain comes around in the middle of the afternoon. Some of the patients who receive Communion have their television sets on, are smoking, or interrupt conversation with their visitors only while

the priest is in the room. Is this informality what our Lord wants? There seems to be no preparation, nor even any awareness of the wonderful thing that is happening. I can't help questioning why the Blessed Sacrament is brought day after day to someone who in ordinary circumstances would not be receiving Holy Communion daily. Is it accomplishing anything?

You have reason to wonder about this situation. The time is all right. Communion in the afternoon is a legitimate option. In some ways it is preferable in hospital practice. Normally the patients stand a better chance of being alert and attentive in the afternoon than they do at six-thirty in the morning after a deep and often drugged sleep.

However, the reason for wondering comes from the fact that the alert patients are so little attentive to the Lord they receive. Receiving the sacraments should not be a somber thing. The event should be a joyful celebration. But the joy should be a joy in the Lord, not a joy in the afternoon ball game.

Communion is not a matter of merely swallowing the sacred host — there should be communication. Spiritual food should be eaten spiritually, that is, with the spirit of man open to the Lord in intelligent faith and devout self-giving love. This requires an atmosphere of recollection. And recollection in this case means that a person gathers all his energies together to respond to the Person who is so totally giving himself through the sacrament.

There is no new theology that can sanction the kind of informality you refer to. It smacks of ignorance or irreverence rather than the free familiarity of the children of God. At a time when the best sacramental theology of our day speaks of the sacraments as being privileged moments of personal meeting with Christ, the practice you describe reduces the Blessed Sacrament to a kind of sacred aspirin which is thought to do its work automatically whether one thinks and prays or not.

One thing that your hospital experience shows is how poorly we have preached Jesus Christ and his love to our people. Perhaps we have been too preoccupied with having a smoothly running church organization and too eager for the comforting statistic of having huge numbers at Communion, when we should have been teaching the people how to contact our Lord through their Communions and how to live in his presence. How often do we hear a sermon that helps us to know Christ better and moves us to converse with him when he is closest to us? Where is the parish that ever has a problem in its parking lot because those who have received Communion want to stay in their places to commune with their Lord?

While working for the genuine renewal that the Vatican Council sought to initiate, we have to take people as they are — as we have helped them to become. I don't think that we should say that only those who regularly go to Communion every day are to be allowed to receive daily when they are sick. However, we should be very careful lest a zealous devotee of the spiritual numbers game give the impression that daily Communion is part of the expected routine of a Catholic hospital. It is a privilege, freely available to all those who genuinely desire it. Many hospital chaplains do a fine job in helping new patients to desire it with reverent faith. Let us hope that their good work becomes even more effective. It will keep abuses at a bare minimum.

Daily Mass

The priest in our parish does not have daily Mass or even a regularly scheduled Mass other than one on Sunday morning. In response to the request of the parish liturgy committee, he said that he will provide a weekday mass each month — but he does not want to have it in the church but at different homes, because enough people will not come to fill up the church. Is it unreasonable to expect a regularly scheduled Mass other than on Sunday? Does there have to be a required number of people to make it worth while?

If the situation is exactly the way you describe it, there is something wrong here. It is not my place to provide the snowballs for you to throw at your parish priest. However, I can reflect the thoughts and attitudes that prevail in the universal Church.

Most priests consider it a privilege to celebrate the sacrifice of the Mass every day. Most of us also consider it a personal spiritual need to share in the Body and Blood of Christ each day in the sacrament, as well as in prayer and the apostolate. Most who have a parochial responsibility think of providing frequent opportunities for weekday Mass as part of the spiritual service of their people which no other Christian can provide. In addition, there is also the objective consideration that the Pope, whose job it is to express the sense of the Church's living tradition, has repeatedly urged all priests to celebrate the Eucharist each day.

With all these considerations converging on the one point, I don't think it at all unreasonable for people to expect a regularly scheduled Mass during the week.

There is no required number of people who must be present at the celebration. Since it is a liturgy, and therefore an action of the community, it is normal that a group of people be present to participate devoutly and fully in the action. But the church building need not be filled. The Mass is always eminently worthwhile as the public action of the Church's worship. The only requisite to make it worthwhile for us is that the hearts of the worshipers, be they few or many, be filled with desire for the Lord.

Your present awkward situation, a situation in which members of a parish cannot fathom the thinking behind their priest's practice, is likely to increase this desire and bring about the happy result of making the people ready to flock to weekday Mass once it is restored to your section of the Church.

Communion Once a Day

Since there have been so many changes in the Church — all good — I wonder about the possibility of another change. Each Sunday and holyday, I assist at a second Mass and sometimes on other days too. My problem is that I may receive Communion at only one Mass and therefore feel that the other Mass is incomplete. How I wish that the bars would be let down so that I could receive our Lord every time I take part in a Mass. Do you think this will ever be possible?

It's a great pleasure to read a communication like this. The spirit of the renewing Church is with this questioner. With all our fumbling, he perceives the aim of all the adaptations in the Church and sees that they are good. No complaint. No despondency. He finds them a stimulus to a closer union with our Lord. It is heartening indeed. But will he ever get his wish? There are indications that we are coming nearer to this. The principle is clear. The most perfect participation in the Mass is had when a person filled with faith and love and desire receives the Body of the Lord sacramentally. And the aim of the liturgical renewal is to bring the people to a full and active participation in the sacred liturgy. Likewise, the precedent has been set for receiving Holy Communion more than once a day. For instance, those who go to Communion at the Easter Vigil and the

Christmas Midnight Mass may receive again at one of the daytime Masses. Similarly, those who participate in the Bishop's Mass of Chrism on Holy Thursday may receive a second time at the regular evening liturgy. Where the Mass of Sundays or holydays is anticipated the evening before, those who participate may receive Holy Communion, even though they already received the same morning. There may be further changes in the same line.

I think, though, that the Church authorities will move slowly in this direction, if at all. You will notice that none of the above exceptions to the rule of Communion once a day concerns the case of participating in the identical liturgy or mystery. In each case, it is a new event that we celebrate with new Mass texts which is completed by receiving the Lord's Body. Then there is always the possibility that an opening of this kind will be an opening to superstition. And it would smack of superstition if some of the faithful began circulating from Mass to Mass trying to receive as many times as possible each day. An effort towards repeated reception of the sacrament on the same day might get in the way of the Lord whom the sacrament communicates.

Don't expect your change right away. And meanwhile, make your desire to receive at the second Mass be the base of an intense spiritual Communion rather than a source of frustration.

Holy Communion—How Frequently?

If one receives weekly Communion without weekly confession, is it not wise to take advantage of daily Communion?

When we try to think of the advantages of daily Communion, we should not fall into the error of trying to solve the question by simple mathematics. The things of the spirit are not like material things that we can weigh and count. It is not necessarily true to say that if 52 Holy Communions are good, 365 are seven times better.

The Church believes that *the* advantage of Holy Communion is that it is the most privileged form of contact we have with the Person of Christ. Through a Christian's contact with the sacramental Body of Christ, the community of Christians is drawn together in closer unity by the bonds of love, the life begun in baptism is brought to maturity, and man is more and more healed from sin and the effects of sin.

If these effects are to take place, our contact with Christ in Holy

Communion must be personal. Eating the Body of Christ is not like swallowing a pill, which then goes on to produce its medicinal effect almost automatically. St. Augustine said, "We eat by believing." Our physical act of sharing the consecrated bread and wine has no spiritual value unless it is the sign of a deeper personal communion with the Person of our Lord — a communion that consists in our real wanting to surrender ourselves to him in faith and love. Spiritual life exists on this level of personal openness to the Lord in faith. It is present, in a minimum degree, in the person who is firmly determined to exclude anything that would wholly separate him from the love of Christ. It can grow to the point that every moment of a person's daily life is stamped with a God-centered, self-effacing concern for others.

A person who is trying to live his baptismal union with Christ through service of the brethren will increasingly want to take advantage of every opportunity to make this union explicit. That is, he will want to express all that this union means to him in the inner communion of prayer and in the sacramental communion of the Eucharist. And in this explicit union with the Lord, he will find the strength to live out what it implies in his daily life.

Frequent Communion, or better, frequent, full participation in the Holy Eucharist, is indeed desirable and to be recommended. It is to the Christian life what a man's desire to come home to his wife is to family life. His whole workday may be an implicit act of love for her — but love is apt to fade into routine unless it is nourished by personal closeness. Similarly, a life spent in the service of Christ and his Kingdom needs the nourishment of frequent contact with the Person of Christ.

Daily? Some can't do this all the time. For them, it might be a shirking of the responsibilities of their vocation rather than a sign and deepening of true love and communion with Christ. But most of us just need to get out of a rut. Why not get started this Lent? Lent is a time for renewal, and the principal task of the Church in renewing itself is to deepen the personal communion with Christ that leads to and flows from the Eucharist as its summit.

On Chewing the Sacred Host

Must one chew or swallow the Host, or can one make a fruitful Communion if he lets the Host dissolve entirely in his mouth? I have trouble swallowing the Host, and if I chew it, parts sometimes get into my teeth.

The Lord said, "Take this and eat it." (Matt. 26:26; cf. Mark 14:22; Luke 22:19). May we chew? Must we chew? Must we swallow? These questions arise from time to time as people analyze what is necessary to complete the sacramental sign-action of eating. There seems to be general agreement that the Sacred Host should be swallowed. Hard candy is "eaten" by melting in the mouth, but bread is usually swallowed. And the Eucharist is given to the Church in the form of bread.

When I was a boy, people in the Northeast had a thing about chewing the Host, or even about letting it touch the teeth. Why this misplaced reverence, I could never understand. In some churches, with the use of more substantial altar breads, it is almost impossible to swallow the Blessed Sacrament unless there has been some chewing. In this situation the proper thing to do is to chew and swallow.

Recently we have seen an increasing number of clerics making quite a production out of chewing with a hyperactive jaw motion that most parents would correct in their children as smacking of bad table manners. Their reason, apparently, is based on a literal interpretation of the Greek word for "eat" (grind with the teeth) that is used in John 6:51, in the discourse on the Eucharist. A fundamentalist biblicism is no more warranted here than anywhere else.

We should eat the sacramental Body of the Lord — and do whatever is necessary to eat — with as little fuss as possible over how we eat. A fruitful Communion depends far more on the spirit of faith and love we bring to this sacred moment. It is a time to cherish and deepen, first of all, a sense of oneness with him who is the ultimate source of meaning in our lives; and then to heighten our awareness that in him we become more fully one with all our brothers and sisters in the faith. A fruitful Communion is not just the moment of swallowing, but the whole life of prayerful communing and active concern that is enlivened by this contact with the real Body of the Lord. I long for the day when our sense of what the Lord has done for us in giving us his flesh to eat will bring us to see the need for a genuine personal, prayerful preparation for the communal act of Eucharistic worship, and a period of silent communing with the Risen Lord-with-us after the liturgical action has come to an end.

The Mystery of Faith

In William Buckley's first book, "God and Man at Yale," he quotes

a Yale professor as saying: "After many days of argument, I said to those Jesuits: 'I'll tell you how you can convert me and the rest of the world overnight. Submit the wine to a chemical analysis after the Consecration, and then see if you've gotten any hemoglobin out of the grape juice.'" I'd like to see a theological answer to the professor's scientific questioning.

Gee, the Jesuits get all the sticklers! Really, I'm amazed that we have expressed our faith so badly that a learned man could have so distorted a view of what we believe. Of course, he is inexcusable for using his position to shake up undergraduates.

A misunderstanding similar to the professor's occurs in John 6:61. In a clearly Eucharistic passage, our Lord had proclaimed the necessity of our eating his flesh and drinking his blood. This scandalized many of his disciples. They seemed to have understood that Jesus meant to give them pieces of his flesh and part of his blood to be eaten in cannibalistic fashion. This is not the understanding of the Catholic Church, nor of any Christian body that has links with orthodox Christianity. A view like that of the scandalized disciples at Capernaum has cropped up from time to time in periods of theological decline. It is because of an almost superstitious realism that some have hesitated to touch the Eucharist with their teeth lest they bite the body of Christ. Whereas, in actuality the communicant never touches the real body of Christ, he touches the appearances of bread which constitute the sacrament of his body.

The belief of Catholics concerning the Eucharist has always pivoted around two points. The first is faith's conviction that it is truly the body and blood of Christ that we eat and drink. The second is our undeniable experience that nothing apparent to the senses has been changed by the words of Consecration.

If the consecrated wine is now truly the blood of Christ, then it follows that it is no longer truly wine. Yet, if to all appearances it looks like wine, tastes like wine, and can intoxicate as wine does — this is a fact not only for unaided senses but also for aided senses. And all the elaborate technology of a laboratory is but a way of aiding our sensory powers of observation. The very terms of our faith lead us to expect that the most sophisticated chemical analysis would discover sugars and alcohols rather than hemoglobin and platelets.

The change we believe in is not a change of chemical or molecular structure. It is not a change of anything that can possibly be observed or measured. In the terms of the ancient philosophies, the "accidents" remain unchanged. The real change occurs on the level of the inner intelligible reality of bread and wine — what the ancients called "substance." The reason why the Church still clings to the awkward word "transubstantiation" is that it expresses this unparalleled and mysterious change precisely.

Our belief in the Blessed Sacrament does not imply that we have the appearances of the blood of Christ and its measurable chemical components together with the appearances of wine. If such a thing ever did take place, it would be wondrous, but it would not be a sacrament. A sacrament is always a sign. And the efficacious sign of the blood of Christ given for us and really present is the unchanged volume of wine in the chalice with all its special qualities and characteristics.

Eucharistic Heresy?

I'm a student at a state university, and I'm presently taking an ecumenical course in the religion department. One of my fellow students in the class is a Brother, and the other day he got up and explained the Catholic view of the Eucharist. Much to my dismay, he said he couldn't really accept the traditional teaching and feels that instead of "transubstantiaton," we should think of it as "transignification."

Since the Brother blatantly displayed his dissension in front of all those non-Catholics about a subject that is dear to my heart, I really felt annoyed — unjustly so, perhaps. I can't understand, if Catholics claim to believe in the teaching authority of the Church, how they can develop their own ideas of how to explain doctrine and still feel that they are loyal members of the Church.

How do we categorize such people? Are they heretics? That seems like such a strong word, and yet, aren't they proposing things that are against the teaching of the Church?

A heretic is a person who obstinately contradicts a truth of faith which has been defined by the Church. The awful thing about heresy is that it really is the abandoning of *all faith*. The content of faith is a package deal. There is no such thing as a "selective faith." If a person is a true believer in Christ, he accepts everything which the Church teaches has been revealed by God. If he picks and chooses only those things which are congenial to him or which seem reasonable to him, he no longer is submitting his own intelligence to the light which comes from God.

We should be very careful, though, about labeling persons as heretics.

Some people with a genuine faith in Christ do not accept the whole package of revealed truth proposed by the Church, because they are blamelessly unconvinced of the authority of the Church to speak in the name of Christ. This is the position of many very fine non-Catholics. One cannot accuse them of the sin of heresy.

Others reject a formula of the Church because they don't really understand what it means or because it seems to them to say something other than what the Church intends to teach. This happened immediately after the Council of Nicaea (325), and St. Athanasius showed himself to be very flexible with people of this sort. He had fought to have the orthodox belief of the Son's total equality with the Father in the one divine nature expressed by the technical word "homoousion" (of one substance). Yet he was willing to omit the word where it caused confusion, provided that the truth of faith it signified was maintained.

"Transubstantiation" is a technical word. Some people have difficulty with it. They think of the substance of a thing in terms of its mass or molecular structure. Consequently, the idea of the special sacramental change of the substance of bread and wine seems to mean that the molecules of bread and wine are invisibly changed into the molecules of the body and blood of Christ. So they want another way to express the mystery that takes place during the sacred sign of the Eucharistic consecration. "Transignification" seems to offer a way around the difficulty. By this term they hope to avoid language which smacks of chemistry or physics and to remain in language appropriate to sacraments — for sacraments are first and foremost *signs* of a divine reality. And they intend to express the reality of a mystery by affirming that the consecrated bread, which undergoes no molecular change, is freighted with a new meaning that communicates the real body of Christ to the faithful.

Their kind of objection to "transubstantiation" seems to me to be based on a misunderstanding of what the Church teaches. In fact, the Church's teaching on transubstantiation positively excludes the idea of any kind of change which can be measured — and a molecular change is capable of being observed.

By the dogma of transubstantiation, the Church affirms that what was bread is now no longer bread after the consecration. The bread has been changed into the body of Christ. This is true in objective reality — it is not merely "true" in the minds of believers who place a new value on bread by their belief. Contained under the unchanged appearances of bread is the true reality of the Risen Lord Christ, whole and entire: body, blood, soul, and divinity. There is no question of a mere symbolic presence of the power of his saving love. The consecrated appearances of bread have a new significance, and hence we can speak of a "transignification." But they mean something new because, in fact, they do contain a new reality. After this real change, our Lord remains really present as long as the appearances of bread and wine remain. For this reason, the Blessed Sacrament reserved in the tabernacle is to be treated with reverent adoration.

If a Catholic rejects this belief, which is at the heart of the dogma of transubstantiation, even when he has been shown that such is the teaching of the Church, I would not hesitate to consider him a heretic. If he merely has problems with the technical expression "transubstantiation," it is still possible that he is my brother in the faith. But all of us who hold fast to the faith must recognize our obligation to use words correctly, lest we "occasion the rise of false opinions regarding faith in the most sublime of mysteries" (Pope Paul VI, *Mysterium Fidei,* September 3, 1965).

The Eucharistic Fast

I heard a priest state in a sermon that when the Church reduced the period of fasting required before Holy Communion it was done only for the aged, sick, and infirm. He said that others took advantage of the change contrary to the instructions of the Church. Is the instruction of the Church regarding the above change available in any document that I may buy?

I think that the priest overstated the case. The requirement that a communicant be fasting from all food and drink from midnight was in effect until 1953. On January 6 of that year, Pope Pius XII issued a document that began the process of mitigating the Eucharistic fast. This process was concluded on November 21, 1964. Pope Paul VI, in the course of his address concluding the Third Session of the Vatican Council, reduced the required period of abstinence from all food and drink to one hour before Holy Communion. This is the law of the Church. It was not brought about by the abuse of persons wrongly taking advantage of concessions given only to the sick and the infirm.

At the same time, we are free to observe the norm of the old law and fast from midnight before receiving Holy Communion. In fact,

Pope Pius XII exhorted all of us to do so when he freed us from the strict obligation of doing so. He made a practical pastor's and law-maker's decision.

Two values had to be weighed in the balance. One was the all-important value of making it possible for all Catholics who are rightly disposed to participate fully in the Mass by receiving Communion. The other value was that of surrounding the Eucharist with those things which would foster the reverence due the Blessed Sacrament.

Fasting from all ordinary food and drink before sharing in the spiritual food of the body and blood of Christ certainly expressed the second value. However, the Pope saw that, in the changed conditions of life in our time, the rigor of the full Eucharistic fast was keeping a number of people from Holy Communion. Far better, then, to ease up on the requirements of the fast. This he did, while encouraging all of us to prepare for Holy Communion by fasting from midnight if we are able to do so.

This is not double-talk. It is entirely appropriate in laws whose purpose is spiritual. The law establishes a clear minimum for all healthy communicants. At the same time, it urges us all not to be content with a legal minimum if we are able to do more.

I presume that the priest you heard was hoping to inspire his congregation to greater generosity in this matter. However, we should be careful. The spirit of the "generous" is a questionable spirit when it looks with condescending disapproval at those who are following their own consciences and doing what they are asked to do.

I'm not familiar with any book in print that includes all the documentation on the mitigation of the Eucharistic fast. There is a good, brief article by A. M. Carr in Volume V of the *New Catholic Encyclopedia* (p. 847a), which should be in your local public library.

Announced Masses

What is the latest on Mass offerings? At one time our pastor accepted whatever was offered. But today, unless it is a solemn high Mass, the name of the person prayed for is not mentioned at all. The parishioners are becoming baffled.

I don't know if "the latest on Mass offerings" is really going to help you. Your problem is a practical one — a matter of parish policy and parishioners' feelings. It is something that should be handled in the privacy of your own parish by the kind of relaxed communication that can issue in mutual understanding.

The latest on Mass offerings is a somewhat theoretical discussion — though it has practical ramifications. There are, basically, two views in this matter. One may be called traditional, in the sense that it is the view that is followed in practice almost everywhere in the Church. According to this view, the priest who celebrates the Mass has a privileged place in applying the spiritual benefits of the Mass to the person or group of persons he chooses. This special role as intercessor is his because he acts in the place of Christ and in the name of the Church. It does not depend on his personal holiness or lack of it. He has but to offer the Sacrifice of Christ rightly with some particular intention in mind, and the prayer of Christ and of the Church embraces this need in a special way. The practice of Mass offerings attests to the conviction of the faithful in this matter. In effect, they ask the priest to make their own intention his, and in deference to him they make a donation for his support and for the expenses of the altar. (A Mass stipend is this kind of donation. You do not "buy a Mass.") According to the theological principles that underpin this practice, there seems to be no good reason why the Mass can be offered for only one person's intention. However, according to the good sense of canonists, who wanted to avoid the suspicion of commercialism, a priest may accept only one stipend for each Mass, and it is the intention of this donor that is announced.

There is another view of this whole matter. There are theologians who question whether the priest celebrant has any special privileged position in disposing of the fruits of the Eucharistic Sacrifice. They argue that our present practice arose rather late in the history of the Church and depended on historical factors rather than on a developed insight into the meaning of the Mass. They do not deny that the sacrifice is offered to benefit the living and the dead. They question whether there is any spiritual value that comes to the Church that is independent of the real spiritual condition of those who are offering the Mass. In this view, it is hard to maintain that the intention of the priest celebrating the Eucharist guarantees a greater spiritual benefit to a person than does the intention of the person who requested the Mass or that of the participants who enter into this supreme act of worship with faith and devotion. If this view should come to be accepted, there would be even greater reason for publicly announcing the intention of the person who contributes to the altar. Thus, the whole community would be made aware of his need and could consciously recommend it to the care of our heavenly Father.

Intercommunion—Path to Unity?

In our town, a group of seminarians came out in favor of having common Eucharistic celebrations with Protestants during the Church Unity Octave. How can they even think of such a thing? I believe that nobody should be allowed to receive Holy Communion who does not believe in the Sacrament and Sacrifice or who does not believe that he is receiving the real body of our lord.

You're in good company. St. Paul wrote: "A man should examine himself first; only then should he eat of the bread and drink of the cup. He who eats and drinks without recognizing the body eats and drinks a judgment on himself" (I Cor. 11: 28-29). The Eucharist is not just a common meal that expresses our feeling of closeness with one another. It is the Lord's Supper — Christ's gift to the Church. It is to be shared only with a person who believes and who has been baptized. This cannot change. To invite an unbaptized or unbelieving person to receive Holy Communion is to be guilty of serious sacrilege and to fail in the respect due to the person we invite.

But there are many baptized persons who are not fully one with us in the Church. Can we share the Eucharist with them? In certain circumstances, yes. The Council noted that the sacraments are both signs of the real unity of the community which celebrates them and sources of grace. Now, grace itself is the source of unity. Normally, the lack of full visible unity will stand in the way, preventing us from admitting Protestants to our sacraments. However, in special cases of urgent need, if the separated brother asks for the sacraments, believes in them, and is rightly disposed, a Catholic priest may give them to him. This is already authorized.

What the seminarians are asking (and they are not alone in this request) is that the meaning of "urgent need" be extended. Don't confine it merely to the urgent need that an individual may experience. The purpose of the Eucharist is to make the Church perfectly one. Isn't the need that all Christians be made one sufficiently urgent? They recognize the fact that all Christians are not visibly united in the one Church of Christ. But they suggest that this is itself the reason why we should share the Eucharistic Body of Christ on some very special occasions. In this way, we would be made open to the power of Christ, who is really present to make us one in him.

The idea is fascinating. It is not the path the Council pointed to as normal. Nor is it the road that most ecumenical groups have previously trod. For the most part, ecumenists have seen a value in having us experience the pain of our division by not being able to share the very sacrament of unity. Thus we might be impelled to work and pray more earnestly to cure the sickness of disunity.

Before we embark on the suggested new path, there are all kinds of practical difficulties that must be taken into account. Not the least of these is the matter of reciprocity that we refer to in the next question. Briefly, it is this: Can Catholics accept with good faith receiving communion at the Eucharistic celebration of their separated brethren? Where there is no mutual intercommunion, the offer of the Eucharist to our separated brethren could easily seem to be spiritual colonialism.

Apart from these practical difficulties, you're asking if there is sufficient agreement in faith for us to give the consecrated bread to Protestants. Don't presume too quickly that there isn't. It's true that there are real differences in the expression of Eucharistic faith between Roman Catholics and the other Western Churches (though the Episcopalians, Lutherans, and Catholics are more in harmony than many imagine). Yet I wonder if there is really a significantly different faith. I wonder if the faith which recognizes in our Mass a form of carrying out *what the Lord gave the Church at the Last Supper* might not be sufficient. Isn't this able to be taken as an implicit acceptance of the whole mystery of the Eucharist? A person might be blamelessly in error about the special nature of the enduring real presence of Christ in the sacred species of the sacrament and yet firmly believe that this is the great gift through which Jesus gives himself as food.

I have heard the situation of such a person likened to that of a Catholic raised in a racist environment. His background may be so dominant that it is really impossible for him to recognize a Negro as his brother. Objectively, this is a more serious heresy than an error about the nature of the real presence. Yet, for years our pastors have admitted people like this to Communion. This doesn't mean that they ignore the heresy of white supremacy. But should they cut off the person blamelessly infected by it? Even while they are trying to help him break free from his error, they give him the help of the body of Christ.

The hierarchy must judge whether the advantages of the seminarians' suggestion outweigh its real difficulties. But if the pope and the bishops respond favorably to this petition, they will not be abusing the sacrament or giving it to unbelievers. They will be ministering it to Christians whose real belief is often far richer than their formulation.

Discrimination at the Altar Rail

At a nuptial Mass I recently attended, the Protestants in the wedding party received Holy Communion. Why must I, as a Catholic, meet various criteria before receiving, but these Protestants apparently did not?

The only conditions that are absolutely and in all circumstances required of a communicant are that he be a baptized believer and that he be in the state of grace.

The first requirement is based on the Church's conviction that a person comes to exist in the sacramental world of worship and life only through the door of sacramental baptism. Apart from this, even though a person may be bound to Christ by the bonds of grace and love, he is incapable of receiving any of the sacraments as the signs of his worship and the vehicle of deeper divine life. To share the Blessed Sacrament with an unbaptized person would be to empty it of meaning, and to do it knowingly would be sacrilegious.

The second requirement flows from the special meaning of the Eucharist itself. When a person receives the Sacrament of the Body of Christ, he professes that he is seeking to deepen his personal union with our Lord. If he is conscious of having alienated himself from the love of Christ by a sinful refusal to keep His commandments (John 15:10), the act of taking the Blessed Sacrament is a fraud. In effect, his external profession is at odds with his life and inner attitude. This is what we mean when we speak of a "bad Communion."

There is no permissible exception to these requirements. Even in those rare circumstances where the Church authorities judge that there is sufficient reason to offer the Eucharist to those who are not fully united to the Church, these conditions must be complied with. There is no difference between the Church's approach to Catholics and Protestants in this matter. The fulfilling of the second condition is so private and personal a matter of conscience that neither pope nor you nor I can determine the fact of the matter. "Let a man examine himself" is St. Paul's injunction to the Church (I Cor. 11:28).

In addition to these requirements that can never be dispensed with by anyone who would "eat this bread and drink the cup of the Lord" worthily, Church law adds another. It requires that a person who is conscious of having committed a personal mortal sin since his last confession must *ordinarily* receive the sacrament of penance before communicating. Note the word *ordinarily*. Exceptions to this law have always been recognized. And when there is a situation where the competent authorities extend the privilege of Holy Communion to separated Christians, this legal requirement of sacramental confession is waived — though the divine requirement of inner conversion and repentance is not.

The only further point I would make is this: the intercommunion that you witnessed is not a usual and normal thing in the Catholic Church. There has been a great deal of somewhat official discussion between the churches on this point. There is much hope that the day will soon come when the sacrament of Christian unity will be shared in a way that will lead to the unity of all Christians. But at the moment, it would be rare to find a situation where intercommunion is appropriate, where its good effects would clearly outweigh its bad ones, and where it will genuinely contribute more to unity in Christ and in the Church than to a scandalous religious indifferentism.

The Eucharist in Other Churches

How does the Church view the "Lord's Supper" celebrated in the churches separated from Rome? Do they have the real Holy Sacrifice?

The official teaching of the Church is that the validity of the Eucharist depends on the validity of priestly orders in the Church. There is no question but that the Eastern Orthodox Churches have a validly ordained priesthood. As Vatican II put it in the *Decree on Ecumenism*: "Although these Churches are separated from us, they possess true sacraments, above all — by apostolic succession — the priesthood and the Eucharist . . ." (no. 15).

The question of valid succession of orders in the Anglican or Episcopalian Church was answered negatively by Pope Leo XIII in the papal bull *Apostolicae Curae* in 1896. However, the issue is not dead. A new theological literature is still raising the question. So also is Pope Paul's manner of acting with the Archbishop of Canterbury, which obviously goes beyond the requirements of gentlemanly civility in an ecumenical age. Apart from the question of the correctness of the 1896 decision, the cooperation of Orthodox bishops as co-consecrators of the present hierarchy of the Church of England has apparently restored the link of apostolic succession, if it was in fact interrupted.

As for the "free," or nonepiscopal, churches, Vatican II expressed the situation this way: "We believe that, especially because of the lack of the sacrament of orders, they have not preserved the genuine and total reality of the Eucharistic mystery" (*Decree on Ecumenism,* no. 22). For this reason, the Council speaks of them as "ecclesial communities" rather than as "churches," for the Church is the community where Christ's worship of the Father is perpetuated in the Eucharist. Note that at the same time, the Council denied that they have the "total" Eucharistic mystery. There is some partial Eucharistic reality that is shared by these communities in their celebration of the Lord's Supper. What is it? It is at least that spiritual communion with our Lord and with one another in him which is the ultimate purpose of the sacrament of the Eucharist. For when a community comes together in faith and love and with the intention of following our Lord's invitation to "do this as a remembrance of me" (Luke 22:19), can we imagine that the Spirit of Christ does not refresh the hearts of those who open themselves to him to the best of their ability?

Is there any more than this? Our present understanding of God's designs for men and for his Church forbids us to say a clear yes. This is one of the reasons why Catholics are forbidden to share in the Communion service of these churches — lest they appear to be saying by their actions that it is the same as our Eucharist. Similarly, this is why we are forbidden to have a Protestant clergyman concelebrate Mass with us. At the same time, theologians (part of whose job it is to reach to the outer limits of our present understanding and beyond) are raising tentative hypotheses. Is it not possible that a special divine Providence provides in these communities of the baptized for the lack of a normal sacramental succession of clergy? Where the lack of the sacrament of orders is no longer something that can be blamed on the culpable rebellion of a believing Christian community, might not God provide for the validity of its Eucharist in an extraordinary way? It is possible. However, we cannot assume that it is a fact and act on it. If God is acting this way among them, we can believe that he is providing them with a means that is working toward the perfect unity of the Church — for this is the special grace of the sacrament of the Eucharist.

Experimental Masses

When is a Mass still experimental? How can you tell whether a parish or group of people is genuinely experimenting or merely going too far? We've seen Masses under quite a few different circumstances. For example, we've seen where the priest offers up a large loaf of bread, consecrates it, and passes it around to everyone. We've seen circumstances where little children are crawling all around the altar area (sometimes sitting on the poor priest's foot!). Many times the priest is dressed in a sweater outfit for Mass, everyone very informal, some smoking. We are open-minded about all this; it doesn't actually upset us. Yet we aren't sure whether the pope is opposed to this and we do want to know if we are going to things not yet acceptable.

A genuinely experimental Mass, ideally, would come about like this. Competent men — men well versed in the history of ritual, the theology of the liturgy, the psychology and sociology of celebration, and the cultural patterns of our own time — would work together at creating new texts, ceremonies, and gestures. They would be careful to preserve the changeless elements of the Mass and try to communicate these more effectively to various groups of people. Ideally, field testing would follow. Responsible communities would be authorized to celebrate in these new ways to see if they worked — to see if the people would more easily understand the holy things the rites signify and would be led through them to a more faith-filled life. These experiments would be reported upon and evaluated. The best elements would be preserved. Less effective things would be dropped. Finally, there would come a time when a decision would have to be made. Authorized field-test types of experimentation would be discontinued, and a final form of the Mass would be issued by the authority of the pope and bishops.

This would have been the ideal way to proceed. To a certain extent, this kind of research and field-testing experimentation has gone on in the years since the Council. Unfortunately, however there wasn't a great deal of it. And so the apparent lack of authorized and controlled experiment, combined with many other factors, led a number of priests to "do their own thing" while calling it an "ex-

perimental Mass." Their good will was oftentimes unquestionable.
They generally met their congregations just where they were and
reenlivened a faith that was slipping. They also served as catalysts
to move more conventionally minded churchmen to take a second
look at what kind of changes were possible.

However, these ventures into unauthorized liturgical change were
sometimes very ill-advised. The innovators did not have the scientific
or artistic competence to create a liturgy. Even when the men were
competent, there was something questionable about these unauthorized experiments. It is not proper for an individual priest or group
of people to set up a *liturgy* in opposition to the bishop. Liturgy
is always a public act of the whole Church. It is authentic when it is
celebrated by a priestly people, presided over by an ordained minister
who acts in harmony with the episcopal leadership of the Church.
A priest is no more free to make his own rules for celebrating the
Mass than a citizen is to bypass the courts and set up his own Mafia-
like justice.

One thing that disappointed me during these years was the failure
of so many concerned priests to use creatively the variants that were
open to them in our authorized Latin Rite ceremonies. Here was a
way to involve the people in more relevant celebration that would
be unmistakably linked with the larger Church community. Was it
really necessary to move so quickly into liturgical anarchy?

At any rate, we are now at the final phase of the revision of the
Mass that Vatican II called for. In 1970 we began to use the newly
revised rite of the Mass that is the result of years of study and
limited, authorized experimentation. For this reason, Rome has said
that the time for experimental forms of the Mass is past.

The present rite is not a monolithic structure. There are many
flexibilities built into it. A priest and people who work together to
mine its potential can find the ways to combine religious spontaneity
and appropriate celebration capable of being the prayer of any group.
Our present and urgent task is to try to make this work well.

The new forms of the Mass are authentic — they have the full
approval of the hierarchy of the Church. The new forms are orthodox
— they do not lose sight of any aspect of the complex reality of the
Eucharist: sacrifice; communion with Christ, source of unity of the
Church; and community of celebration. The new forms are reverent
— undisciplined casualness is not the way a redeemed people should
approach the sacred mysteries of redemption. The new forms are
prayerful — the Mass is not just a meeting with friends; it is a
meeting with God. The new forms are easier to understand and to

share in — this is the reason why any change was made at all.

The things you describe are not yet acceptable, nor are they apt to become so. There is no question but that an ordinary loaf of bread could be the matter of consecration. But why do something like this? Does it increase the sign-value of the sacrament? Does it make the person more gratefully conscious that the Lord is feeding him with his flesh and blood in order to change his mind and heart and make it like his own? Does the casual breaking of a loaf of bread with its inevitable scattering of crumbs, help me to believe that Jesus Christ is here whole and entire in every piece that looks like bread?

Personally, I don't mind children sitting on my feet, nor am I opposed to smoking in a friendly gathering. But there are times and places for everything, and the Mass is not one of them. The ordination rite urges the new priest to be aware of what he is doing. At the moment when I am trying to be conscious of offering all the joys and sorrows of mankind to God and of lending my whole personality to Christ to be his instrument in making his one sacrifice present to this community of believers, I think it rude or obtuse to encourage this kind of distraction. Religion should not be somber. Worshipers should not emulate the rigidity of plaster statues. But, at the same time, a religious community of joyful and prayerful worship is not the same thing as a fun-gathering of a happy family.

The Forms of Altar Bread

I have noticed that some churches are using different kinds of altar breads. Would you please explain what this change is all about and how far it is apt to go?

As you go about the country, you will notice some groups are moving away from the white, coin-shaped wafer of bread that has been in use for a long time in the Roman rite celebration of the Eucharist.

These variations will include brown wafers, made from whole-wheat flour, or particles that are puffed into larger pieces by a new baking process. At times you will even find some groups using the leavened bread of the Oriental Churches.

The reason why parishes and other groups have been moving away from the tiny white wafer is based on the principles of sacrament theology. The Vatican Council pointed to these principles when it said: "The purpose of the sacraments is to sanctify men, to build up the body of Christ, and, finally, to give worship to God. *Because they are signs, they also instruct"* (*Constitution on the Sacred Liturgy,* no. 59). The paragraph went on to emphasize the need for the symbolic elements of the sacrament to instruct effectively, to be genuinely intelligible: "It is therefore of capital importance that the faithful easily understand the sacramental signs."

Many people have come to be dissatisfied with the tiny white host. It does indeed convey the essential meaning of the Eucharistic sacrifice and meal. But it is not a strong sign of some important elements of that mystery. Since the Eucharist is a shared sacred meal, it would be better if the consecrated elements looked and tasted more like real food and if they lent themselves to the symbolic action connected with the Eucharist from early times: the breaking of bread.

These desires were reflected in a recommendation that has come from Rome in the official directives on the Order of the Mass promulgated in 1969 and put into effect in 1970: "The nature of the sign demands that the material for the Eucharistic celebration appear as actual food. The Eucharistic bread, even though unleavened, should therefore be made in such a way that the priest can break it and distribute the parts to at least some of the faithful" (no. 283). Two elements seem to appear here: (1) the bread should be easily recognized as food, and (2) the principal bread of the celebration should be large enough to be broken and distributed as a sign of the unity and love of the Christian family.

There are technical problems involved in making bread that is a strong sign while still conforming with the serious requirement of the Roman rite that the bread be unleavened. Unleavened bread must be baked from a batter of wheaten flour and water without the addition of any natural or chemical materials to make it rise. It is difficult to bake this mixture in a way that will make it "appear as actual food" without its becoming too hard or unpalatable.

Some are solving the problem by avoiding it. These are the groups who are using ordinary table bread or making special breads with leavening and moistening elements.

As far as I can see, this "solution" raises significant theological problems. The Eucharistic liturgy is not merely the private celebration of the faith and devotion of the group assembled around the altar. It is always the public action of the whole Church. Hence, it should conform to the public and official requirements of the Church. Docility to law of this kind is not a legalistic fetish. It is an act of faith in the Church universal, whose leaders have the right and duty to establish the guidelines that bring each local church's celebration into harmony with the great act of worship of the whole Church.

How far is the change apt to go? It is hard to predict. At present there are some who are at work to solve the problem of providing a strong sign in unleavened bread without bypassing the problem. It may well be that these efforts will be successful and will be widely accepted.

Another possibility is that the Roman authorities might modify their requirements and permit the use of leavened bread on special occasions when pastoral reasons suggest that this would be appropriate. Meanwhile, I think it is greatly to be desired that all priests and liturgical committees consider themselves bound by the directive of the Vatican Council: "Absolutely no other person [apart from the proper authorities], not even a priest, may add, remove, or change anything in the liturgy on his own authority" (*Constitution on the Sacred Liturgy*, no. 22).

Communion in the Hand

What is the official ruling on receiving the consecrated host in one's hand and communicating oneself?

The official ruling that is in effect in the United States is that an authorized minister must place the consecrated host on the tongue of the communicant. This custom has been reconfirmed by an Instruction issued on May 29, 1969, by the Vatican office that is charged with regulating the liturgy, the Congregation for Divine Worship.

Throughout the centuries there have been different ways in which Holy Communion was given. All the evidence indicates that in earliest times the consecrated bread was broken and then handed to the laity, who "took and ate." In time, the practice disappeared in large segments of the Eastern Church and through the West. The reasons were different in both regions.

In sections of the East, Communion under both kinds began to be given by means of a consecrated bread soaked in the precious blood. When this happened, it was no longer convenient or considered reverent to take Holy Communion in one's hand.

In the West, theological questions were raised about the nature of the consecrated bread — with some churchmen diminishing the

Church's faith in the real presence of Christ's body, reducing the sacrament to a merely symbolic thing. It was about this time, when the faith was called into question, that the practice of receiving the consecrated host directly into the mouth began. Very likely it was intended to emphasize the especially sacred thing which the Blessed Sacrament is. While the very nature of the Eucharist requires that it come into contact with the body of the communicant — otherwise it could not be eaten — bodily contact was reduced to the bare minimum.

In recent years, with the renewal of full participation in the liturgy, the desire has grown in a number of places to restore the ancient practice of taking Communion in the hand and eating it in a more normal manner. Those who favor this procedure see it as a better expression of some genuine Christian values. The practice shows more clearly that Holy Communion is a sharing in the Lord's Supper, for adult diners feed themselves. By baptism, the whole person is consecrated as a temple of the Holy Spirit — his hands as well as his tongue — and the Christian people are reminded of their sacred status by a procedure that does not make their touching the Blessed Sacrament seem to be a profanation.

In a number of places, there was much more than a mere desire to receive Holy Communion in the hand. Priests were going ahead with the practice without any authorization. A number of bishops and some regional bishops' conferences asked the Holy See to approve the practice. In an exercise of collegial responsibility, Rome polled the bishops of the world for their opinion. Three-fifths of the bishops opposed any change. But that left a sizable minority of two-fifths who favored some modification.

The Instruction of May 29, 1969, was the result. While reconfirming the present custom as a general norm for the Church, Rome left the way open for exceptions to the general norm. It was prepared to grant this if two-thirds of the bishops of a region voted to have their bishops' conference request it.

Requests have been made and granted. In fact, it was only eleven days after the date of the Instruction that the bishops of France had an exception made for their country.

Where an exception to the general rule is authorized, Rome is insistent on very wise pastoral rules: (1) nobody who wishes to receive Holy Communion is to be forced to take it in his hand; (2) there is to be nothing casual about taking the host — it is to be given by an authorized minister who addresses to each person the formula that expresses the faith in the real body of Christ; (3) a careful instruction is to be given to the people before they begin with the optional manner of receiving Communion.

Instruction is extremely necessary. There have been real problems of faith and devotion in recent years. And during this same period, there have been some erroneous opinions making the rounds on the question of how the body of Christ is present in the Blessed Sacrament. It would be tragic if the new practice were to be introduced where it might be misinterpreted, as if the Church's faith in the real presence had changed.

Are there any other legitimate exceptions to the general rule of receiving the consecrated host on the tongue? A number of theologians think so. Since there is nothing wrong, in itself, with the practice, they would consider it proper to anticipate a legal authorization on special occasions where its contribution to Eucharistic devotion is foreseen to outweigh the undoubted value there is in following the direction of liturgical authority. These occasions would occur only in special groups where there is no scandal nor fear of the practice's being misunderstood, nor danger of disrespect to the Blessed Sacrament, and when the circumstances would make this manner of communicating a more evident sign of the Lord's Supper.

It is interesting to note that when the Roman Instruction leaves it up to the episcopal conference to judge whether it should ask for an exception to the general norm, it prefaces the directive with these words: "If the contrary usage, namely, of placing Holy Communion in the hand, has already developed in any place. . . ." Does this simply refer to a past situation which can now be regularized by a dispensation from the rule? Or does the Holy See anticipate that the usage will probably spread before it is officially authorized and tacitly acknowledge that this spontaneity is not necessarily wrong or abnormal?

In any event, it is unlikely that the practices that are authorized in a fairly large part of the Catholic world this year will be forbidden to the rest of the Catholic world for very long. For my part, I would prefer to wait for the *desire* to grow in our country, and when the people are ready for it, the practice could be begun with approval.

Layman Minister of Holy Communion

I have been very upset at the sight of laymen distributing Holy Communion alongside the priests in our parish. How did this come about? Can we still believe in the Lord's real presence in the

Blessed Sacrament if ordinary, unconsecrated laymen are allowed to handle it?

On April 30, 1969, the Congregation of the Sacraments, one of the Pope's Roman offices, sent an instruction to each of the Bishops' Conferences throughout the world. It granted the bishops power to authorize religious men and women, as well as lay people, to administer Holy Communion in case of need.

There are several situations in which it is foreseen that this faculty will be used. The most obvious is at Mass, when a great number of people are coming to Communion. I have helped out in parishes where five priests were engaged in giving Holy Communion and the distribution took between five and ten minutes. Few parishes can call on so many priests, and it really is not right to have the Communion procession last so long that the Eucharistic celebration is thrown out of balance and becomes a burden.

Also, there are situations where the priests of the parish cannot satisfy the desires of the sick who want to be nourished more frequently with the Blessed Sacrament.

There are also communities where a priest is not available every Sunday to celebrate the Sacrifice of the Mass. Here an authorized layman could lead the people in the readings and in prayer and give them Holy Communion from the tabernacle. What a tremendous help this would be to the spiritual life of Christians in remote places.

This adaptation does not imply any lessening of faith in the reality of the Lord's presence in the Eucharist. Nor is it the thin edge of the wedge for doing away with the distinction between the layman and the ordained priest. Only the ordained minister presides at the Mass. He alone can consecrate the bread and wine so that it becomes the Body and Blood of Christ.

After the Consecration, it is the sacrament of His Body and Blood. No matter who presents it to the communicant, it is the Lord who is giving himself. We should not let the person of the minister come between him and ourselves.

This new arrangement is not something unheard of in the Catholic Church. The practice was not unusual in Christian communities right up to the eighth century, especially for bringing Holy Communion to the sick.

I'm sorry about the shock you were exposed to by all this. Really, there should be a gentle pastoral preparation of the people before beginning a change like this. You should have been shown the reasons and the authorization before the practice began.

The French hierarchy has prepared a beautiful ritual to be used when a layman is designated as a minister of Holy Communion. It is celebrated publicly before the community. The person chosen is asked if he is willing to accept this ministry of giving the Body of the Lord to his brethren for the service and growth of the Church, if he desires to live profoundly by the Bread of Life and pattern his life on the sacrifice of Christ, and if he will perform his duty with the greatest care and respect. The blessing of God is called upon him to help him faithfully fulfill his service of the Body of Christ.

In this setting, faith and reverence for the Blessed Sacrament should grow rather than be broken down by extending the privilege of this ministry to the laity.

Confession and Communion

Is it permissible to receive Holy Communion if one hasn't the opportunity to go to confession? That is, can't one make a sincere act of contrition, receive Holy Communion, and then go to confession as soon as possible? In the prayers at the beginning of Mass there is a public confession and absolution of sins. With all the changes in the Church, perhaps this public confession will enable the whole congregation to receive Communion together — unless someone is conscious of having been guilty of a grave sin which will need the immediate attention of a priest.

It is permissible to receive Communion without first going to confession. In fact, this is not only permissible, it is and should be the more usual and normal procedure.

It may be that you got the opposite impression a few years back. Some of our practices and instructions were colored by a pessimistic view of man that carried over from the Jansenist heresy. Jansenism assumed that the normal condition of the ordinary Christian was a state of sin. If this were in fact the case, then each communion should be preceded by sacramental confession.

However, the ordinary and normal situation of one who is trying to live a Catholic life is that of being fundamentally at one with our Lord — what we speak of as being in the "state of grace." This is the basic requirement of anyone who wants to receive Holy Communion. The very meaning of sacramental Communion requires that the communicant be already united to Christ by faith and love, that there be no major inconsistency or lived lie in his life. It makes no sense to profess in sacramental action that I am seeking to deepen my relationship with our Lord and with his Church if I know that I am, in fact, cut off from a living relationship with him by reason of unrepented serious sin. Such a Communion would be a sham.

If a person has failed our Lord by mortal sin, he must sincerely repent before he can receive Communion without sacrilege. And, in ordinary circumstances, the Church requires that this repentance be expressed in the sacrament of penance before the person receives Communion.

However, for the ordinary Catholic who is not conscious of being guilty of serious sin, there never has been an obligation of going to confession in order to receive Holy Communion.

This does not mean that the sacrament of penance should be neglected. Nor does it mean that the daily life of Catholics is so totally under the guidance of the Spirit of Christ that it is practically sinless. Rather, it stems from the Catholic view of the Eucharist, which sees the body of the Lord as the source of a better life and a remedy healing us from our daily sins. The sincere act of contrition and the public prayers of the Church for forgiveness that are part of every Mass are helps to dispose us to closer oneness with Christ by sloughing off the shabbiness of our petty jealousies and meanness and selfishness. It will take no change in the action of the Church to bring the congregation to the altar. It will take merely an inner renewal in ourselves — a realization that the Lord invites even us struggling sinners to share a closer union with him.

Penance

Confession—How Frequently?

I would like to see a long answer to the question, "Confession — How frequently?" It is a very important pastoral question, for many confusions and false ideas have been created and exist in the minds of Christians, including priests.

A long answer! That's the kind of invitation I really don't mind.

I think we all know that, at the very least, a Catholic should receive the sacrament of penance before going to Holy Communion if he has been guilty of a serious sin. And since Communion once a year is obligatory, it is generally urged that those whose sacramental life is this minimal should also go to confession once a year. In the present Canon Law, members of religious orders and priests are urged to receive the sacrament of penance frequently. Up until recently, the general practice urged for "good Catholics" was to get to confession at least once a month, and very many went every other week.

Recently there has been a noticeable change. People are staying away from confession in droves. Weekly communicants more and more begin their confessions, "It is three months since my last confession." Saturday afternoons and evenings are very quiet in most of the parishes I am familiar with. Many people have obviously reappraised their religious practice and, for various reasons, have decided against frequent confession. I sometimes get the impression that those who shouldn't come do, while those who should come don't. The confessional is still frequented by those poor, anxious souls whose wounded psyches are sometimes even more shaken by the use they make of the sacrament of pardon and peace. Yet it's the well-balanced and fundamentally wholesome Catholic who could benefit most from the sacrament of penance.

Why are they staying away? Some have been told by priests that they should not come unless they are conscious of serious sin, that the penitential acts of the early parts of the Mass are an equally adequate and effective expression of the Church's ministry of the forgiveness of sins. This kind of advice certainly runs counter to the pastoral teaching of the Vatican Council. In the *Decree on the Bishops' Pastoral Office,* priests are urged to work hard to bring their people to use the sacraments frequently. And they are expressly reminded of "the immense value of the sacrament of penance for growth in the Christian life" (no. 30). The conviction of the Church comes through in the *Decree on the Ministry and Life of Priests,* where, among the helps for fostering an intimate union with Christ, there is "the fruitful reception of the sacraments, *especially frequent sacramental confession.* Prepared for by daily examination of conscience, this contributes enormously to that indispensable conversion of heart to the love of the Father of mercies." (no. 18).

These quotations highlight what I think is another principal reason for the increasing rarity of confession: the sacrament did not seem to be fostering the growth promised, people did not experience it as enormously helpful to a profound turning toward their heavenly Father. This probably stems from defects on three levels: the rite, the confessor, and the penitent.

That the ritual of the confessional is defective is so obvious that the Council contented itself with a direct statement ordering a revision that will make the meaning and effect of this sacrament more evident. Very likely we will one day see more communal celebrations of this sacrament that will make us aware that our sin injures the community and that God reconciles us to himself by reconciling us with the community.

I've often heard people complain about the defects of the priests who hear confessions. They speak of a deadening impersonalism, a sense that they are being turned out on an assembly line. This does not help them to feel that our Lord is personally forgiving and healing them through the sacrament.

It may be some time before the ritual is revised. And the ministers of the Church will probably continue to come in every variety of personality. But meanwhile we can do something about the defect that lies within each of us as penitents. If we go to confession out of routine, if we think of it as a speedy dunking in a spiritual detergent, if we look for "automatic" results, then no wonder we save it for emergencies. A person can grow through the sacrament of penance only if he brings to it an openness to growth, only if he comes as one who wants to uncover the depths of his personal sinfulness in the presence of the Lord in order to beg his healing mercy. Luther remarked. "You cannot preach the Gospel to men who do not know they are sinners." And it is equally true that no one will be helped to grow through this sacrament who does not know he is stunted. The grace of penance works through an awareness of man's sin and God's mercy, and it brings us to turn ourselves in repentance to our Father's love. Even with a poor ritual and a confessor who does not show the interest we would like, the person who prepares with prayer and faith and examination can find each confession enriching him.

There is no special advantage in long confessional lines — they might serve to lull us into thinking we have a flourishing Christianity. But those who are eager to be fully Christian should be in them frequently.

Weekly Confession

I have been told by a number of friends that going to confession

weekly is not necessary and that they have been told this by their confessors. That is wrong in my book, because I learned early in life that confession is a sacrament. What is your answer?

There is a very delicate and personal element implied in the judgment whether weekly confession is advisable or not for a particular person. I don't think that the casual conversation of friends and the second-hand opinion of other people's confessors are very helpful in making that judgment.

Certainly, weekly confession is not "necessary" in the sense that a person who does not go to confession every week is a poor Catholic. In fact, for a person who would confess this regularly out of a sense of anxious self-punishment, the practice could be positively harmful.

Nor is the question resolved by a simple appeal to the fact that penance is a sacrament — as if four celebrations of this sacrament a month were automatically four times better than one would be. The sacraments of faith are never automatic!

Whether weekly confession is genuinely helpful for me is something that no casual acquaintance can decide. I must weigh in the balance my own faith and devotion, my own sense of sin and repentance, and my readiness to use the sacraments of the Church as a special way of drawing closer to our Lord.

I ought also take into consideration the thought of the Church universal as she reflects on the meaning of her faith and practices. The thought — not just the feeling of many contemporary Catholics. Not every trend that begins to develop among Christians has the guarantee of reflecting the guidance of the Holy Spirit. There are unwholesome trends and retrogressions, as well as genuine evolution and progress.

This thought of the Church was strikingly expressed in Pope Pius XII's encyclical on the Mystical Body of Christ (June 29, 1943). His teaching is not outdated. Its sense was repeated in the pastoral documents of Vatican II. He wrote: "To ensure more rapid progress day by day in the path of virtue, we will that the pious practice of frequent confession, which was introduced into the Church by the inspiration of the Holy Spirit, should be earnestly advocated. By it, genuine self-knowledge is increased, Christian humility grows, bad habits are corrected, spiritual neglect and tepidity are resisted, the conscience is purified, the will strengthened, a salutary self-control is attained, and grace is increased in virtue of the sacrament itself. Let those, therefore, among the younger clergy who make light of or lessen esteem for frequent confession realize that what they are doing is alien to the Spirit of Christ and disastrous for the Mystical Body of our Savior" (no. 88).

To sum up, I believe that weekly confession can be extremely valuable for most Catholics. Whether it has been or not, I'm not ready to say. I have the impression, however, that many weekly confessions have smacked of deadening routine or anxious obsession. The truly valuable confession is the sorrowful accusation that expresses the Prodigal's genuine desire to return more fully to his Father's house. This totally personal act is rich in its capacity to produce growth and ought to be encouraged as frequently as possible.

The Sins of Children

When one of my children commits a deliberate venial sin, should I punish him each time or simply remind him that he did wrong? I'm afraid that if there is no punishment, he will grow up with no discipline.

I've never raised any children. Yet even from the "vantage point" of my bachelor quarters, something sounds a bit out of focus in the way this question is put. Isn't it too negative a view of the problem of how best to bring children to Christian maturity, to be saints? The religious man matures in his relationship with God in a way that meshes rather closely with human maturation.

A baby starts out as eight pounds of selfishness. He is a bundle of wants and needs, and he demands (sometimes very vocally) all kinds of attention. The process of education is a process of making it easy for His Majesty, the Baby, to abdicate his imperious throne in favor of deeper personal satisfactions and goals. This he can do well only if he is supported by an atmosphere of love and acceptance. There may be need of the proverbial "rod," but he must be able to feel that it is wielded by the hand of a person who cares for him and is not merely annoyed at him. Otherwise, he may learn to conform in order to avoid pain and rejection, but he will not learn to give himself and to give up his selfish interests in behalf of others — he will not learn to love.

It is even more difficult to help a child grow into Christian maturity. God does not put his arms around a child. The conviction that God is real and personal and that he loves the youngster grows more slowly. Our principal concern ought to be to develop this sense of loving faith in the child. If every time he is naughty or mean, we punish him for "sin" or threaten him with God's judgment, he is apt to grow up with the idea that God is a cruel and demanding tyrant. This happens, in fact, and all too frequently. A psychiatrist friend tells me that a major component of the neuroses of many of his Catholic patients is that they have a seething anger against God!

I wonder how often we find a deliberate *sin* in a child. He may be studiously rebellious — but is he kicking up his heels against God or against something he resents in his parents or companions? The act may be "sinful" — the refusal of love to one's neighbor is a refusal of love to God. But is it good to call God in on the act in a way that risks making him into a social control to whip hostility into line through fear? This is what punishment for "sin" might indeed do. Wouldn't it be far better to grapple with the human problem of selfishness and resentment on a strictly human level and help the child gradually to see that this difficult work of self-control is a way of responding to God, who is all love and mercy?

To bring a person up with the notion that the willfulness of childhood is a significant offense against God is apt to create a backlash. Will he as an adult take seriously the real horror sin is, if, when he was a child, sin was the failure to put away his toys?

Sin and a Seven-Year-Old

We've moved into a parish where children are expected to go to confession before their First Holy Communion. I can't see the theological sense in this practice, and I don't believe it's good psychology. Why should I have to teach my child something I believe is wrong at this time? What do you think of conscience, sin, and a seven-year-old?

Your question illustrates the kind of pastoral problem parish churches face in this era of changing emphasis and mobile populations.

I imagine that you just came from a diocese where a lot of soul-searching went on about first confession and Communion, where a new policy was implemented, and where an intensive indoctrination program succeeded in convincing you that the practice we had lived with since the turn of the century no longer makes "theological sense." The stage is perfectly set for conflict when a person like yourself moves into a locale where the cultural patterns and convictions are at variance with your own.

What can a parent like yourself do? There are two clear choices. You can choose to conform to the prevailing custom of the parish, or you can handle this most important moment in your child's religious life privately. However, you should consider carefully what the consequences might be before you choose.

If you are not going to go along with the practice of the parish, there is nothing to prevent you from preparing your child spiritually for his First Communion and taking him to the altar when you judge he is ready. Particularly in big city parishes, no one would question the parents who bring their seven-year-old to receive the Lord's Body with them as a family.

However, bear in mind the consequences for the child. Will it help or hurt him to be so isolated from the other seven-year-olds when they make their First Communion in the parish? Is it really good to make First Communion so private that the Christian community does not have the chance to rejoice in the addition of another member of the parish family at the table of the Lord's Supper? Is the mentality of your area such that your initiative might result in some future embarrassment for the child when he begins to go regularly to Communion — not having gone through normal procedures in your parish? The initial step of independence is easy — but I wouldn't take it, unless I were quite sure that there is no danger of spiritual or psychological harm coming to the child as a consequence.

Supposing you do conform to the practice of your present parish, will it mean that you will be untrue to yourself in a significant matter? You seem to think so, but I'm not so sure. I think we are dealing with the kind of gray area in religious practice where good reasons can be given in favor of either alternative. I cannot see it as a case where one is right and the other wrong, where one makes theological sense and the other is theological nonsense. In matters of this kind, either choice can be right. But if a public policy is being made, one or the other has to prevail as a general rule.

No matter which practice is in vogue, none of its proponents will insist that all seven-year-olds are bound by Church law to confess their sins before going to Holy Communion. The only time a person is obliged to go to confession before receiving the Blessed Sacrament is when he is conscious of being guilty of mortal sin. No one presumes that the average seven-year-old has made such a shocking choice against God and conscience.

Basing themselves on the work of developmental psychologists like the great Piaget, a number of pastoral theologians have questioned the very possibility of so young a child's committing a mortal sin. However, if you grant this, you must also say that such a child is incapable of any real love or holiness. For the condition of both sin and love is the ability to prize another for himself and to see one's actions in relationship to that unconditional prizing.

Those who favor confession for the very young believe that the growth toward love that makes Communion appropriate implies that there will also be failures in this initial love which can be healed in the sacrament of Christ's merciful forgiveness.

They are aware of the risks involved in preparing children for confession. It would be hideous if a child were made to be afraid of a God who is eager to punish every childish foible. It could severely damage his delicate psyche if he thought that each of his petty self-assertions was another blow on the nails pinning Christ to the cross. Religious educators are careful to avoid any such exaggeration and to emphasize the positive motivations of love.

Surely, to provide a child with a child's way of saying "I'm sorry" to God and of receiving an effective assurance of his understanding acceptance is not theological nonsense, nor need it be psychologically harmful.

If, in your own case, you have good reason to believe that it would harm your child to follow the pattern of the parish and yet you want to have him join his group in the parish, I'm sure your parish priests would be willing to consider making an exception in his case.

My own views? I think we have enough examples of quite well-developed consciences in the very early years of Christian saints to make me hesitate to generalize. I would hate to see the sacrament of penance denied to children until they were well into their teens. At the same time, I favor separating First Communion and confession. I would prefer to focus the attention of seven-year-olds on what God is going to do for them in the Eucharist, rather than on what they must do and say in the new experience of going to confession. In the year or two following, they can be prepared at leisure to understand and receive the sacrament of pardon and peace.

The Law of Annual Confession

Are Catholics obliged to follow Canon 906 in the Code of Canon Law, which calls for confession once a year for those who have reached the age of reason? My nine-year-old son has not made his confession, and I am supposed to be preparing him for it by using

a new religion textbook. The impression I get from this book is that there's no such thing as sin and that parents are wrong if they teach their children that sin is more than merely selfishness and lack of consideration.

Canon 906 still obliges. But it does not require us to receive the sacrament of penance as such. It binds "all faithfully to confess *all their sins* at least once a year." The sins that must be confessed are mortal sins. If a person is not guilty of any mortal sin, there is no obligation to go to confession. In this case, the law simply does not apply. There is no law obliging the generality of the Christian people to make a devotional confession.

You are undoubtedly concerned that the practice in your parish has been a violation of this law in your son's case. There are a number of reasons supporting the practice they are following in your locale, and I'm sure that they have been presented in the literature you have, as well as through meetings in the parish. They all boil down to the feeling that it is quite unlikely that the sins of a nine-year-old are mortal sins. Therefore, the parish or diocese makes the judgment that the law of the Church is not certainly binding on the youngsters.

Some seem to give the impression that a child is *incapable* of any serious sin. They base their view on psychologists' observations that tend to push back the age at which a person is mature enough to make a responsible and free personal choice — and mortal sin is a free personal choice of something that is incompatible with loving God.

In my judgment, this is a dangerous conclusion. I would agree that mortal sin is improbable in so young a child, but not impossible. If it is impossible, does it not follow that a genuinely free choice to love is likewise impossible — real holiness, then, too. This does not seem to accord with the experience of the Church, at least in the lives of some saints.

The conviction of the Church — a conviction grounded in the Gospel and confirmed by the sad experience of centuries — is that sin is a reality. It is not mere indiscretion or impoliteness. It is an offense against God, a refusal to live in harmony with his will as it is made known to us, a refusal to love which throws man and society into disorder and alienation. Its real horror can be plumbed only against the background of the sufferings and death of Christ.

I'm sure that your book does not deny this. The concern of the experts in religious education is to emphasize the positive, to draw children to hand themselves over to Christ and to a life lived in union with him out of personal love. It is hard to gainsay the fact that too many people have lived crippled lives in the name of religion because they were taught a negative religion of fear. They came to sense the presence of God principally as an oppressive force ever ready to plunge them into eternal fire for breaking a law. That's hideous.

To see one's life in terms of love or the lack of it is not an escape from the difficult task of living up to the commandments. It is rather to see to the very heart of the commandments. Each sinful violation of a commandment is a selfish refusal to live out the inexorable demands of loving God. And the person who genuinely loves is a person who has that wholesome esteem for God, for himself, for others, and for society that the commandments sanction.

In every man there lurks a measure of unregenerate selfishness that leads him daily into sinful refusals to love. Sometimes it erupts in the destructive rebellion which mortal sin is. God's love shows sin for what it is and leads the sinner to repentant confession of his sin. There is always matter to confess — not merely once a year but much more frequently — for the man who would be more fully healed to respond to God's love.

Mortal Sin Obsolete?

Up until now, I have always thought that the Catholic Church was clear about what is right and wrong, what is mortal sin and what is venial sin. Now I'm reading things that seem to me to imply that there is no such thing as mortal sin. Have things changed that much?

No, they haven't. Let's see if we can get to one of the roots of this confusion.

We grew up with the understanding that a mortal sin is a human action that is in serious violation of the law of God. We were taught, and rightly, that a person was not guilty of a mortal sin unless his action dealt with a matter of grave moral significance and unless it was performed with sufficient insight and full consent of the will.

There are two basic elements that are contained in this brief teaching.

One is the objective element. It is based on the kind of being man is — a creature of God who is rational, free, responsible, and purposeful. Because of what man is, we can speak of certain kinds of voluntary behavior as good or bad inasmuch as they are appropriate or inappropriate for his nature.

The other is the subjective element. It is based on the realization that loving is never an accident. No one refuses to love or seriously offends one who loves him unless he knows what he is doing, sees his action in relationship to that love, and freely chooses this course of action.

In a universe that seemed quite fixed, the understandable tendency of the Churches was to focus on the objective — to proclaim clearly what is right and wrong. It was not only a Catholic tendency. Methodists, Baptists, Orthodox Jews, and others also emphasized the norms and rules as they saw them. In this climate, we found very clear listings of the kinds of sins that said which actions are mortal sins and which are venial sins. These were useful. They showed us what kind of behavior significantly violated the special dignity of man as a child of God and hence offended God, who wanted man to be true to his vocation.

This approach, however, ran a number of risks. Good but anxious people saw serious sin everywhere. A number of people equated mortal sin with the breaking of a law and lost sight of the personal dimension of the relationship with God to which they were called. Too easily could they come to see sin and grace as something mechanical. The moral life of many seemed to teeter-totter on a precarious brink: they thought of it as a life that was in and out of the state of grace as they broke a law or fulfilled the requirements of a law. I know that this is a bit of a caricature, but it points to what tends to happen when we concentrate excessively on objective sin — the kind of actions that are wrong — in our personal moral life.

If the recent past was the era of the objective, today is the era of the subjective. Everywhere in the world men concentrate much more on motive and purpose than they used to. Our present understanding of how complex a thing freedom is in any human person is far more sophisticated. Our awareness of the personal relationship involved in love, whether it be the love of God, of friends, or of spouse, is sharper. The universe we live in no longer seems to be so fixed. We see the possibility of evolution even in standards of human behavior. The tendency today is to ask what an action means, rather than what it is.

Hence, the concentration today is understandably much more on whether a person sees his action as destroying his basic relationship

with God. This is what the catechism called "sufficient reflection."
Likewise, now that we recognize more of the interior hindrances
that burden us as we struggle for genuine freedom and true maturity,
pastoral guidance takes more account of a person's diminished freedom; it wonders if this person's bad action really involved his taking
a stand against God. The catechism also took this into consideration
when it required "full consent of the will" if a person were to be
guilty of a mortal sin.

When you read that it is difficult to commit a mortal sin, recognize
that the author is focusing your attention on the subjective elements
that must be at work if a person is to make his objectively wrong
action expressive of his choice to cut himself off from God. Such an
author is reminding us of how stumbling is the march to any genuine
commitment — be it to the love of God or to unadulterated egoism.
He is also presuming that his readers are the kind of people who
are interested in questions about sin — hence, people who have some
kind of prevailing wish not to offend God.

Like any reaction, this reaction against a kind of excessively objecti-
fied and codified view of sin runs the risk of being extreme. It is
important to encourage people to struggle on, to reassure them that
some of the faltering they experience is perhaps less than the catastrophe of abandoning their heavenly Father through mortal sin. However, it would be an even worse catastrophe if people were to conclude that adultery and murder and abortion and hatred and injustice
and stealing were not the horrible crimes they used to think they
were.

The man who, under a drug-induced hallucination, mutilates and
kills another person may not be guilty of mortal sin — but mutilation and murder are "mortal sins." The girl who, under the pressure
of fear and influenced by the scandal of a relaxed climate of public
and legal opinion, aborts her child may not be guilty of mortal
sin — but abortion is a "mortal sin."

Human life is not lived on the level of objective considerations
of right and wrong. But neither is it a thing so personal and subjective that the teachings of a Church and the insights of centuries
have become irrelevant — as if each man is licensed to create his
own standards independently of every other consideration.

The Catholic Church holds fast to the conviction that there is an
objective moral standard that endures and measures the rightness or
wrongness of men's actions. Whether any particular person who acts
at variance with these standards has committed a personal mortal
sin is for God to judge. But it is of extreme importance to the quality

of human life that we recognize this objective standard for what it is and try to bring ourselves and our society in harmony with it. In our accustomed — and sometimes confusing — terminology, this means acknowledging that certain actions, attitudes, and omissions are "mortal sins."

Perfect Contrition

I've read lately that a person could be saved from hell even though he neglected the practice of his faith for years, provided that he said an act of contrition and was really sorry for his sins. In my time, we were taught that Catholics had to confess their sins to a priest to get absolution. Would you please explain in words I can understand? I have a catechism here that states that a person who dies in mortal sin goes to hell.

There are three clear points here. First, the person who dies in mortal sin — for example, the person who is deliberately a rebel against God, who clearly refuses to accept the mercy of God — does indeed go to hell. Second, the normal means for the forgiveness of sins is through the sacrament of penance. Third, there is no forgiveness of sins unless there is true personal repentance for sin, and whenever there is true repentance for sin, there is forgiveness.

Repentance always implies that the sinner is ready to do whatever God asks of him. Hence, true repentance will include some reference to the means which the Lord has established for the forgiveness of sins. A Catholic knows that this means that he must come to Christ, who is present in the Church and who forgives our sins through the sacrament of penance.

But suppose he cannot get to confession. Is he simply out of luck? Does he remain in his sins? Not if his sorrow is that true repentance which your catechism calls "perfect contrition." But isn't perfect contrition rare? Isn't it something only great saints have? I hope not — or else we are all still in our sins. Whenever sins are forgiven, whether in the sacrament or apart from confession, the state of the former sinner is one of perfect contrition. The person who turns away from sin and is determined to love nothing in a way that will shut God's love out of his life has perfect contrition.

We sometimes misunderstand the Catholic teaching on contrition. What we call "imperfect contrition" is never enough to free us from our sins. It is enough to move us to come before our Lord in the sacrament of penance confident that the power of his grace will make our repentance "perfect." Don't be startled at this. The teaching of the old catechism encouraged us poor sinners to come to seek our Lord's forgiveness in the sacrament. But when the Lord forgives, he transforms us from sinners into lovers — he makes us perfectly contrite.

What you've read lately is really the same thing we have always been taught and believed. God is mercy. He is always seeking us, to turn our hearts from sin to himself. That he sometimes accomplishes this conversion at the last minute for a person who has neglected him all his life is something that brings joy to the hosts of heaven. It is not a warrant for us to continue to live in neglect and rebellion.

Examination of Conscience

I have been using an examination of conscience which I find contradicts the teaching of today. The following used to be mortal sins: Have I affiliated myself even for a short time with a non-Catholic sect or religious body? Have I seriously expressed the opinion that all religions are equally good or true and equally pleasing to God? Have I attended meetings or listened to speeches or sermons which I knew would destroy or weaken my faith? This whole chapter called "Faith" is apparently wrong. Could you recommend another examination of conscience?

If you find your present examination of conscience helpful, keep on using it. Things have changed, but not that much. Whatever used to be a mortal sin against faith still is. It is still apostasy and serious sin for a Catholic to abandon his allegiance to his Church by joining another religious body. It is still wrong to maintain that all religions are equally good or true. It is still wrong to listen to speeches or sermons that are apt to destroy your faith.

Today we recognize that "some, even very many, of the most significant endowments which together go to build up and give life to the Church herself can exist outside the visible boundaries of the Catholic Church" (Vatican II, *Decree on Ecumenism*, no. 3). We recognize other churches as the means God uses to bring their members to salvation. But this recognition does not imply that a Catholic can, without fault, abandon the fullness of divine truth and means of grace he has in his Church, in order to join another Christian church. As the same decree says, ". . . it is through Christ's Catholic Church *alone*, which is the all-embracing means of salvation, that the fullness of the means of salvation can be obtained" (no. 3). Obviously we are not ready to concede that all religions are equally good and true. For a Catholic deliberately to run the risk of losing the faith in God by which he holds the truth of the Church is as wrong as risking suicide.

In using a printed examination of conscience, remember that it is a help for your judgment not a substitute for it. It ought to make you face up to the fundamental issues in your own personal life — the points where your loyalty to Christ and to his Church are really tested. Ideally, it should be tailor-made for you.

An examination that I have found helpful is printed in the little book *The Sacrament of Penance* (New York: Paulist Press, Deus Books, 1966). The whole book is very worth while.

General Absolution

My question concerns the subject of open confession. I know for a fact that such confessions are held at a church in New Jersey. As I understand it, the priest begins with prayers and meditations on sin and repentance. This is followed by general absolution of all present desiring forgiveness. People are free to confess to the priest privately, but it is not a necessary part of the sacrament. I would like to know why such confession is not administered to people in other parts of the state. Must I travel for this type of religious experience?

The reason why the sacrament of penance is not administered in this way to people in other parts of the state is that most priests recognize that they have no right to do so.

General absolution, according to the present discipline of the Church, may be given in certain emergency situations when it is impossible to hear the individual confessions of those who desire to receive the sacrament. Besides the difficulty of hearing the confessions and the genuine desire for the sacrament, another condition must usually be verified if a priest is legitimately to give general absolution: there must be a real danger of death. This is what our troops will remember when the chaplain gathered them together, helped them to examine their consciences and to come to a repentant desire for God's mercy, and gave the sacrament in a single absolution to all who were properly disposed. It is because Catholics are aware of this that we priests are made to feel so welcome on scary airplane flights. We're useless as good-luck charms but good to have aboard to be ministers of God's pardon through general absolution should danger escalate to terror.

There are other situations in which it would be beneficial to be able to administer the sacrament of penance through general absolution. For instance, when a great number of people want to receive the sacrament and have only a limited time in which to do so. This happens in mission territories that have no resident priest. It can happen when a group assembles at a shrine or place of pilgrimage. Missionaries find themselves faced with the dilemma of either rushing penitents through in a way that helps very little to develop a sense of penitent conversion or taking adequate time with each one with the practical certainty that they will not be able to help all. Where this condition happens frequently, some missionary territories have sought authorization to use general absolution, and, I believe, some of them have obtained it.

The procedure your letter describes is not motivated by a judgment that a real emergency is present, nor is it based on any permission or authorization of the Church. The motive of the priest who is doing this is, I imagine, pastoral. He rightly sees that his people should be brought to realize that even the most secret sin has a social dimension, that all the sacraments, including the sacrament of penance, are the public liturgy of the Church. One of the most obvious ways to deepen our awareness of these values is to conduct a public celebration of the sacrament, bringing together the community of the parish, the community of those who seek God's pardon. In this context, it is far easier to see that sin is a wounding of the Church, that the sinner's quest for forgiveness is made through the Church and with the prayerful support of his brethren in the Church, that the forgiving act of Christ is embodied in an act of the Church which reconciles the sinner with the Church and hence with God. I'm sure that it is the view of the priests who are acting like the one you refer to that the group action of a people seeking God's pardon should normally climax in a communal absolution. Their point of view deserves to be heard.

However, it is one thing to raise a point for debate in the hope of discovering which way of celebrating the sacrament will be most helpful to the people and most in accord with the nature of the sacrament. It is an entirely different thing to innovate without any authorization.

I have referred to this need for authorization several times. This is not stodgy legalism. No priest has a right to take the discipline of the sacraments into his own hands. He is the minister of the Church's sacraments. He ministers properly only when he acts in harmony with the whole Church and in accord with its authorized procedures. If he strikes out on his own independently of the authority of the Church, no matter how effective he might be as a creator of felt religious experiences, there is something defective (almost schismatic) about his administration of the sacraments.

This is true for all the sacraments. But it is especially true in the case of the sacrament of penance. It is not enough merely that a priest be ordained. Normally he can absolve only if he has received authority to do so from the local bishop. His action must be authorized in the local Church if it is to be valid. The service you describe is not known to be authorized anywhere in New Jersey. Consequently, there are grounds for questioning its validity as a sacrament. At the very least, it is a violation of a rather serious law. For the person who is aware of this and still presumes to participate in it, I wonder how he can see his action as that renouncing of personal sin and reentry into the obedience of Christ in the Church that belongs to the sacrament of penance.

What we have said about unauthorized general absolution, with its cavalier ignoring of the divine law obliging the clear confession of all serious sins, does not apply to the growing practice of receiving the sacrament as part of a communal service of repentance. Here private confessions are heard, and absolution is given only to those whose confessions have been heard — but all within the context of a praying congregation that helps the penitent to be more fully disposed to genuine conversion and more realistically conscious of the communal aspect of sin and reconciliation. In most places there is no objection to it. It takes into account the values that belong to the sacrament by God's intention. I think that you would find the elements of the religious experience you rightly seek in this kind of service rather than in the questionable one you report.

Are Sins Forgiven?

When the penitential rite of the Mass concludes with the priest's prayer for forgiveness, are the sins of the congregation forgiven?

First of all, let us be clear that this "absolution" is not the same as the absolution that forms part of the sacrament of penance. Hence, we should not imagine that this humble acknowledgment of sinfulness and prayer for God's forgiveness is the same thing as the sacrament of penance or an adequate substitute for it.

The formula "May the almighty . . . " was the formula used in sacramental absolution around the year 1000. But when it came into the Mass shortly thereafter, its meaning was recognized to be something other than sacramental forgiveness of sin. For words to be part of a sacrament, the minister must intend them to be such. These words are no longer authorized in the Western Church as the words of sacramental absolution, nor are priests regularly allowed to give general absolution to a group in this setting. Consequently, we can presume that no priest intends to confer sacramental absolution before Mass.

Yet we hope that forgiveness of sins does occur in and through the non-sacramental confession and absolution that precedes the Mass. If the person saying the Confiteor sincerely means what he says, he is making a genuine act of contrition. And we can be sure that the united prayer of all for forgiveness is heard by God. Besides the sacrament of penance, God's mercy provides many ways in which we can obtain pardon for our countless daily venial sins.

The Seal of Confession

During recent reading on the sacrament of penance, I have come across the term "seal of confession." Being sixteen and usually up to date on matters, I constantly read in newspapers of betrayed trust, "squealing," and the like — so something like this seems too good to be true. Could you please explain how this practice came about and what it means?

The seal of confession is the most strict obligation to treat as absolutely secret everything revealed by the penitent in the sacrament of penance with a view to obtaining absolution. This information is so private that it is "sealed off" from every ordinary human use.

The obligation of the seal is described briefly in the Code of Canon Law, which states: "The sacramental seal is inviolable. Consequently, the confessor must exercise all diligent care not to betray the penitent in any degree by word, sign, or in any other way, or for any cause whatsoever" (canon 889).

What this means is that it is absolutely forbidden for the priest to identify a person who confesses to him and betray anything that he revealed to him. He can't do this for any reason whatever, whether it be because of a pressure brought to bear on him even by a threat to his own life, whether it be for the good motive of protecting another person, bringing evidence in behalf of an innocent party accused of a crime, or preventing a crime from being committed.

Likewise, a priest is obliged by the seal of confession to be so careful of the penitent's trust that he does not let anything slip which could permit a third party to conclude that a specific person had confessed a specific sin to him.

The basis of the strict obligation is partly natural, but, more importantly, it is based on the special nature of the sacrament of penance.

It is a natural obligation because a person's sin and contrition are normally secrets. Their revelation is a thing that ordinarily would be offensive to the person, and it might be a thing that would seriously hurt him. Normally, a Catholic confesses his sins with the understanding that anything he reveals is to be treated as absolutely confidential. If this trust were to be broken down, the confidence of the people in going to the sacrament would be diminished and this valuable means of spiritual growth would be closed to more and more.

The obligation is even more than a natural one, because it arises from the nature of the sacrament our Lord gave to his Church. By tying the forgiveness of serious sin to the condition of confessing them to a priest, Christ implicitly grants us sinners the absolute right to inviolable secrecy. In a very real sense, the priest receives our confession in the place of Christ. The information he has is God's, not his own; he has no right to use it or share it with others.

The history of the seal of confession is not an easy thing to trace. In fact, the whole history of the development of the sacrament of penance is extremely complicated. In the earliest centuries, the sacrament of penance took the form of public penance and a public reconciliation of sinners. Just how sins were made known, whether publicly or privately, is obscure. Consequently, there is no early reference to the secrecy enshrouding the practice.

At least by the beginning of the fifth century, writers are insisting on the principle that the sins confessed by a penitent should be spoken of to nobody but God. Local churches make provision for the severest of penalties to be leveled against anyone who violates this secrecy. This principle and its sanction were framed into the general law of the Church at the Fourth Lateran Council (1215), and the obligation of the seal of confession has been reinforced by general law ever since.

The history of its observance has few pages. Priests through the ages have been extremely faithful in this matter, sometimes at very great cost to themselves. You need never fear that your trust will be betrayed in the sacrament of penance.

Also, I hope that as you get to be a few years beyond sixteen, you will learn to fear betrayed trust even less. True, there is always room for prudent circumspection in confiding in others — there are some things that you don't tell to just anybody. But I wonder if you will always consider the same things to be "squealing" that you do today.

Personal Confessor

Several new parishes are being carved out of the old one, and I find myself in one of the new parishes. I happen to like going to a confessor who is stationed in the old parish. May I continue to go to him for confession?

If you have found a good confessor, be grateful and continue to go to him. Even at its most restrictive, the Church law has never limited the complete freedom of laymen to shop around for the confessor who would be the most helpful minister of the sacrament of mercy for them.

Penance is the most personal of all the sacraments. Its full potential for helping a person to grow in the Christ-life can be realized only if the penitent is at home with the confessor. The official fixing of so many city blocks as a parish does not carry with it a guarantee that this subtle mix of personal relationship, knowledge, and competence will occur for everyone within these boundary lines.

General Confession

Before making a general confession, should one first consult a priest about it? Is it possible to go into a confessional without prior consultation and simply declare that one is about to make a general confession?

A general confession is a sacramental confession in which the penitent makes a review of his whole life or of a significant part of it. There are different situations in which a person may want to make a general confession.

There is the situation where a general confession is obligatory: when a person is *certain* that his previous confessions have been insincere and hence not a true sign of repentance. Sincere conversion will require the confession of all serious sins committed since the last good confession.

There is the situation where a general confession is desirable: when a person, moved by a wholesome sense of penitential gratitude, wants to mark some special newness in his life by this self-emptying act. This is what many spiritual writers have had in mind when they invite those on the threshold of the seminary, religious life, marriage, or death to make a general confession.

There is the situation where some people want to make a general confession and it would be the worst thing in the world for them. I refer to the anxious person who begins to look at himself too much and to be troubled by all sorts of "funny inside feelings" that "maybe" he didn't confess properly. He wants to open the whole thing up again in order to be on the "safe side." A general confession would only stir up sleeping dogs that are best left to lie in peace. Rather than coming from a wholesome sense of sin and of the mercy of God, this desire to confess comes from a somewhat wounded psyche, which would be liable to be more upset by carrying out the desire.

If you are not already consulting a priest, I would think it easier for you to go directly to the confessional. Usually the priest will ask you why you want to make a general confession. If he discovers that your reasons place you in the first two categories, he will be happy to help you with a general confession.

Scruples

I have a tendency toward being scrupulous at times. I feel I worry excessively whether what I did in the past was wrong or whether it will be sinful in the future. For instance, on bad books and articles. Just what makes them obscene? I subscribe to the popular women's and news magazines. Sometimes they have articles about things like the college students who live together. Am I doing wrong to read this so I can be informed, especially since I now have children of this age group? Should I quit subscribing to magazines because they bring up matters like this?

So here I am, middle-aged, raising a large family, fighting the battle of scruples, and worrying about books now. Pray for us. We need to be understood even if it's hard for you and others to counsel us in our life.

The last lines of your letter are beautiful. Of course you need to be understood. You're really telling me that you know it's silly to be worried about sin in these matters — but still this knowledge doesn't keep you from worrying.

Apparently you've had a number of advisers over the years — in the confessional and out of it, short term and steady ones. I gather that you have felt that the quality of understanding was something rare in these persons. Probably some seemed to reassure you by giving you solutions to each of your anxious problems. Others refused to solve your problems. Instead, they tried to get you to live more comfortably with your own common-sense solutions and endure the measure of uneasiness that goes with not being infallible. I submit that the latter understood you better and were more of a help to you.

No scrupulous person ever solves his problem by having an authority point out the moral rule applicable to the situation or assume responsibility for a decision. For the problem is not one of knowledge or its lack. The problem is one of emotional response — the scrupulous person's feelings are out of kilter. They signal fear where there is no danger, guilt where there is no wrong. Scrupulosity is often a kind of generalized and paralyzing anxiety that latches on to the area of moral precepts. The scrupulous person is incapable of making a comfortable decision in the area of his concern, for he feels he must always be on the safe side, free from any risk. The understanding counselor will not want to reinforce this incapability by assuming the burden of decision-making. Nor will he want to go into subtle refinements of moral theology to relieve the anguish of the moment — for what appears to be the solace of today has a way of becoming the torture of tomorrow for these tormented persons.

Rather than go into any discussion of obscenity with you, I would urge you to open out to the more important areas of our faith. God is not the taskmaster who is waiting to pounce on you and make you pay for every curious indiscretion. He calls us to a full life in his service, not to a worried overexactness that ends up forgetting him whom we serve. When you come upon accounts of rebellious young people who are destroying themselves, don't worry about whether you've sinned in reading the account. Be concerned rather for the youngsters who are depriving themselves of so much happiness and personal dignity. Pray for them and for those of our generation who have sown the seeds of their rebellion. And if the affliction of scrupulosity should continue to plague you, entrust yourself to an understanding counselor. The process will involve considerable pain — but the reward can be a far freer, fuller, and holier life.

Confessions for the Scrupulous

For approximately twenty years, I have been bothered with a very bad case of scruples. I want to die but fear I will go to hell because I can't make a good confession. Could a person simply go into the confessional and say: "Well, Father, here I am, and God knows I'm sorry for all my sins. Please give me absolution"? This would be the greatest form of confession for scrupulous people.

When it is judged to be a real help for a scrupulous person, the form of confession you mention would be entirely sufficient.

As you know, the ordinary requirement for a person seeking God's forgiveness in the sacrament of penance is that he confess all his serious sins, telling both the kind of sin committed and the number of times. The Church believes that this requirement derives from the nature of the sacrament and that it comes from the Lord, and the Council of Trent has so declared.

However, the requirement of this kind of integral confession, while essential, is secondary. It is meant to serve the purpose of the sacrament, which is to restore a person to pardon and peace. The theology and practice of the Church has always recognized that there are circumstances when the penitent sinner is excused from any kind of detailed confession. This would be the case when such a confession would be impossible, as, for example, in wartime when there isn't time to hear the individual confessions of troops going into danger.

A person would be excused from integral confession also if such a confession brought with it the probability of serious harm, whether physical or spiritual. For this reason, a confessor who has to work in a crowded hospital ward will counsel people simply to confess some minor sin and to express their sorrow for all their sins in a general way. Otherwise, there would be danger of the spiritual harm of damaging the penitent's reputation and destroying the privacy of the confession.

For a scrupulous person, the effort to confess all his sins exactly can bring much more spiritual harm than good. This, I think, has been your own experience. You *know,* or at least you feel that you know, that none of your confessions has been adequate. The harder you try, the worse it gets. You always find some aspect that you think should be exposed and fear that it's your own fault that it hasn't been. Hence you feel that your use of the sacrament has been wrong and sacrilegious. This surely qualifies as spiritual harm sufficient to excuse a person from an integral confession of his sins.

Being freed from his burden would bring some relief. No longer would your compulsion to make sure and be on the safe side force you to doubt the adequacy and sincerity of your confessions. No longer would it make any sense for you to feel driven to go over the same thing in confession again and again. Your humble acknowledgment of sinfulness and your sorrowful request for forgiveness would be enough — and these could be present every time you received the sacrament.

Relief, yes, but not cure. Scrupulosity may be a symptom of a temporary spiritual crisis. However, when it lasts for decades and seriously affects a large part of a person's life, it is an infirmity as real as stomach ulcers. Its roots are most often embedded in the structure of a person's adjustment to reality. And the best hope of a cure is to be found in prolonged therapeutic counseling with a competent, trained person. I hope that you will consider taking this step to seek help.

The New Look in Indulgences

The Council of Trent told us that indulgences are to be highly esteemed. Unfortunately, the present regime in Rome evidently takes a different view. They tell us they are eliminating the undesirable features of the indulgence picture, but they have pretty well eliminated indulgences — period. Just what has been set up to replace the "Raccolta," or where can a person find a current list of indulgenced prayers and/or exercises?

Let's take another look at what has happened to indulgences. Up until April, 1967, there was a practically unlimited supply of plenary indulgences available each day to the Catholic who was a regular communicant. But, in practice, what did it mean to gain, let's say, ten plenary indulgences a day? Ten full remissions of the temporal punishment due to forgiven sin are no more effective than one.

Most of us were aware of this, and so we fell back on another teaching of the Church. She teaches that indulgences may be applied to the souls in Purgatory and that this helps them to pass through the cleansing that will admit them into God's presence. However, she never claimed the kind of authority over the dead which she has over the living. The Church can pray for the dead; she cannot absolve them. Her gift of a plenary indulgence to a deceased person does not guarantee his immediate glorification. (This was the horrible error of Tetzel's preaching in the sixteenth century that scandalized the Church in Germany and set the stage for Luther's rebellion.) If it is not full remission for the Poor Souls, how, then, is a plenary indulgence more than a partial indulgence in this case? Honestly, I don't know.

The new discipline of indulgences, announced in Pope Paul's Apostolic Constitution on the matter, is more intelligible to me. According to the new arrangement, a person can gain no more than one plenary indulgence a day (except at the hour of death). Partial indulgences are available in abundant supply. The Church no longer measures their efficacy in terms of days and years. The measure is entirely up to us. It's set up like a federal-state matching fund for road construction. The Church intends to make available an indulgence that is proportioned to the generosity of the love with which we pray or perform the prescribed work. The efficacy of a partial indulgence could be practically unlimited if we are that unselfish with God.

The *Raccolta*, which is the official collection of indulgenced prayers and works, has not been practically abolished. It has been revised and is published as a slender volume with the English title of *Enchiridion of Indulgences* (New York: Catholic Book Publishing Co., 1969).

We still should esteem indulgences highly. The Church is not playing them down. She is reminding us that they are the frosting and not the cake. Her aim in granting them is not only to help the faithful become free from the effects of sin but also to provide them with an added incentive to perform generously the works of piety, penance, and charity that will benefit the whole Church. It is to these works that the Church attaches indulgences. And the works themselves are to be esteemed infinitely more than indulgences.

Marriage

What Is Marriage?

Recently a friend has experienced great difficulty in marrying a

Protestant divorcee in the Catholic Church. How can it be that the two Protestants of the original marriage should be required to obey the same rules of marriage as Catholics? These Protestants entered into a contract with each other to live as man and wife until death — with certain exceptions specifically spelled out in the laws of the state. Those exceptions are part of that contract. It seems that when the Catholic Church tries to enforce its own rules on these people, it attempts to add an element to the contract after the contract has been made and to which the participants never agreed. This is neither right nor just.

I think that our separated brethren would be offended at the view of marriage attributed to them in your letter. You are practically saying that they consider marriage to be like a business partnership — very permanent, but. . . . It is as if the terms of the contract are set arbitrarily by the state legislature, so that the consent of a couple in these days is conditional, whereas it was unconditional for their great-grandparents.

The Church does not admit that it is adding any new elements to the marriage contract. Rather, it is saying in effect: We believe that true marriage exists in all the religious confessions and in civil society. And true marriage is something far greater than an agreement of a couple to share their lives according to bylaws and conditions that they personally make up. It is true that persons enter marriage by a personal consent. But once they have consented to marry, the bond of their marriage is permanent; it is no longer subject to merely human decisions, even those of the state.

In Vatican II, the Church restated her view of what marriage is. The statement includes these lines: "The intimate partnership of married life and love has been established by the Creator and qualified by *his laws*. It is rooted in the conjugal covenant of *irrevocable* personal consent. Hence, by that human act whereby spouses mutually bestow and accept each other, a relationship arises which, by the divine will and in the eyes of society too, is a lasting one. For the good of the spouses and their offspring, as well as of society, the existence of this sacred bond *no longer depends on human decisions alone*" (*Constitution on the Church in the Modern World*, no. 48). The Council is not talking about Catholic marriage only, but about marriage — every marriage. There may be conditions required to enter the marriage contract, but, once contracted, marriage is unconditional.

If marriage outside the Catholic Church were a conditional arrangement, such as you describe it, the Church would have no difficulty in allowing the divorcee to marry in the Church. She would not consider the earlier arrangement to have been a marriage in the first place. There is not true marriage consent — whether the ceremony be performed in the town clerk's office or in the cathedral — if the consent is given only with the prior condition that there might be a way out. Even if a couple does not fully understand all of the implications of their action (and who ever understands fully?), when they consent to marry, they marry in accordance with the Creator's laws for what marriage is. If they consent to live in some type of revocable union, it is not a marriage.

The Dissolution of Marriage

A Protestant Church marriage has been dissolved by divorce. Can the now divorced person, if he becomes a Catholic, marry a Catholic?

There is no simple and direct answer to the question you ask, unless there are many more facts available. The Church does not acknowledge the state's authority to grant a divorce that would perfectly dissolve a true marriage and leave the partners free to marry again. She does claim for herself the right to act in God's name (Matt. 16:18) to dissolve some marriages. But if both parties in the first marriage were baptized, the Church recognizes their marriage as not only a true marriage but also as a sacrament. There is no evidence that the Church has ever considered herself capable of dissolving a valid, sacramental marriage which has been consummated.

When the Church acts to dissolve a marriage, she does so only for some higher value of faith. There are some situations where a genuine convert to the Catholic confession will be declared free to marry by virtue of the special authority of our Holy Father, the Pope. Don't misunderstand this. It does not mean that the Church is ready to allow a divorced person to marry a Catholic if he pays the price of becoming a Catholic himself. This would be hideous. The merits of any such case would have to be investigated and weighed individually.

Valid Marriage

If a Catholic marries a non-Catholic at a side altar, does the non-Catholic have to be baptized for the marriage to be valid?

A "valid" marriage is a true marriage. It is a marriage in which all the conditions required to constitute a permanent, lifetime, life-giving, loving union of a man and a woman are fulfilled. The valid marriage of one who has been baptized in the Catholic Church is a marriage that observes all the essential requirements of the Church law. The law requires that the ceremony be performed in the presence of an authorized witness (usually a priest). If this and the other conditions are fulfilled, the marriage of a Catholic and an unbaptized partner (presuming a dispensation has been granted) is just as valid as the marriage of two Catholics — even though it is not a sacrament. And also, the Church considers the marriage of a couple who are not her own to be perfectly valid, if they observe the requirements of the civil law of marriage in the region where they have been married — whether the official witness be a clergyman or a civil official.

Hence, it is clear that the Church considers the marriage you describe a valid or true marriage. If the non-Catholic partner were also baptized, the Church would consider it a sacramental marriage as well. Years ago, "mixed marriages" were celebrated in the rectory or at a side altar. Nowadays, this event of a lifetime is celebrated with all possible religious solemnity in the sanctuary and sometimes at a nuptial Mass.

Baptism, Yes. Marriage, No.

Why is it that baptism conferred by a minister other than a priest is considered valid by the Church, while a marriage performed by such a minister is considered invalid?

Baptism and matrimony are both sacraments in the Catholic Church. But they are quite different sacraments, each with quite different requirements and quite different histories.

The Catholic Church considers seven of her most sacred rituals to be sacraments, because she believes that the saving power of Christ is made present to the believer in a special way through each of these signs of faith. However, among other considerations, it is only when the ceremony is able to be seen as the Church's own ceremony that she recognizes it as a sacrament. This means that the ceremony must express the faith of the Church and be performed in a way that conforms to her rules.

From the earliest days of the Church's history, the fundamental sacrament of baptism has been recognized as the act of initiation into the faith, provided that natural water was joined with a formula of words expressing the Trinitarian faith of the Church.

Whether the person performing the baptism believed in God or not, his action was seen as being in continuity with the baptism conferred by the Apostles — provided he intended to do what Christians do when they baptize.

The marriage of Christians has also been seen as a sacrament, but its history is far more complex. In earliest times, it seems that there was no such thing as a Church ceremony for marriage. The civil contract entered into by a baptized couple was seen as a "marriage in the Lord" that placed the couple in a new state of grace in the Church. Gradually, as Church organization grew, the official minister of the Church came to be considered the proper witness of the contract in which Christians marry each other and minister the sacrament to each other.

Note that the reason why the marriage was considered a sacrament was not because a priest was present. It was considered a sacrament because two baptized persons entered a valid and permanent marriage. Whenever the marriage contract of a baptized couple is valid, their marriage is a sacrament.

It is the conviction of Catholics that the Church is a social institution with the right to establish conditions that must be fulfilled if the marriage contract of her members is to be valid and binding. She says nothing about ceremonial conditions that have to be observed by baptized persons who are not in communion with her. If they enter a genuine marriage contract, the Catholic Church believes that their marriage is a sacrament. But when her own members marry, their marriage ordinarily must be witnessed by a priest, deacon, or another person who is designated as the official witness by the authorities of the Church if the contract is to be valid.

This requirement could change. It did not exist centuries ago. It could be modified in the future. However, while it remains in effect, we are forced to conclude that the Catholic couple who do not observe the requirements of their Church in this matter do not in fact enter a valid marriage contract and their apparent marriage is no marriage at all.

Marriage in the Orthodox Church

A neighbor's son married an Eastern Orthodox girl in her church. His mother tells me that he can still receive the sacraments. This surprises me. Could it be true?

Yes, it could. Since March 25, 1967, the law of the Church has been that Catholics who marry in the ceremonies of the Orthodox Churches are validly married, provided the other requirements of law (such as the freedom of both parties) are observed. Such a marriage is valid but unlawful, unless a dispensation is obtained — which a bishop can give if there are good reasons for it.

For a long time, Catholics have used the expression "married in the Church" or "married by a priest." These meant that the required form for valid marriage was used. While these shorthand formulae used to be adequate, they no longer are. A Catholic may be married by a Roman Catholic priest, an Orthodox priest, or a deacon. In certain circumstances, another minister may preside. And the place of the marriage may, at times, be in a church other than a Catholic church building. The real requirement is that the official witness of the marriage be one who is designated by the Church. There are a number of flexibilities today that were not present only a few years ago.

The practical upshot of this is that we should be very slow to think that a person has married himself into a state of alienation from the sacramental life of the Church. We ought to be ready to take the word of the couple or their families for the correctness of what they are doing. People will rarely lie about having permission for a marriage in these special circumstances, and quizzing them too closely can be needlessly offensive.

Annulments in the Orthodox Church

The Catholic Church now recognizes the validity of the marriage of one of her members when it is performed in the Orthodox Church. Does she therefore recognize annulments given by the Orthodox Church? For instance, if a Catholic marries a divorced Orthodox Christian whose marriage has been annulled by her Church, is that marriage considered valid?

The pertinent law on this question comes from Vatican II. The Council wrote this decision: "By way of preventing invalid marriages between Eastern Catholics and baptized Eastern non-Catholics, and, in the interests of the permanence and sanctity of marriage and of domestic harmony, this sacred Synod decrees that the canonical 'form' for the celebration of such marriages obliges only for lawfulness. For their validity, the presence of a sacred minister suffices as long as the other requirements of law are honored" (*Decree on the Eastern Catholic Churches,* no. 18).

This decision was extended to cover the marriages of Latin rite Catholics and Orthodox Christians on February 22, 1967. Both decrees have the proviso: "as long as the other requirements of the law are observed." Among the requirements of law is one that considers the marriage tribunals of the Catholic Church as the only courts competent to determine the validity or nullity of a union which had all the public earmarks of being a real marriage. It is not yet the practice of the Catholic Church to accept Orthodox decrees of nullity as sufficient to establish the freedom of a couple to enter marriage.

Whether a marriage such as you describe would be in fact valid depends on whether the previous union was in fact not really a marriage but was null and void in itself. It is the facts and the reasons that would have to be taken into account, not the decree of annulment granted in the Orthodox Church.

All of this creates an unfortunate tension in today's ecumenical dialogue. Everyone is conscious of it and hopes that this barrier can be overcome.

In a joint statement issued by Pope Paul VI and the Ecumenical Patriarch Athenagoras I in October, 1967, it was declared: "The Roman Catholic Church and the Ecumenical Patriarchate are ready to study concrete ways of solving pastoral problems, especially in what regards marriages between Catholics and Orthodox." The question you raise is one of the most tricky of those pastoral problems. The solution is not yet at hand.

Marriage Annulments

What are the reasons for which the Church permits annulments of marriage? Why are we nòt told these things? Today we are either ignorant or half-informed Catholics.

The Church does not "permit" annulments. She judges that in a particular case, in spite of the appearances to the contrary, there was no true marriage in the first place. Rather than annulling a marriage, she investigates and concludes that the marriage was null and void from the beginning. Her intervention is a declaration.

This unfortunate situation can arise from any one of these three reasons: (1) One or both parties failed to give a genuine consent to enter the permanent sacrament of matrimony. (2) The marriage consent was not given in the proper form — usually before a priest and two witnesses. (3) There were invalidating impediments to the marriage which were not or could not be dispensed. The impediments that prevent a valid or true marriage from being contracted are treated in the Code of Canon Law (1067-1080). Among these impediments are the following:

1. Lack of age. (A man must be sixteen and a woman fourteen, in order to contract a valid marriage. This is not an ideal age, but the minimum legal one in the Church universal.)

2. Impotence of either party, that is, the previous and permanent inability to perform the marriage act.

3. The existence of the bond of a previous undissolved marriage.

4. The unbaptized condition of one of the partners in a Catholic marriage.

5. Ordination to the subdiaconate in the Latin Church.

6. The solemn vows of a religious order.

7. The detaining of one of the spouses by force before the marriage with a view to persuading her (or him) to marry.

8. The impediment called "crime." It is rather complicated, but in substance it is present if, during the existence of a marriage, a couple commit adultery and pledge that they will subsequently marry. Similarly, if there was a murder of one of their spouses in order to free the guilty couple to marry, they are impeded from marrying in the Church.

9. The impediments of blood or in-law relationships.

Some of these impediments have been set up by Church rule to protect the holiness of marriage — for example, that of crime or the requirement of baptism. These can be dispensed before the marriage, and, in that case, they no longer stand in the way of a couple's entering into a valid marriage. Others, like the impediment of impotence, are natural impediments to true marriage, and no Church authority can dispense from them.

Besides declaring some marriages null and void, the Church sometimes exercises the power she has from Christ to dissolve marriages that are valid but not sacramental. This is a rare measure used when such an action is judged beneficial to the Christian life of the baptized party. The so-called "Pauline Privilege" is an instance of this.

The Church is really not trying to keep these things hidden. The fact of the matter is that they are rather technical matters that belong mostly to the religious specialist. It is only on rare occasions that they are of special interest to the Catholic laity. There are so many more important things of our faith and of our living a life of union with God that we need to attend to.

Marriage Laws

At the present time, our marriage case is in Rome awaiting a decision after being sent there by an American archdiocese with a favorable recommendation. The priest in our parish has stated that he feels there is no reason why we should not go ahead and go to confession and Communion, as he feels we have waited a reasonable period of time. May we follow his advice?

Since you ask me about the advice that Father has given, obviously you are not comfortable with his advice. You sense that your life together is not yet the sacramental marriage you want and that it cannot be until the legal impediments to marriage are cleared away by the authority of the Holy See. Meanwhile, in spite of the reality of your love and your concern to do what you believe God expects of you, you judge that your life together precludes your making a good confession and receiving Holy Communion.

You must follow your own conscience in this matter. No priest can take the burden of personal responsibility from your shoulders by expressing a permissive opinion.

How can it be that he gives you such an opinion? There are several possibilities.

It may be that what you are waiting for is a declaration of nullity from the Roman courts. A declaration of nullity really changes nothing. It is merely an official declaration that what was thought to have been a marriage was never truly a marriage at all. In spite of appearances to the contrary, such a declaration says in effect that you are and have always been free to marry. Some theologians would argue that, while one should wait a normal period of time to obtain an official judgment of this fact before proceeding, there can be circumstances when the wait is excessive and the hardship too great to ask of a couple. In these cases, they would say that since the couple are already certain that they are free before God to marry, they may exercise their right to marry in the private way recognized by the canon law of the Church for situations where an authorized minister cannot be found to officiate.

On the other hand, it may be that you are waiting for a genuine dissolution of a really existing, nonsacramental marriage bond. This is, in effect, a divorce that is sometimes granted for the sake of the faith of a Christian entering a new marriage. It is more than the official recognition of a fact. Until such a grant is made, the partners are not free to enter marriage. To anticipate the Roman judgment, even though the wheels of law grind slowly, is to take on a second spouse while still legally bound to the first — not merely in appearance but in fact.

Again, the priest may have given you this opinion because he belongs to the growing camp of those who are dissatisfied with the archaic machinery of Roman Catholic marriage legislation. It may well be his judgment that that archaic law is unreasonable law, and unreasonable law is not binding. With such a view, he might tend to substitute an honest appraisal of the facts and your reasons and intentions for the unwieldly mechanics of due process.

At the present time, theologians and canon lawyers are examining problems like yours in articles and forums. They are searching to find a way to help couples in extremely difficult situations to come close to God and set their consciences at peace. Surprising remedies have been proposed. In my opinion, they are not yet mature enough or sure enough for a priest to present them to his parishioners as a practical solution of a problem.

Marriage and Mental Illness

A Catholic man and woman, both recently released from mental hospitals, met while attending Recovery meetings and now plan

to be married. Is it all right for them to do so? Wouldn't the couple have to tell the priest of the situation, since one of them comes from a family with a long history of mental illness?

There are special problems that have to be taken into consideration when a person who has suffered a severe mental illness is planning to marry. The two central questions to be faced are these: (1) Is it really prudent for this person to marry now? (2) Is he truly able to give his full and real consent to marriage?

Every person who intends to marry should face up to the question of the prudence of his intention. That is to say, he should examine his situation with insight into the present and foresight of the future. It is often true that couples repent at leisure for an ill-considered marriage that was entered in haste.

For one thing, a couple who met in the circumstances you describe should weigh carefully whether they have found a real love or whether they are clinging to each other in a kind of immature dependency that is apt to hamper their recovery. Will this be a step forward into the realities and responsibilities of adult life, or will it be a regressive withdrawal from reality?

Again they should, like any couple, look to the future and consider the welfare of the children they might have. You mention a history of psychological disorders in one of the families. Does this indicate a genetic defect very apt to be passed on to a new generation? Or does it indicate that the members of this family learned from one another an unfortunate pattern of coping with reality? If the latter is the case, has the combination of rest, therapy, and new-found love perhaps broken the damaging web? These questions should be faced squarely if the marriage is to be prudent. Yet even though there is a probability that their children will inherit some tendency to their parents' illness, this is not enough to take away their right to crown their love with marriage.

But the most important and most difficult question that has to be raised when there has been a severe mental illness is whether or not the parties are capable of giving their mature, free, human consent to the permanent state of marriage. The fact of having had such an illness or of having been hospitalized is not enough to settle the matter one way or the other. People need hospitalization for all kinds of emotional problems. Many of them recover to resume a wholly normal life. But for some, discharge from professional care means that a severe state of the illness has passed, while the patient remains still quite handicapped and immature. Before he could officiate at a marriage ceremony, the priest must be reasonably sure that both persons are genuinely capable of giving their free consent to the common life of marriage. For this reason, he must be told of the facts of the situation, and in most cases like this, he will need to seek professional advice about the particular case before making his judgment.

All of this is a hardship. Yet it is beneficial, not cruel. Far better to discover beforehand whether a person is capable of consenting to marriage's union of love than to learn after a few months that an immature pair are destroying each other in the appearance of a relationship that they are really unable to establish. To have to stop a person who wants to marry is to burden him with a very heavy cross. But it is far lighter than the continuing cross that such a marriage would be. And it is far more humane and charitable than exposing a marriage partner to the heartbreak of a marriage that never really was.

Can This Marriage be Dissolved?

Since the golf season started last summer, my husband has practically dedicated his life to the game. He absolutely refuses to have marital relations with me. He claims it's my own fault because I'm not being a good wife and am therefore undeserving. This is not a new thing. It happens every year from March or April to November. He does have a potency problem, but it is not serious. Doesn't this behavior constitute grounds for dissolution of our marriage in the Catholic Church? Am I not entitled to receive a paper from my pastor granting me permission to obtain a divorce?

In itself, the kind of frustrating behavior you describe does not constitute grounds for dissolving a marriage in the Catholic Church. The practice of the Church is to dissolve a marriage only in certain fairly well-defined cases, when a profound value of faith is at stake or when it is determined that the apparent marriage was null and void from the beginning because of the lack of some essential element.

Your marriage is in serious trouble, as you know, and you both should work with a competent marriage counselor to try to work out the conflicts that are driving you apart.

There is something bizarre in what you describe, and it is impossible to determine what it all means without really listening to both sides. Your husband tells you that he is punishing you by depriving you of the tenderness you need. The punishment is, of course, hideously out of proportion to any real or imagined fault. But why does he consider you "undeserving"? Is golf widowhood making you into a person who seems to be an unbearable nag?

Or, if you find no basis for his resentment in yourself, could his statement be a rationalization that provides him with a way of avoiding a relationship in which he feels inadequate?

Of course, I don't know that either of these is the real reason. I merely suggest that the unfortunate deterioration in your marriage could stem from a number of different motivations. It is not an easy thing to unmask the real reasons so that a couple will be able to cope with them.

Might you eventually discover in this process of searching that there are legitimate grounds for seeking a dissolution of your marriage? It is possible, but it is a remote possibility. The possibility would hinge on the question of whether the present behavior might not be an indication of a much more profound lack of maturity. Certainly the recurrent, annual, nine-month's abdication of responsibility that you describe is a serious indication of immaturity. But, was it always there? How pervasive a thing is it? Is it so severe that it would stand in the way of ever giving genuine consent to the kind of stable, life-giving union of love that marriage is? No one can answer questions like these without a real knowledge of the persons involved and a professional understanding of our very complex human psychology. And then you may discover, with the help of marriage counseling, that there is no reason to raise this kind of question at all.

It is a sad thing when the ardor of a man and woman who pledged undying love to one another is so cooled that divorce seems to be the only way to survive. Try to get your husband to join with you in seeking help to preserve the common life in which you have already invested so much of yourselves.

May Cousins Marry?

Is the marriage of first cousins prohibited by Church laws? What is the reason for such law? Is it dispensed easily?

The Church law, presently listed as Canon 1076, prohibits the marriage of relatives descended from the same stock to the third degree. This excludes the marriage of brothers and sisters and first and second cousins. The historical roots of the law are older than the Bible.

Among the reasons for the law are these: (1) conservation of morals — those who are apt to live in close contact with one another in a family situation are discouraged from considering marriage as a possibility; (2) social benefit — the law fosters warm contact with other families and relatives and breaks down clannishness; (3) physical good of children — the children of close relatives are more prone to inherit genetic defects.

Since the impediment barring the marriage of cousins is a Church law, it can be dispensed. The bishop of the diocese is empowered to do so when a request is made accompanied by very good reasons.

To Marry an In-Law

Why was it necessary to get a dispensation for Catherine to marry Henry VIII after her first husband, Prince Arthur, had died? Since he was dead, wasn't she free to remarry without any dispensation?

Catherine of Aragon was not free to marry Henry after the death of her first husband. The reason was that Arthur was Henry's brother. Church law forbids a widow to marry her brother-in-law. This impediment to marriage is called that of "affinity." The present law of the Church concerning this matter is contained in canon 1077.

In sixteenth-century Europe, Arthur, Henry, and Catherine were chessmen in the game of international politics. The marriage of Arthur and Catherine was arranged when they were children, in order to seal a blood alliance between England and Spain. His death in 1502, after four months of marriage, raised the issue of another political royal marriage in England.

Pope Julius II granted Catherine a dispensation to marry Henry, even though such a dispensation was almost unheard of at the time. Henry delayed the marriage till 1509. Eighteen years later, when Henry was already enamored of Anne Boleyn, he began to have "scruples" about the validity of the dispensation and hence about the validity of the marriage. Those great ecclesiastical schemers, Cardinal Wolsey and Thomas Cranmer, the Archbishop of Canterbury, arranged a suit against the King for having lived in incestuous union with his brother's wife! Henry never thought of divorce in the sense of dissolving a valid and consummated marriage. He wanted his marriage to Catherine declared null on the grounds that Julius' dispensation was worthless.

Excommunication

A close friend of mine, who is a Lutheran, invited me to her wedding. I knew beforehand that the groom was a Catholic and attended Mass every Sunday. To my surprise, they were married in the Lutheran Church, and he received Communion from the minister also. Is he now excommunicated from the Roman Catholic Church?

I only attended the wedding because the girl is a friend of mine. Was this sinful because I am a Catholic and I know the Church doesn't recognize this sort of marriage?

The man is not excommunicated. Under the former law, he would have been for celebrating marriage before a non-Catholic minister. However, this legal excommunication was abrogated by the Sacred Congregation for the Doctrine of the Faith on March 18, 1966.

More important than the problem of excommunication is his real situation as a Catholic. Because his marriage was not celebrated according to the form required by the Church for her members, it is not recognized as a valid marriage. Since he was a practicing Catholic prior to his marriage, I would imagine that he had to do violence to his conscience to take this step and seal it with full religious participation in a Lutheran ceremony. A serious violation of conscience brings with it a far more serious break in communion than Church excommunication does — it breaks man's bond with God. Pray that he receives the strength to restore it.

Did you commit sin? This is the sort of question we should ask ourselves before the fact rather than afterward. Whether presence at a wedding like this is wrong or right depends on what your presence or absence will mean. If being there is apt to be taken to mean that you support the couple in a choice you consider to be wrong, then you should politely excuse yourself. If your presence cannot be interpreted as condoning the marriage, then there may be reasons that could move you to attend. But your decision on this should be made before you attend.

How Can I Tell the Children?

I am married to a divorced Catholic, and we have two children. They have been baptized and attend parochial schools, and we go to Mass regularly together. Now the older child wants to know

why we don't receive Holy Communion. Where can I get help in answering this question honestly, as it will be cropping up again?

First of all, I want to congratulate you for the loyalty to your faith that has impelled you and your husband to share that faith with your children. I am sure that it has not always been easy to stay loyal during these years when you felt cut off from your Church.

There is, of course, no easy way of answering the child's question honestly. It seems to me that the following points are the things that would enter such a heartbreaking conversation. Explain to the children that the Church does not recognize divorce, that their father had been unhappily married and divorced before you met, and that you fell in love and were married outside the Church. Then I think you should impress on them that this is your secret and they shouldn't talk about it outside the family. Ask them to pray for both of you and to remember you in every one of their Communions that the day will come when you can join them. I know it sounds cold in this outline. It needs the warmth of a mother's understanding to find the words that are truly right for your children.

You might also use the occasion to tell the children that there is one question they should never ask anyone: "Why don't you go to Communion?" This is too personal and private. Parents and teachers and friends may encourage those close to them to receive this sacrament. But they should never put them on the spot or exert any kind of pressure to receive, even the gentle pressure implicit in asking the question.

One last point. Your child's question has made you think. May I suggest that this might be an invitation of God's grace for you and your husband. Why don't you both reexamine your own situation? Has any new fact come to light that might make him free to marry in the Church? Do you think you could face the challenge of deciding to live in continence? With the help of God's grace, couples in your situation do find their love great enough to make such a decision and come back to full communion in the Church.

Zeal or Pressure?

The answer to "How can I tell the children?" (p. 204) is slightly fearful or twisted; no? The part where the children shouldn't ask "Why don't you go to Communion?" is puzzling to us. Why shouldn't they ask? Sure, it's personal. But the parents are personal

to the children. How do we get family and friends to do or undo certain things that are very important if we don't get personal?

I guess you're right. Out of the mouths of babes there has often come that probing, personal question which is the source of grace for us complacent adults. It can make us reflect and decide to "do or undo certain things."

On the other hand, if a person is in a vulnerable position or has a fearful desire to please, a question like this can exert a tremendous pressure. Most priests have encountered persons who have been badly damaged because they felt obliged to conform to others' expectations in this matter when their own consciences reproached them. Call it "human respect" or what you will, it is a fact of the human condition that we have to take into account. This is what I had in mind. It is more likely to apply to teachers' and parents' questions to the young than to children's questions to their parents. The highest authorities in the Church have been at pains to remind educators and superiors not to exert any pressures that will take away their charges' liberty in refraining from receiving Holy Communion. It takes a very understanding person to be able to manifest encouragement and concern without exerting undue pressure.

Reconciliation after Divorce

A friend of mine was married in the Catholic Church fifteen years ago. There are children. Several times, the husband left home to live with another woman, but each time she forgave him and took him back. However, the last time, she divorced him. Now he wants to come back again on account of the children. Where does their marriage stand? Do they have to be married again?

Human affairs are often very complicated. Your friend's unhappy situation is especially so. You want to know where their marriage stands right now. On the level of Church law there is no special problem if your friend agrees to another reconciliation with her divorced husband. In other words, there is no need of a new Church marriage. Divorce does not break the marriage bond between two baptized Catholics. The sacrament of matrimony continues to endure as long as the parties continue to live.

On the level of civil law, there may be all kinds of legal entanglements. It would be well for a couple who planned such a reconciliation to consult the lawyer who helped them with the divorce proceeding. He could help them to avoid running afoul of the legal and financial complexities.

On the level of that most important personal union of love, neither you nor I can know where their marriage stands. We pray that this will not be like the other times, that somehow or other both the husband and the wife have grown to the degree that they can now nurture their battered marriage into a union where self-forgetful love is the bond. A reconciliation that is merely an "arrangement" for the sake of the children or because of the pressure of alimony is not even a good counterfeit of Christian marriage.

Counterfeit Marriage

You amaze me, Father. "A reconciliation that is merely an 'arrangement' for the sake of the children or because of the pressure of alimony is not even a good counterfeit of Christian marriage." Many of us are living in "counterfeit marriages" without love because none exists. And you seem to imply that they are not worth continuing. We endure them because we were taught "until death do us part." What about it? One feels one is doing God's will by remaining in a marriage which is a daily cross — especially if defecting would embitter a husband without religion.

I see how this sentence could be open to misunderstanding. It could be literally a scandal to a couple who are struggling to maintain a fidelity to one another in spite of the conflicts and alienation that sometimes do spring up in a life together. I admire the persons who stay together because of their sense of the enduring bond of their marriage. I most certainly am not advocating that these shaky, sometimes unhappy unions would be better broken up. Such a loyalty to God and to one another, in spite of excruciating difficulties, is a mature Christian's way of handling this situation. And it provides the ground of a hope that love will be reenkindled when the storms are past.

What I was referring to as a counterfeit of Christian marriage had little to do with God or loyalty or fidelity. I was referring to the kind of social arrangement dictated by "good manners" or by financial security. It has nothing of those deep loyalties you speak of. Nor was I urging a couple in this situation to break up. I was musing about what a belated reconciliation might mean.

The enduring of a loveless marriage, when every effort to revive its spark has been made in vain, can be the shape of the cross. The cross in any Christian's life can be the product of tensions and circumstances that are beyond a person's power to control or alleviate. For those who are under the burden of such a cross, its patient endurance can be an act of love for God and a prayerful act of love for the one who hurts us and whom we unwittingly hurt.

The Duties of Husbands

It has been made very definite to women through the years about "their duties." Women are supposed to be "subject to their husbands," look after them in sickness and in health, et cetera, et cetera. What about the duties of husbands? Will you please add some words of advice to them about their duties?

The reminder that wives are to be subject to their husbands comes from St. Paul. He never intended his words to be used to keep women in an inferior place in a man's world. He spoke to husbands in almost the same breath and reminded them of an even more demanding "duty." "Husbands should love their wives just as Christ loved the Church" (Eph. 5:25).

However, the apostle wasn't primarily concerned with duties. He was reflecting on the new reality that marriage had become for those who live by the life of Christ. He put before men and women a very high ideal. He reminded them that marriage can only be fully what it ought to be when both husband and wife submerge their self-seeking interests in the community of loving care for one another that is a miniature reliving of the mystery of the cross.

The model of a husband's love for his wife is Christ's love for the Church. Christ's love made Him empty Himself even to death on the cross, that He might woo and win and enrich His bride, the Church. When He brought the Church into existence from His open side, she became not merely His "better half" but His other self, His Mystical Body. The basic relationship between Christ and the Church is not one of rights and duties but one of love and service.

Husbands and wives bring this ideal to the level of practice in the strength and delicacy of real human love. To love as Christ loves, a husband must be sensitive to the needs and desires and tastes of his wife. His relationship is not an extension of the kind of casual comradeship that might be suitable with the boys in the clubhouse locker room. The psychology of women, at least in our culture, will not tolerate this. A husband must set aside every free-wheeling self-assertiveness that threatens to injure the bond of love's harmony. Unless a man is trying to grow up to this ideal, he is failing in his basic duty as a husband.

Self-gift rather than fulfillment of duty is the norm. A few years ago, the bishops of the world assembled in the Vatican Council wrote about marriage in this way: "Such love, merging the human with the divine, leads the spouses to a free and mutual gift of themselves, a gift proving itself by gentle affection and by deed. Such love pervades the whole of their lives. Indeed, by its generous activity, it grows better and grows greater" (*Pastoral Constitution on the Church in the Modern World,* no. 49).

This may not be the answer you wanted. The real problems in marriage will not be solved by drawing up a contract or code of rights and duties. Where a husband and wife are working at growing in love and maintaining real communication, there is no need to remind them of duties and obligations. When a couple have given up on one another, words of advice about duty are a flimsy support to make a bad and lonely situation tolerable. It would be better to sit down together and try to recapture the heart of your relationship than to have a distant columnist write about the minimal ground rules.

Divorcee Excommunicated?

I have been noticing a woman in our parish going to Communion regularly, even though she has been divorced recently. Is she not automatically excommunicated by getting a divorce?

No. A divorce always has the note of tragedy for the persons involved and for society, but procuring a divorce may be the only practical remedy to a situation that is destroying the lives of the couple and their children. It may be that there were a number of personal failures and sins leading up to the decision to get a divorce, but taking the legal step that ends the civil effects of a marriage does not mean excommunication. In many cases there is no sin at all in this painful choice.

Consequently, the fact that a person has received a civil divorce does not exclude her from the privilege of receiving our Lord in Holy Communion. In the personal upset that is very often part of a divorce, the poor lady may have even more need of receiving strength from the Body of the Lord than many others do.

To take this question one step further — I'd like to suggest that we all be content to rejoice with those who join us in the bond of eating "the one bread," without pausing to wonder how they dare join us. Each of us has enough to do in examining his own conscience and his state of preparedness. We should presume that our neighbor has done likewise. Even if we know that there has been something irregular in the past, the healthy thing to do is to take it for granted that our fellow communicant has rectified it and is coming forward in good conscience.

It Takes Three?

Because of all the discusssion on birth control which has followed the publication of the encyclical, "Humanae Vitae" (Of Human Life), a question has been bothering me. I have always felt that the creation of a new human life required three-sided cooperation — that of a human couple and that of God. In view of the distressing and miserable conditions under which children frequently are conceived, born, and raised, is it possible to say that every child born into the world is born as the result of the direct will of God?

Whenever we speak of the cooperation of God and man, we are always in an area that is extremely difficult to cope with. We have to use human words filled with human associations when we speak of God — who is the unspeakable. We make comparisons and borrow analogies from the things we daily experience and apply them to God in a way that is true enough in what is said but that can be extended only with a real risk of misunderstanding.

What do we mean when we say that God and the parents cooperate in the begetting of human life? For one thing, we mean that the new being that has come into existence depends ultimately on the Author of all being. In this sense, however, we can say that God cooperates in the coming to life of malarial mosquitoes and disease-producing organisms, as well as human babies. Beyond this, we also mean that the new human being has a special kind of life and a capacity that, in its spirituality, goes beyond the power of biology and chemistry and genetics to explain. The Christian speaks of this by referring to the special creation by which God brings each immortal soul into existence.

This last statement can cause a problem. If there is a special creative act, then it must be free and responsible. Consequently, God comes on as utterly insensitive to human misery, if not downright cruel. He appears to will directly the hopeless lives of so many infants who are thrust into conditions that trap them into a continuing and hopeless cycle of depravity and degradation. Certainly, if you or I were to cooperate decisively in putting a man into such a hideous existence, we would rightly bear the blame.

But is this the kind of "cooperation," the kind of special "free act," we mean when we speak of God's work in the creation of new human life? Not really. If the biological process of fertilization takes place, it does not take another divine, free act to decide whether to create the human soul. Wherever human life exists, its inner spirit is already uniquely dependent upon God. Fertilization depends on the free, human cooperation of a man and a woman, who are responsible for their actions, and on a set of circumstances that are purely natural and, to some extent, observable and predictable. We should not imagine God as if he were a third partner manipulating the chemical and biological processes. Nor is he one who oversees things in a way that he stands ready to exercise a veto power by refusing to create even when all the conditions for fertilization are perfect. Granting the order of nature that he established in creating man, male and female, if he were to refuse the creation of the human person in these circumstances, it would be a miracle. And God has not led us to expect that he will compensate for our mistakes and greed and lust by miracles.

The begetting of some babies can hardly be called that which God directly wills. He does not directly will the issue of a casual coupling or of a sinful weakness or of already overburdened parents — at least not in the sense of being an independent partner who must bear the responsibility of his choice.

On the other hand, God does directly will the life conceived. To our new brother, as to all of us, he offers the destiny of being with him forever. He calls each person to share in his life and love. He calls on all of us to spend ourselves to change the conditions of society in a way that will make the life of all who come to share the human condition a life that is filled with the possibility of temporal and eternal happiness.

Responsible Parenthood

The Church is now stressing "responsible parenthood." How in the world can we be responsible when we have no control over the number of babies we can have (rhythm never works for us)? When I asked a Catholic doctor to explain it better, he replied, "You mean Vatican roulette." Boy, was I surprised! I think the Church errs on this birth-control subject. She has great sympathy but little else to offer. Perhaps our interpretation of Onan spilling his seed is wrong. As part of a priest's seminary training, I wish every one of you would take care of a large brood twenty-four hours a day (and night) with hardly any sleep and only one bathroom in the house and then come and tell me how wonderful the rhythm system is.

Yes, the Church is now stressing responsible parenthood. This emphasis is the result of a considerable development in her thinking about what marriage is meant to be. And it is people like you who have spurred this growth by generously sharing your anguished experience.

Marriage is undoubtedly designed by God for procreation and to provide a stable home, wherein children may grow and be educated in an atmosphere of love and harmony. And the Church has been right to champion this truth in the face of a campaign that would try to obscure it. But marriage is much more than a means of making babies. It's trite to say it but theologically important all the same: marriage is characterized by a tender human love, a mutual self-gift of a man and woman that is marked by fidelity and totality.

The reality of marriage is badly distorted when we see it only from the viewpoint of procreation. It's too narrow a view of a very complex reality. We went through this narrow phase on a folk level in the American Church. Remember when all you had to do was just count the children and you knew it was a "good Catholic family." It might well have been. But not simply because of size. Goodness is not a numbers game.

The really important thing is the real love that binds the family together in the love of God. The truly "good" Catholic couple is the one which lives in love. Examining the real needs of their love, a couple may find, at times, that God is asking them to share that love with another child, be he the third or the thirteenth. At other times and in other situations, they may honestly discover the opposite — that it would not be real love nor a response to his will to bring another child into the world. In both situations, they are trying to grow in love. Both decisions are efforts to *respond* to what God asks of them here and now. Both decisions demonstrate the responsibility the Church refers to in exhorting to responsible parenthood. Responsible parenthood does not automatically mean fewer children.

And yet there is a terrible problem. How is a couple to maintain their bond of tender love when they see that a genuine response to God means avoiding conception? Theirs is a married love, not a monk's love. For many years, the Catholic Church has seemed agreed that any kind of artificial interference with the reproductive process is forbidden by the law of God. This was never taught infallibly with the fullness of the Church's authority. Yet it is official teaching of the Catholic Church, reaffirmed by Pope Paul VI. We will discuss it later.

Meanwhile, I think that a Catholic physician who gives his patient the flip remark about "Vatican roulette" is both irresponsible and un-informed. Rhythm is better than its "press" would indicate. Where it is used with guidance and control, it is often a real help to conjugal tenderness, and an extremely dependable means of regulating con-ception. Misericordia Hospital, Bronx, New York, has provided a Thermal Rhythm Clinic since 1963. Their records show that, in the first four years, 967 women used the service. Only 52 undesired conceptions have occurred. And, on review, 46 of these resulted from a personal error, not from a fault of the method. With informed medical guidance, the rhythm method is better than 99 per cent effective.

As for the ill-fated Onan (Gen. 38:8-10), no reputable Catholic Scripture scholar sees this story as directly telling us what God thinks of contraception.

I so admire the heroism of my married brothers and sisters in Christ that I know they must have it as the fruit of their sacrament. Without that blessing, I don't think our seminarians could stand the gaff!

Ill-fated Onan

Your answer "Responsible Parenthood" (see p. 212) has this line, "As for the ill-fated Onan (Gen. 38:8-10), no reputable Catholic Scripture scholar sees this story as directly telling us what God thinks of contraception." Pope Pius XI saw it this way, and so do a flock

of books and pamphlets I have read and preachers I have heard on the subject. Who's kidding whom?

I'm not trying to kid, really. It is true that Pope Pius XI appeals to this text as a witness that "the Divine Majesty pursues this unholy crime with intense hatred and has sometimes punished it by death" (*On Christian Marriage,* no. 56, December 31, 1930). It was thus that St. Augustine interpreted the text, and Pius cites him in support. So, of course, it was to be expected that the anti-contraceptive literature of the thirties and forties would make a great deal of this "proof" from Sacred Scripture.

However, there has been a revolution in Scripture studies since 1930. It received the enthusiastic encouragement of Pope Pius XII in his epoch-making encyclical of September 30, 1943, *Divino Afflante Spiritu.* Supported by this mandate and armed with the tools of a greater knowledge of the Bible than either Augustine or Pius XI could have had, scholarly interpretations have made a number of our old "proof texts" no longer as forceful as we once thought.

The text tell us that Onan's older brother had died childless. In keeping with the Semitic practice of "levirate marriage" (cf. Deut. 25:5-10; cf. Matt. 22:23-28), Onan was obliged to give his sister-in-law a child who would legally bear his brother's name and be his brother's heir. Out of selfish resentment, whenever he had intercourse with Thamar, Onan interrupted the act in order not to build up his brother's family (verse 9). What was the evil he did in the sight of the Lord? Was it his selfish refusal to fulfill the requirements of the levirate custom? All scholars agree that it was at least partly that. Was it also because of the contraceptive means he used? Most Catholic scholars, very cautiously, say that this too is part of the evil thing but that it is not the direct concern of the sacred author. If it is not the direct concern and teaching of the sacred author, how can the text tell us directly what God thinks of contraception?

It is significant, I think, that Vatican II nowhere makes use of Genesis 38 in its discussion of marriage and parenthood. Nor does Pope Paul VI appeal to the story of Onan as a direct scriptural support for his opposition to artificial contraception.

Contraception and Natural Law

I cannot understand why birth control is against the natural law. It frightens me, because, all of a sudden, I see no sin involved in

this practice. How do I know that it is against God's plan for married love?

Don't be surprised if you find it hard to understand why artificial contraception is opposed to the natural law. Very few people can follow the arguments. And, among those who understand them, there are many who do not find them convincing. I remember reading a book in which the author laboriously expounded the reasons why contraception is wrong. And when he had finished, he confessed that these arguments would convince the convinced but would probably not persuade those who did not share intuitively in the same mentality to begin with.

I spoke of arguments and reasons. As you know (and it might be good to review this for our readers), the natural law is not a code of statutes arbitrarily enacted by God for human living. Catholic moral theology uses the term to designate the binding norms of human behavior that men can discover by reflecting on the nature of the human person and his acts. The conviction underlying this view is this: there is a reflection of God's plan built into the very structure of the human person. This plan can be discovered through rational analysis. Those actions that are fully in harmony with man's nature are seen to be permitted or commanded by God's design and, therefore, right. Those actions that are contrary to man's nature are recognized as forbidden by God's design and, therefore, morally wrong. Thus, from a study of the nature of man and his acts, even if there were no biblical teaching on the matter, we can know with certainty that murder, disrespect, adultery, fraud, and many other deviant acts are wrong.

What is the thinking behind the Church's conviction that birth control is against God's plan for married love? It is based on an insight, which is admittedly subtle and elusive, into the basic structure and personal character of the conjugal act: *it is a life-giving act of love.* It must be an act of love. A conjugal act that is forced on one's partner without concern for his or her reasonable wishes is a violation of God's plan for marriage and, therefore, wrong. It must be life-giving; that is, an act of true conjugal love must have an inherent relation to the begetting of human life, at least in the sense that there is no interference with the fullness of the act. To act otherwise is also to violate God's plan for marriage and, therefore, wrong. Underlying this is the conviction of the unique value of human life — so valuable that man is not fully the master of human life. When a man holds fast against the temptation to destroy himself, he acknowledges that he is not the arbiter of his own life and that he holds it in stewardship. When a man respects the laws of the generative process, he acknowledges that he is not the arbiter of the sources of human life. Rather, he is the minister of the design established by the Creator. Here is the way the pope in his encyclical *Humanae Vitae* concludes his brief sketch of the reasons for his teaching: "Just as man does not have unlimited dominion over his body in general, so also, with particular reason, he has no such dominion over his generative faculties as such, because of their intrinsic ordination toward raising up life, of which God is the principle" (no. 13).

In the limited space of these pages, I cannot go into this thinking in any depth. I would like to emphasize, however, that it is not based on a simple biological analysis of animal sexuality. The natural-law theologians are reflecting on the nature of the specifically distinct reality that sexuality is in human persons. Nor are their conclusions equivalent to urging couples to have as many children as they possibly can. They recognize the ideal of responsible parenthood, but, they argue, contraceptive procedures are not a proper means of achieving this control, because they destroy the nature and meaning of the marital embrace, which must always be a life-giving act of love.

In addition to this fundamental reasoning, the pope's encyclical pays a great deal of attention to the probable consequences that might follow should the Church withdraw her objection to contraception. For example, if governments did not have the moral pressure of the Catholic stand to contend with, would they feel freer to avoid the burden of radical social and economic reforms and tend to take the easy way out by interfering with the personal integrity and the rights of couples who want more children? Again, even the most liberal pre-encyclical opinion would grant that the use of contraceptives was acceptable only for a couple who were quite pure in their love for one another in Christ. Otherwise, the risk grew that a contraceptive mentality would infect their marriage, that their life together might degenerate into mutual exploitation that would stop their Christian growth. Is this genuinely self-forgetful love, this capacity for self-criticism, this authentic holiness, a common endowment in our time? Would it be more likely to develop or to diminish in the climate that would follow on the heels of a lifting of this restraint?

Both of these lines of argument are ways of discovering the requirements of natural law. If these two forms of argument are taken separately, two different conclusions will emerge. The first concludes that the use of artificial contraception can never be good in itself.

The second concludes that artificial contraception is something which is always morally dangerous. The encyclical *Humanae Vitae* joins these arguments and uses the second only as a persuasive support for the first.

All of this may sound unconvincing. Subtle and elusive conclusions of natural-law morality are not everybody's cup of tea. This is why God's providence has provided mankind with an authoritative interpreter of natural law in the teaching office of the Church. Although there are some theologians who challenge this concept sharply, Pope Paul reaffirmed it clearly in his encyclical on human life: "No believer will wish to deny that the teaching authority of the Church is competent to interpret even the natural moral law" (no. 4). In other words, if I lack the leisure, the expertise, or the clarity of judgment to follow the rational arguments against contraception, I can learn of their binding conclusion through the teaching of the pope.

One last point: If the natural law prohibits contraception now, is the question settled for all time? Not necessarily. The specific directives of the natural law are arrived at by a process of human insight into the reality of human nature. Though the fundamental nature of man is changeless, there is always the possibility of change occurring in human social institutions (and the family is a social reality) or the development of new insights into the nature of the human person and his acts. Change in either of these elements could conceivably result in a change of what is commanded, permitted, or forbidden by the natural law. This hypothetical possibility of future change does not, however, authorize us to consider ourselves already exempt from the requirements of God's plan for married love that our Holy Father's teaching has proclaimed.

What Now about Birth Control?

A year before the encyclical "Humanae Vitae" was issued, I received permission from my confessor to use contraceptive pills. It was a very relaxed and wonderful year. Now I'm awfully upset. The pope's encyclical has outlawed the use of the pills. Does this mean that my husband and I were in sin all that year? What can I do now? The conditions that led the confessor to give us the permission are no better. I don't know if I will be able to live up to what we are asked.

Thank God for the wonderful spirit of faith that impels you to ask this question. There have been such loud voices raised to reject the guidance of the Holy Father in the very personal and delicate matter that I find it is as heartening to hear of such loyal fidelity as it is saddening to share your present anguish.

Let's review what the situation was when you raised the question. For many years, Catholics had been in agreement that every kind of artificial interference with the reproductive process was a serious violation of God's plan for married love. During the time of the Council, this agreement was publicly challenged and the pope reserved final judgment on the matter to himself. He established a commission of experts to look into the matter — and most of mankind interpreted this action and the pope's prolonged silence as a sign of unsureness. The Church seemed no longer certain that it was truly a changeless requirement of God's law that contraceptives could not be used in the expression of married love and the pursuit of responsible parenthood.

By 1967, a great many Catholic theologians had come to admit in practice that the Church was uncertain about the guiding force of the former teaching. They recognized that the pope had asked Catholics in *loyal obedience* to follow the norm of the past and refrain from using contraceptives.

However, the obligation was seen to be one of law and obedience. When an obligation is merely one of obedience to a directive made for good order it is not unusual that a person can find a good reason that excuses him. It is something else again when the obligation flows from a law of God that tells us that an action is always wrong in itself.

In view of the prevailing view of the theologians in 1967, I'm sure that the decision you made with your confessor's help and advice (he cannot give "permission," he can only help you form your conscience) was prudent, conscientious, and good. Your difficulty was truly extraordinary. You were led to believe that you had a real option. And you exercised your liberty in a way that was not a refusal to do what God was clearly asking of you. Certainly your decision was not sinful, nor was your way of life.

Now, however, there is a crucial new element that modifies this picture substantially. There is no doubt about what the pope, as supreme teacher, is telling us. Every contraceptive procedure, whether mechanical or pharmaceutical, is declared to be wrong in itself, that is, opposed to the design and will of God revealed in the very nature of man. The obligation is no longer set on the level of obedience to a practical pastoral directive.

Painfully aware of the heroism he is asking of his married brethren, the pope affirms that one cannot justify the use of contraceptives in the name of the true requirements of Christian marriage. The general principle is now clear and binding. The kind of doubt that many theologians appealed to in 1967 no longer exists. In the application of this moral principle, as in the application of any moral principle, there is still room to consider the uniqueness of the individual person and the complexity of particular cases. And this is where individual conscience and personal pastoral guidance still have an irreplaceable role to play.

You fear that you won't be able to live up to the demands of this teaching. The wonderful thing is that you want to, that you intend to try. There may be times when human weakness will be overpowering. This is no reason to despair. The saints experienced many a slip in their effort to be perfectly faithful to God. Will such a failure be a mortal sin? Only God knows, but the quickly regretted sin of weakness is more often a misstep on the path than the complete turning from God that a mortal sin is. Our Holy Father urges husbands and wives to persevere in seeking God's healing mercy in the sacrament of penance. And his directive to the clergy is to manifest the patient and gentle mercy of Christ. You have the right to expect the help of the ministers of the Church, and of God, "who does not command the impossible, but by commanding urges us to do what we can, and pray for what seems beyond our power" (St. Augustine, *On Nature and Grace*, c. 43, no. 50).

Permissible Uses of "the Pill"

I have never been an advocate of birth control. But my last two pregnancies were horrible, involving complications. My doctor gave me a good warning. I am forty-one now, and my periods are changing. This poses a problem, as I am fearful beyond words of the outcome of another pregnancy. What help is there for us women on the brink of the "change of life"?

From the time the ovulation-inhibiting medications came to the attention of Catholic moral theologians, a distinction has been made between using them for a simple contraceptive purpose and using them for a therapeutic purpose. Pope Pius XII acknowledged this fundamental difference, and Pope Paul VI has repeated it in his encyclical *Humanae Vitae*. The use of these synthetic hormones merely to prevent pregnancy has been judged wrong. Their use for an appropriate medical purpose has been reckoned to be purely the doctor's business.

While not intending to get into the business of prescribing drugs, the moralists wrestled with the problem of determining what conditions could justify the use of these medications. It was obvious that there was no moral objection to them if there was a serious physical disorder that these drugs could correct. From this, they reasoned that the pill could be used if a physician hoped he could regulate an irregular cycle thereby and thus make the use of rhythm practical. Their thinking was that such medication would be assisting the designs of nature — not violating nature.

At this point, a number of moralists began to look more carefully at what could be considered "assisting the designs of nature." They thought they found evidence of a design of nature to delay pregnancy and space babies in the probability that the hormones that inhibit ovulation continue to be produced naturally when a mother nurses her baby. They thought that they found another design of nature in the fact that there is a distinct lessening of fertility in women who are entering the time of menopause.

So they raised the question: Is it morally permissible for a woman to take the pill in order to assist the designs of nature, which indicate that she should be free from a new pregnancy during these times? A number of them answered, "Yes, it is." The opinion concerning the case of the mother of the newborn child has been published in professional theological journals. I can find no literature on the second case, though I know the opinion mentioned has been held by very reputable theologians. This discussion was during a time when no Catholic moralist would admit the possibility of using contraceptives — a time when all were conscientiously remaining within the guidelines set by Pope Pius XII.

To the point then. If you can accept the logic of this position, you can with good conscience ask your physician if he would prescribe this medication for you. You must make your own judgment in conscience on this matter. I can tell you that I think that is an honest opinion, though I know that others would object to it strenuously. And, of course, you will have to leave the medical judgment on the advisability of using these drugs up to the professional skill of your physician.

The Anguish of Women

I am disturbed — deeply disturbed, by your reply "What Now about Birth Control" (p. 217). I think of the millions of women who share this unhappy world of ours — women who daily witness the horror of death in the eyes of their starving children. These people cry out to Mother Church. The only sympathy they seem to be getting is the recent encyclical on birth control and "Rome has spoken." I and countless other middle-class, thinking Catholics still have some faith left. Today, that faith is in grave danger. Please, give us an answer we can believe in.

In the same mail I received this letter from a lady in Westfield, New Jersey:

"I read with much interest and concern your answer to the question 'What Now about Birth Control?' My heart goes out to the lady who sent in the question. and I feel compelled to write to you and ask you to convey my message to her.

"You will please forgive me, Father, if I say you have not helped her. You gave her no tangible help — just spiritual. In as important a matter as this, Father, practical information is necessary, and you priests must have the answers *now*.

"I have solved my problem, if I may call it that, and God, in his goodness, has rewarded us for our faith and trust in him. Pope Paul is right, and God bless him in his efforts to lead us to heaven.

"Now, how can we follow his teaching? For a beginning tell her to read D. and H. Kanabay, *Sex, Fertility, and the Catholic* (Staten Island, N. Y.: Alba House, 1965). Tell her that the rhythm method adds a dimension to marriage that complete freedom can never give. It brings romance and dignity to sex and creates a period of longing and delight (when properly practiced) that recalls the days before marriage. You are truly 'lovers' again. It takes patience, understanding, and love for a few months, and I am sure she will find, as I have, that you long to be pregnant again.

"I also think she should be told (since she lives in the Bronx) that St. Vincent's Hospital (Seventh Avenue and West Eleventh Street, New York) has a rhythm clinic and does wonderful work. It is free! I have friends who have solved problems with their help.

"I, too, had a priest tell me and my husband that we had done our bit, that Christ was in our house, that we shouldn't wait for Pope Paul to make a decision. We could not follow his advice — we read the book and have made a good marriage, a marvelous one.

We fall in love again every month, and I want the world to know.

"Father, this can work. Mother Church (pardon the expression) is right. Please get Catholic doctors working for us. Encourage them to be understanding and helpful to people — not to brush us off.

"The penmanship is frightful, the grammar not the best — but I could not let this moment go by. Anyway it is time to prepare dinner for my nine little darlings."

So you see, I get it from both sides. I'm glad I didn't mention anything about rhythm in that reply. Otherwise, we never would have received this marvelous first-person account. If a celibate had written a thing like this, he'd be dismissed as an idealistic dreamer. Incidentally, there are a number of first-rate rhythm clinics throughout the country. A call to the Family Life Bureau of the U. S. Catholic Conference in your diocese could provide specific information. In the New York area, we have another clinic at Misericordia Hospital, 600 East 233rd Street, Bronx, New York 10466, whose high rate of success I referred to in the item "Responsible Parenthood" (p. 213).

Rhythm is an answer this couple can believe in. An answer you can believe in? Please believe me. I am not trying to give you heartless double-talk. I appreciate the depth of your anguished groping for faith. But I cannot tell you that the pope is just another theologian — one who is less well-informed, more rigid, and less competent than others in the Church. I believe that he is performing his God-given duty to the Church when he reminds us that contraception is always a disorder, that it can never become a good thing in itself. Is it always a serious sin? I indicated before this that the answer to this question could not be given in clear blacks and whites. Let me clarify the point still further in the next question.

Birth Control or Ruined Marriages?

Over the past twenty years, my husband and I have found that the only reliable method of birth control allowed by the Church is absolute abstinence. We have five living children, and since the birth of our fifth child nine years ago, we have had no intimate relationships.

For the first few years, we were highly motivated in denying each other normal tenderness, and I feel our marriage suffered no ill effect, but this is no longer the case. I'm now convinced that abstinence practiced for a long time without any relief in sight has a damaging effect on a marriage. It's an insidious effect, too, as unfortunately the wife, at any rate, hardly realizes what is happening until it's too late.

My husband and I desperately need that intimacy we enjoyed the first ten years of our married life if our marriage is to survive. But, in fairness to our living children and to each other, we cannot chance another pregnancy. So if we are to remain within the Church, we will have to continue on a course which is wrecking us and our marriage.

I, for one, don't think I can remain in the Church and reject the teaching of the encyclical. Yet it is impossible for me to accept it when I'm so well aware of its insidious effect upon a marriage in a case such as ours. Can you comment?

Don't think I overestimate the value of sex in marriage. I still feel that it is emphasized out of all proportion to the part it plays in a happy married life, but it is an integral part of a good marriage. For years I've been underestimating its function in marriage and, maybe only too late, have come to realize that this view, too, can be catastrophic.

I have printed so much of your letter because I think that you have expressed very well the most serious problem of generous Catholic couples as they confront the teaching of Pope Paul VI in his encyclical *Humanae Vitae,* on the regulation of human birth. No one can accuse you of seeking an easy way out of a minor problem nor of trying to bend the requirements of the Gospel to fit into a self-serving or pleasure-seeking mentality.

The elements of your problem may be boiled down to this: two duties force themselves on you, and both of them seem to indicate what God is asking of you.

One is the duty of following the teaching of the pope. According to this teaching, there is always something wrong in itself about contraception. It never is a truly good solution to any problem, because it distorts the act of life-giving love that is at the heart of marriage, because by it man usurps a dominion over the sources of life which does not belong to him.

The other duty is that of preserving your marriage. And your own experience has proven that the continual denial of marital tenderness is driving you and your husband into an impossible situation. Yet, at the same time, there are most serious reasons why you consider yourself conscience-bound to avoid another pregnancy.

The duties seem to be in conflict. Is there any way to harmonize them? For most women, the use of the rhythm method *under the direction of informed medical guidance* (which, unfortunately, is often available only in a clinic) does provide a harmonious solution. It provides the opportunity to give full expression to marital affection, thus fulfilling the duty of preserving and deepening the bond of marriage, and it provides a reliable means to avoid jeopardizing the welfare of the family by a new and probably harmful pregnancy, while fulfilling the duty of observing the directives that flow from the Church's understanding of God's plan for married love.

There are some couples who find that mutual love can grow in their marriage while they deny themselves the full expression of married love. Yet there are other couples whose problems become intolerable under the regime of abstinence and for whom rhythm is unreliable because of a physical irregularity or a traveling husband's work schedule. For these, there can be a genuine conflict of duties which results in "agonizing crises of conscience," as the American bishops noted in their pastoral letter of January 21, 1968. From the tone of your letter, I would judge that this is how it is in your case.

Traditional moral theology has always taught that when a person is confronted with a genuine moral dilemma in which *some action must be taken,* he must follow that course which he judges before God fulfills the more important duty. Even though this involves a failure to fulfill the conflicting duty (and, therefore, doing something which is objectively wrong), this does not mean that the person is necessarily guilty of sin. In the sight of men, it may happen that you're "damned if you do and damned if you don't" — but God does not play with us in this way. The violation of the lesser duty does not become a good thing — it always remains an objective evil and, at best, a regrettable necessity. Nor is it a case of doing evil that good may come of it — rather, it is a question of choosing which is the greater duty.

In their pastoral applications of the teaching of Pope Paul's encyclical, the bishops of France have applied this venerable principle of Catholic moral theology to cases such as the one you present. It would seem that the bishops of Canada make reference to the same principle. They do not challenge the pope's teaching. There is no claim that contraceptive intercourse is a good and appropriate means of fostering conjugal love and achieving responsible parenthood. They simply recognize that some couples risk destroying the life and harmony of their homes if they forego every expression of tenderness in their effort to avoid the evil of contraception. As the Canadian bishops express it: "In accord with the accepted principles of moral theology, if these persons have tried sincerely but without success to pursue a line of conduct in keeping with the given directives, they may be safely assured that whoever honestly chooses that course which seems right to him does so in good conscience."

The couple who find themselves constrained to make such a choice are not rejecting the teaching of the Holy Father nor his right to teach. They should not blow up the dilemma into a question of either leaving the Church or destroying the marriage.

Yes or No for Simple Peasants

Your advice to the couple whose question is given on p. 222 seems to indicate that birth control is OK. The OK seems clear to me and to everyone to whom I have shown your answer; however, no one wants to believe that a priest in a so-called "Catholic" magazine is saying that birth control is OK. In plain, simple language, so that we peasants can understand exactly what you mean, please state if you go counter to the Holy Father and say that birth control is OK for Catholic couples to practice.

No. I don't go counter to the Holy Father. Artificial contraception is never a good thing. Express it another way: artificial contraception is always a bad thing. It is always something objectively bad.

Is it something that is always a personal sin? No.

How can an objectively evil human act be subjectively not a personal sin? When there is a genuine impediment to freedom in the action. And the point of the laboriously worded and carefully worked-out reply to the above-mentioned husband and wife was to ascertain whether a particular couple could be in a situation where they are not free to find an objectively good alternative to two objectively bad choices. I may be wrong, but I see this view as remaining within the limits of the teaching of the pope.

Intimacies of the Married

My husband and I are trying to practice rhythm. Our baby is young, so we are being careful, abstaining for longer than three weeks at a time. It is very difficult. What is permissible regarding our sex life during this period of abstinence? If either of us lose control, do we both have to confess it? At times I almost feel resentful that I have to worry about such things. After all, we are married, and surely

we don't have to conduct ourselves as single people do. We are confused and perplexed but certainly want to do what is right. I think this fact of married life should be included in the Pre-Cana Conferences.

You're right. You should not have to worry about such things. For one thing, the most modern methods of periodic continence rarely require a couple to abstain for three weeks in order to have the security you honestly need. I hope that you are getting good medical assistance in using these more sophisticated and dependable methods.

Several times, I have referred to rhythm in these pages and have urged women to take advantage of good rhythm clinics. Actually, it might be better to drop the word "rhythm." The original rhythm method was a very crude and chancy way of determining the time of ovulation and the fertile time. There were so many factors that could throw off the rhythm of the menstrual cycle that the method of depending on a calendar was basically unreliable. Research done here and in Melbourne, Australia, has uncovered more accurate ways of recognizing when ovulation is about to take place. Some of this help should be available to you. The only thing these new methods have in common with rhythm is the fact that they require periodic continence for effective family planning. And, I hope, the research being funded by the American bishops will soon result in even greater refinements and simplicity that will make safe, effective, and unobjectionable family planning readily available to women everywhere.

Meanwhile, you want to know what is permissible in your intimate expressions of affection when you are abstaining from intercourse. For the married, conjugal tenderness is right not only in the immediate context of an act of intercourse but also and especially in times when the couple does not intend to have intercourse. Father Bernard Häring has a paragraph in his book *Shalom: Peace* (New York: Farrar, Straus and Giroux, 1968) that answers your question well: "[conjugal caresses] are expressions of love given to one another in the intimacy of married life by two persons who belong to each other in an indissoluble bond. The caresses are part of 'knowing' one another and loving one another. As long as the prevailing motif and attitude is conjugal love and not mere sexual exploitation of the other person, the couples should not be disturbed on this score if an orgasm occurs outside the conjugal act while they express their tenderness. Of course, the spouses must strive for a fuller control of strong passions at such times but not by way of anguish and fear. This, in my opinion, is surely a 'probable opinion' and can be followed by all spouses who, in their own conscience, consider it right" (pp. 216-217).

The only thing one has to tell in confession is serious sin. Honest mistakes are not matter for confession. And I, too, hope that this aspect of conjugal chastity is clearly explained to young people preparing for marriage. Too many married couples have been too pressured by an anxiety over possibly and unintentionally "losing the seed."

Blessing after Childbirth

Shouldn't we do away with the old custom of churching women? It seems to me to be connected with a superstitious idea that there is something unclean about becoming a mother and that this taint must be purified before she is fit to return to church. The whole concept is repugnant to modern women.

The idea you associate with this blessing of the Church is repugnant to modern men, too. But have you ever read the prayers of "churching"? The Ritual calls it the "blessing of a woman after childbirth and of her child." The ceremony begins with a joyful procession of the mother and her baby into the church. All join in saying the pregnant Mary's hymn of gratitude: "My soul magnifies the Lord." More brief prayers climax in this lovely request: "Almighty, everlasting God, by the child-bearing of the Blessed Virgin Mary, you turned the pains of child-bearing into joy for your faithful. Look with kindness on this your servant who comes rejoicing to your holy temple to give thanks to you and grant that after this life she and her child may, by the merits and intercession of the Blessed Virgin Mary, attain to the joys of everlasting life. Through Christ our Lord. Amen." Not one word about an implied evil to be purified!

Yet the very setting of the ceremony does have overtones that associate it with the Jewish ritual purification that Mary submitted to after the birth of Jesus (Luke 2:22-39). Some may feel that this is passé and distasteful. But take another look. Granted that there is a complex of many factors that gave rise to these symbolic purifications, some students of Israel's customs have noted a profound religious intuition in the idea of purification: the idea that man is unworthy of any contact with the divine. Whenever he comes into contact with the sacred, this sense of creaturely unworthiness becomes conscious and makes it fitting that he seek purification. It is in line with this intuition that the ancient rabbis would speak of a book as "soiling the hands," when they meant that it was a holy book — not a dusty one. This would seem to be the sense of the Catholic expression of "purifying" the chalice and ciborium at the end of Mass, so that nothing of the sacred species remains. And so, also, the purification of a woman after childbirth in Judaism is a testimony to a belief that the new mother has been in intimate contact with the creative power of God!

So think it over again. I can't find anything degrading in the beautiful custom of praising God for the gift of sharing his power in the making of a man nor in seeking the blessing of God in and through the Church on this joyful occasion.

Holy Orders

The Christian Priesthood

Can the office of priesthood in the Catholic Church be compared to positions of leadership in business or government? That is, can the leader of the Church's worship be the person who is simply elected or chosen by the faithful?

Not according to Catholic doctrine. Some Protestant communities disagree, and this is one of the doctrinal problems that stand in the way of perfect Church unity.

According to Catholic teaching, ministry in the Church is hierarchical. Even if a democratic process were used to select bishop, priest, or deacon, the man would not yet be able to act as a Christian minister. He must be ordained — that is, he must receive the sacrament of holy orders by the bishop's imposition of hands. His ministry is not derived directly from the congregation's call, nor does it last only as long as it consents to it.

All Christians agree that there is only one priesthood in the New Testament, that of Jesus Christ. All similarly agree that the whole community of the baptized have been constituted as a priestly people, united to Christ, and offering the worship of their lives to God on behalf of all mankind. Consequently, theology speaks of the common priesthood of the faithful.

But, in addition to this share in Christ's priesthood, the Catholic Church recognizes another kind of share in the priesthood of Christ, and this belongs only to the ordained. It is a question of kind, not merely one of the degree of sharing. The difference is not like the difference between men who have different degrees of skin pigmentation making them white or brown or black men. The difference is like that between automobiles and furnaces.

The ordained minister can act in the person of Christ in a way that no other member of the priestly people can. He alone can make the sacrifice of Christ present in the Eucharist. He alone can exercise the sacramental ministry of reconciliation in the confessional.

Yet his position is one of total service to the priestly people. He does not stand outside the Christian community as some kind of super-Christian. He is within it as a member. He lives its life as a man equally dependent on the grace and mercy of God. His greatest glory in the final analysis will not come from his special role in the priestly people as minister of Christ's word and sacrament, but from the fidelity with which he fulfilled the vocation he shares in common as a baptized member of the Christian Church.

We like to hope that the priest's leadership of his people is such that he would be the people's choice, but his privilege of ministry depends on ordination and not on such a choice.

The Celibacy of Priests

The celibacy of the clergy has been under attack for some time now. Where did the idea of celibacy come from, and of what real value is it?

The idea of Christian celibacy is deeply rooted in the Gospel. It is not that the Gospel considers celibacy as *the* way of living the Christian life, in the sense that it alone is the ideal and marriage is tolerated as a kind of inevitable and unfortunate compromise for the weak. The Gospel sees living in celibacy as one possible way of living as a Christian. It is presented as a way that is especially significant and meaningful for the whole Church.

There are a number of places in the Gospel where radical renunciation — even the renunciation of marriage and family — is indicated as the response that some of Christ's followers will make to His call.

Perhaps the most forceful expression of this is contained in Jesus' words: "Some men are incapable of sexual activity from birth; some have been deliberately made so; and some there are who have freely renounced sex for the sake of God's reign. Let him accept this teaching who can" (Mt. 19:12). A very strong word is used in this passage, "eunuchs," which the translator interprets in three contexts. Addressing himself to normal men, Jesus suggests that God's grace will be experienced by some in such a way that they will be psychologically incapable of entering marriage.

In other words, the religious value of serving to bring about the reign of God and concentrating totally upon it can lead a person to dedicate his whole life to this value in such a way that he is willing to forego marriage. It is not a question of prefering divine values at the expense of human values, nor of rejecting natural goods for the sake of supernatural ones. Marriage in a redeemed universe is not an inferior and unblessed thing. The celibate makes a positive choice, not a negative one. He chooses a way to live his life in Christ that is valuable and fruitful. It is valuable if it is chosen as a way of expressing his personal dedication to Christ and making himself available to the apostolate. By the very fact that he chooses celibacy for these motives, the celibate becomes a sign to the whole world of the seriousness with which every Christian ought to take the kingdom or the reign of God.

St. Paul proposed the celibate way of life to his communities as an optional and desirable way of following Christ (I Cor. 7:7-8; 28-35). In addition to its meaning in reference to a personal relationship with Christ and to the apostolate, Paul saw celibacy in relationship to the completed kingdom of God — an anticipation of the state where there will be neither marrying nor giving in marriage.

How did celibacy, which the Church always recognized as a special gift of the Holy Spirit, come to be linked to the official priestly ministry of the Church? Apparently the Spirit stirred the movement himself. It began spontaneously. By the end of the third century Tertullian writes that innumerable clerics before him had remained unmarried for the sake of the Lord.

There was a profound religious intuition at work here. These early priests recognized that it was particularly appropriate for the men who were officially and totally given to the religious service of the community to remain unmarried in the name of that service. They would not merely be functionaries bestowing word and sacrament, their lives would be on the line witnessing to the reality of the kingdom.

Mingled with this Gospel intuition, but separable from it, were some unfortunate rigorist tendencies. In the early exhortations to the celibate life there are evidences of a frankly unwholesome attitude toward marriage as a form of Christian life in holiness. However, it is a distortion of the facts to maintain that these ideas that crept in from paganism were the dominant force in the movement for priestly celibacy.

What had begun spontaneously as the religious choice of many clerics started to be regulated by church laws in the fourth century. Some local churches required celibacy of their priests, and throughout the whole Church, East and West, it was urged as an ideal. However, it was not until 1139, at the Second Lateran Council, that celibacy became the law for all priests in the Western or Latin Church. Since this time, the practice of this church has been that only those who freely accept celibacy for the sake of the kingdom of God are admitted to the ministry of the Priesthood.

There is no essential reason why the Church has to restrict priestly ordination to celibates. There is an inherent appropriateness in this, but no necessary and changeless reason. Today, as you indicate, the pastoral wisdom of this requirement is being questioned. There is nothing wrong with this, but we should be careful not to ask the wrong questions, or to question the discipline of the Church for the wrong reasons.

There is no question but that the Church has the right to give her official priesthood only to the man who tells her that he feels called to celibacy. There is no "vocation" to the priesthood that compels the Church to ordain any man, and the hierarchy of the Church may indeed determine to ordain only those who show signs of the special vocation to celibacy as well as the vocation to ministry.

Nor should this decision of the Church be seen as forcing celibacy on a man. No one comes forward for ordination unless he comes freely. Once ordained a man is bound to persevere in the celibacy he freely accepted as long as he wishes to remain in the active ministry. If one should say that this is forced, the same would have to be said of the fidelity of marriage which restricts the choice of spontaneous and vagrant love by the moral obligation of a faithfulness that must sometimes be fought for strenuously.

Some change may come if the Church finds that other values and considerations are more urgent than the values that are fostered by ordaining only those who freely choose celibacy. It may be that at a particular time or in a particular place there will not be enough men who feel inspired to choose celibacy. Then it may be argued that the essential need the church has for an adequate supply of priests is more important than confining ordinations to celibates.

For me it is unthinkable that the celibate way of life will ever cease to exist in the Church. I think that God will always inspire men and women with the determination to dedicate their whole being to Christ and his people. And this not because of a distaste for marriage, much less because of a disdain for the holiness of this way of life. The Church needs, for her fullness, the complementarity of those who are married in the Lord and those who remain celibate for the sake of the kingdom.

That the clergy will continue to be drawn from the ranks of those who freely choose celibacy is the present intention of the leaders of the Western Church. This policy is being debated especially because of sociological, psychological, and spiritual problems that are making it difficult to live this way of life today. However, it is hard to gainsay the fact that celibacy is inherently appropriate for the man whose whole life is meant to point dramatically to the reality of the kingdom of God (cf. Vatican II, *Decree on the Ministry and Life of Priests,* no. 16).

If you want to read further on this question, I recommend the beautiful little book of E. Schillebeeckx, O.P., *Celibacy* (Sheed & Ward, N.Y., 1968), and the chapter on "The Celibacy of the Secular Priest Today" in K. Rahner, S.J., *Servants of the Lord* (Herder & Herder, N.Y., 1968).

All Right for a Priest to Marry?

When is it all right for a Catholic priest to marry? Does he also receive the sacrament of matrimony?

I wouldn't say it is ever "all right" for a priest to marry. There is always something sad, something that injures the Church and society, when an ordained priest comes to the decision to go back on his solemnly pledged word and seeks permission to marry.

The Catholic Churches of both East and West long agreed to consider that sacred ordination is an impediment that makes it impossible for a priest to enter a marriage. The difference between East and West was this: In the West the Church has maintained the policy of ordaining only those young men who judge before God that they have been gifted with the grace to remain unmarried in special dedication to God's interest — and whose relative maturity gives us reason to hope they are not deceiving themselves. In the

East, the Church has always ordained both single and married men; but she has not allowed priests to marry. The Eastern Rite priest who loses his wife cannot marry again.

Up until quite recently, this law and practice of the Church was maintained most rigorously. The Church refused to dispense the impediment to marrying that she has established by law. There were practically no exceptions. If a priest found it spiritually impossible to continue to function in his ministry, she would release him from active duty, but she would not permit him to marry. If he took a wife, it could only be in a civil ceremony — and, just as is true for any Catholic, this liaison was not considered a marriage.

During the past several years, the Church authorities have been dealing more gently with priests who request to be relieved of their ministry and freed from the legal consequences of their priesthood. Now, in fact, they do dispense the "impediment of sacred orders" and make it *legally* all right for the Church's beloved and troubled sons to receive the sacrament of matrimony. There is no doubt that the Church can dispense the impediments she has herself created (such as that which prevents first cousins from marrying, or a Catholic from marrying an unbaptized person) when there is a sufficient reason for doing so.

The man who receives a permission like this remains a priest forever. A declaration of the Church cannot change the profound, unseen change that has taken place within him by the power of Christ. But for all practical purposes, the laicized priest has reentered the layman's world. His way of life and his problems are not unlike those of any layman in the parish. He is even forbidden to exercise his priesthood, except in the extraordinary case where the need of a dying person to be helped by the sacraments requires him to assist.

Holy orders is irrevocable, but the legal obligation not to marry is not. The pope has definitely stated that he intends celibacy to be joined to the priesthood in the Western Church. But since it is a rule of the Church, not a law of God, the Church can dispense a man from this obligation. She does this only when she judges that such a dispensation is necessary for the salvation of his soul and that, without it, he will be unable to live any kind of Christian life.

The desire of these priests is to live a genuine Christian life in the layman's world. When the step has been taken, it falls on all of us to accept them and to help them to live at peace. It is horribly un-Christian to cut them off or to hound them with malicious gossip or to keep them from holding a job. The priest who has been permitted to marry in the Church may be very conscious of the need of great penance. But it is not for the self-righteous to determine its form.

If Priests Can Marry . . .

If priests can be relieved of their priestly duties and allowed to marry after receiving the sacrament of holy orders, why can't divorced (with Church permission) Catholics be allowed to remarry, although they have also received the sacrament of matrimony? I know of several couples that are in this position and are living up to Catholicism but feel they should be able to change in view of the Church's outlook on priests being able to marry.

Your problem is a real one. Is not the priest's pledged word (and, for that matter, the religious' pledged word, given by vow) as binding as the pledged word of a married couple? In a sense, yes. To pledge something to God is to oblige oneself to eternal fidelity. If there is a breakdown of this sense of fidelity in one area of the Church's life, it affects every other area. Someone has remarked cynically that the religious vow of chastity is beginning to seem as if it means this: I will stay single until I change my mind! Obviously, all this makes it far more difficult to accept the Church's teaching that marriage is for keeps.

Hard though it is to accept, especially in the anguished situation of those whose unhappy marriage has ended in a shambles, the Church sees herself obliged by fidelity to Christ to differentiate between the breakable permanence of the pledged word attached to an office in the Church and the unbreakable permanence of the pledged word that forms the stuff of this sacrament in the Church.

Holy order is for keeps. Marriage is for keeps. But a priest's promise not to marry is different from the sacrament of his priesthood — there always have been married priests in the Church — while a husband's promise not to marry another woman is at the very heart of the sacrament of matrimony. In a special case, the Church may permit a man to cease to function as a priest — she cannot take his priesthood away. In a special case, the Church may permit an incompatible couple to separate — she cannot undo their sacrament of matrimony.

Why? Because the Church believes that the true and perfect sacrament of matrimony is unbreakable by any human power. No new arguments have demonstrated that she can do any more than suffer with the suffering of those who are in the lonely state of this unwanted singleness.

More—If Priests Can Marry . . .

I still don't understand how a man who has received holy orders can marry in the Catholic Church and receive the sacraments, while a woman who has had an unfortunate marriage and, after all kinds of efforts to save the marriage, has separated is forbidden to marry again?

I'm very sympathetic to your difficulty. The theory is quite clear: practices, laws, and even the external obligations of public vows and pledges can be changed by the authorities of the Church. The Church does not acknowledge that she has any such authority over the life-long fidelity that belongs to the essence of a consummated, sacramental marriage.

A number of people are dissatisfied with the seeming inequity of this whole thing. They see both marriage and holy orders as comparable package deals involving similar lifelong obligations. They are not comfortable with distinctions that talk about things that belong to the nature of the two sacraments (over which the Church claims no authority) and things that are appended to the sacraments by Church law and personal pledge.

This difficulty of the people suggests two things to me.

One is the responsibility of priests in crisis. A priest cannot attend solely to his own personal anguish. He must also weigh in the balance the impact that his request for a dispensation from his obligations will have on those who cannot distinguish between changeable legal obligations and changeless sacramental obligations, and he must do everything possible to avoid any injury to his brethren in the Church.

The other is a concern that the anguish of unhappily married people must be taken more seriously. The Church takes it for granted, and operates on the conviction, that complete sacramental marriage can never be dissolved. Hence she does not consider the partners of such a marriage free to remarry should there be a divorce. But should every Church marriage be considered an indissoluble sacrament unless the opposite can be proved by absolutely compelling evidence? Are there not some — even many — "unfortunate marriages" which are unions that were never the result of a free, mature choice? Even though force or fear or immature impulse cannot be satisfactorily proved in a chancery marriage court, are these things therefore to be presumed to be nonexistent, even when a couple know in their hearts before God that they were present? In other words, might it not be true that a number of marriages that end up in the divorce courts today were never truly indissoluble marriages in the first place?

Compassionate churchmen are asking these questions today. They are concerned to make the law and practice of the Church reflect, as perfectly as possible, the real situation of men before God. They are anxious lest an understandable desire for good order and the protection of the institution of Christian marriage should end up imposing intolerable burdens on sincere and generous persons who are caught in the web of the law.

The Faith of Priests

Regarding those priests who have left their ministry, many claim they do not go to church any more. Is it possible that these men do not believe or never have believed in their power to consecrate the body and blood of Christ at Mass or their power to forgive sins in the sacrament of penance? Have their priestly lives been one grand charade?

The shock that you feel at the number of priests who are abandoning their ministry is shared by most Catholics. The reasons why these men leave are manifold. Each case is unique. But the case of the man who was simply an unbelieving jobholder is almost nonexistent.

A couple of studies have been made to help us understand the phenomenon of priests leaving their ministry. One was done in Italy. The author interviewed seventy-two "ex-priests." It is most significant that, in citing the elements that influenced their unfortunate decision, sixty-nine said they had given up praying, sixty felt a torment of conscience from living in a way opposed to their state, fifty-five spoke of the love of a woman, but only one said he had lost the faith.

A man who does not pray can lose the sense of the specialness of his dedication to our Lord. A man who is living at odds with his conscience must sooner or later repent or give up his ideals. A man who finds the spiritual dynamism of his life disappearing is understandably vulnerable to the promise of fulfillment in a human love. But the roots of faith are hardy.

Among the men who have set aside their calling are those to whom we are personally indebted. They gave us Christ in his word and in his sacraments. Their priestly lives enriched the Church. It was no grand charade. They believed in what they did in the name of Christ.

Many of them yearn to be able to act as his ministers again.

Pray for them and for the Church that aches at their loss. Pray for the tempted and the lonely priests who are even now struggling, that they may be strengthened to hold fast to their vocation.

The New Deacons

I've heard of a man in the office who is studying to become a lay deacon. Would you please tell me what this is all about? What are these lay deacons to do, who picks them, why do we need them?

Your use of the expression "lay deacon" is interesting. When a man is ordained deacon, he becomes a member of the hierarchy. He receives the sacrament of holy orders — diaconate being one of the three sacramental orders in the ministry of the Catholic Church. Hence he will no longer be a layman but an official minister in the Church.

However, the average American Catholic doesn't ordinarily think in theological and canonical terms. For many of us the word "lay" refers to a style of life rather than a theological state in the Church. Since many of our new deacons will be married men who will continue to hold their secular jobs and raise their families, it is understandable that people will tend to think of them as "lay deacons." It would be better, though, to drop the expression as something that is apt to create more confusion than clarity.

It was in 1964 at the Second Vatican Council that the way was opened to restore the rank of permanent deacon to the ministry of the Catholic Church. For centuries prior to this, diaconate had been little more than an intermediate step on the way to the priesthood. It was not always so. The Acts of the Apostles, chapters 6 to 8, shows the apostles choosing seven men to assist them in the works of caring for the poor, in preaching and instruction, and in baptizing. Through the first centuries, deacons served in various ways to assist the bishops. Eventually there were conflicts and power struggles between priests and deacons and changes of mentality among the people that reduced the diaconate to the relatively unimportant state it had held up to the present.

Vatican II declared that "the diaconate can in the future be restored as a proper and permanent rank of the hierarchy" (*Constitution on the Church,* no. 29). In 1967 this decision was implemented by Pope Paul VI, and in the following year the American bishops received permission to establish the permanent diaconate in the United States.

The Council's decision was an authorization, not a mandate. It was left to the bishops of each country or region to judge whether having deacons in the service of the Church would meet their needs.

The question of authorizing the reestablishment of the diaconate created a great deal of interest at the Council — seventy bishops spoke on the matter, pro and con. Their concern was practical and theoretical. Theoretically, some felt that without deacons the Church's hierarchy was like an army without sergeants. The overriding practical concern at the Council was that a diaconate could provide for the pastoral care of Christian people who were leaderless.

This practical consideration would be especially applicable in mission territories. It often happens on the missions that a priest can visit a Christian community only about once a month and then only for a very short time. Catechists and religious brothers and sisters have done marvelous work in teaching, leading, and helping these communities to grow in faith and holiness. But a deacon's presence would be an official presence of the Church in the person of an ordained minister.

The official character of his service to the believing community is probably the most important thing that distinguishes what a deacon can do from what a dedicated layman can do. Laymen could be authorized to do all the services that ordained deacons can do. They can administer communion, baptize, preach and teach, and lead the people in prayer and apostolic activity. But unlike the deacons they do these things as authorized individuals rather than as members of the official leadership of the Christian Church.

How are deacons picked? The way priests are picked. Men who feel themselves called to serve God's people present themselves. Their vocations are nurtured and scrutinized by a process of direction and education. When the candidate and the bishop agree that the step is wise, the bishop ordains. Any man who feels a desire to serve the Church as a deacon should speak to his parish priest or diocesan vocation director as a first step in discovering whether he should go ahead.

Why do we need deacons? Each local church must answer this question for itself. Some may need deacons to make up for a genuine shortage of priests. Others may judge that the Christian leadership of a man will be more effective if he is more closely identified with the official Church establishment. There is no single answer. In some situations, identification with the Church establishment might be a barrier rather than a help to effectiveness.

So, the Church is taking a first step on a new path in restoring the permanent diaconate. How this will serve the Church and the world in the long run, we don't know. We don't know what shifts in attitude will take place, nor what the interaction between priests and laity and deacons will be. But in an effort to be responsive to the call of the Holy Spirit and the invitation of the Church generous men are becoming deacons. It is our job to welcome them and help their ministry to be fruitful and satisfying, while we leave it to the future to show how the new ministers will contribute to the renewal of the Church.

Diaconate—a Holy Order

I thought a man could receive the sacrament of holy orders only once. Is not the diaconate, which is received prior to the priesthood, also a sacrament of holy orders?

Right on both counts. But the conclusion doesn't really follow. The clue to the solution of your difficulty is contained in the name of the sacrament, holy orders — in the plural.

The sacrament of holy orders is unique among the seven in that the sacred gift of being minister to the Church has various degrees. The fullness of the sacrament of holy orders belongs to the bishop. Lesser shares in the same sacrament belong to the priest and to the deacon. Whether the minor ministers also share in the sacrament is disputed. A person cannot be ordained deacon twice — once he is ordained, his ordination is forever. But a deacon may be, and usually is, ordained a priest.

Reversing the Orders

It is very clear in the Acts of the Apostles that the first deacons were elected by the early Christians to handle the financial affairs of the Church to free the Apostles for spiritual things. Why has the Church now decided to do the reverse — ordain married deacons to preach and administer some of the sacraments while leaving finances in the hands of the priests?

Your point is a cute one. It reminds me of a friend who became a

Signpost

yeoman in the Navy and felt that his special value to the nation was that he freed a Wave for active duty. However, my friend knew that he was oversimplifying and kidding — I hope that you can see your own oversimplification.

The intention of the bishops at the Vatican Council in restoring the order of diaconate as a permanent thing in the Church is not to free priests to take care of the building and finances of the Church. Where deacons are ordained, their job *as deacons* will be that for which the sacrament of their order has prepared them — a ministry of word and sacrament. This is also the principal care of the ordained priesthood, whom the deacons will assist.

Meanwhile, someone does have to keep the store, and it usually is the responsibility of the parish priest in residence. Perhaps the day will come when the parish council or the laity in the parish will be ready to assume the burden of caring for the fabric of the Church and the balancing of the books. Any volunteers? It's a far bigger job than that of secretary for the Holy Name Society.

7
Questions
of
Conscience

Liberty of Conscience

Where does Vatican II teach that man must be free to accept God or reject him according to the dictates of his conscience? What is the effect of this teaching on Catholics who reject some of the doctrines the Church teaches?

The Council does not teach that each man is absolutely free to reject God. Such a teaching would be equivalent to declaring the Church and Council quite irrelevant, since the whole mission of the Church is to bring God to men in such a way that men will open themselves to accept God and the full human life that they can find only in union with him.

Man, in fact, has a duty to accept and worship God. It is the conviction of the Catholic Church that "God himself has made known to mankind the way in which men are to serve him, and thus be saved in Christ and come to blessedness" (*Decree on Religious Freedom,* no. 1). The individual person does not have a right to reject God's designs. His obligation is to seek to know them and to follow them of his own free choice. In this very personal adventure of the free conscience, not all men will come to the same knowledge of the truth. Some will lead a life in ignorance of God, devoid of any sense of loyalty to him or religious worship of him. Others will express their faith and dependence on him in ways that Catholics consider more or less defective.

History records the efforts of men through the ages to force a conformity of belief and religious expression by means ranging from physical torture through legal disabilities to psychological pressure. Vatican II has rejected every such effort as being opposed to the fundamental dignity of the human person, and consequently to the will of God, who calls men to respond to his call as free sons in the Only Son. This is the meaning of religious liberty as defined in the Council's *Decree on Religious Freedom.* It declares the "civil rights" of all men in the matter of professing their religious belief. No one has the right to force a person to act contrary to his conscience. No one has the right to prevent a person from acting in accordance with his conscience, whether in private or public, except in keeping with the demands of public order.

In this sense, freedom of religion is a basic human right. It is likewise true that each man's conscience is free and inviolable. Does this mean that each Catholic is free to take or leave the doctrine of his Church in the name of his "free conscience"? No!

While championing the freedom of each person's conscience, the Council reminds all men of their personal duty to form a *right* conscience. Conscience is not a blind impulse or a funny inside feeling. Conscience is an act of my mind. It is a judgment, based on facts, that affirms that in these circumstances I must do or avoid such and such if I am to be faithful to the will of God for me. Among the "facts" that a Catholic has to consider in the formation of his conscience is the "sacred and certain doctrine of the Church" (*Decree on Religious Freedom,* no. 14). This is not a crimp on the Catholic's liberty. It is a guide to that liberty. It is the consequence of that supremely free act of faith by which I accept the whole reality of the Church as the continuing presence of Christ in our time.

While all are equal in the Church in possessing the Spirit who leads them to holiness, all are not equal in possessing the gift of the Spirit to teach and direct the faithful into the fullness of the truth of Christ. It is not an act of the free conscience to reject the "sacred and certain" teachings of the pope and bishops. It is an act of anarchy.

Love, and There Is No Sin

Is it the privilege of Catholics, as individuals, to formulate their own opinions about such controversial questions as premarital sex and contraceptive birth control? Also, how do you answer the argument that "where there is love, there is no sin" with reference to the above question?

Catholics are not free to approach these questions as if they were wide open. The Church has a moral teaching on these matters. She teaches that they are objectively wrong, that these actions can never be good in themselves. Whoever gives his loyalty to Christ in and through the Catholic Church is no longer free simply to ignore its moral teachings. He must try to understand the teachings and their intent and form his own conscience in the light of the values contained in these teachings.

Suppose, however, that a Catholic has taken very seriously a particular ethical teaching, that he has studied the matter and weighed all the reasons given for the teaching and even tried to find more cogent ones — and has failed to be convinced that the teaching is correct. Is it possible for him to maintain his own view and still be a good Catholic? Yes it is. Responsible dissent is possible in the Church.

Responsible dissent is a precious and difficult thing. It isn't akin to the easy rationalization of the teen-age couple who whisper to one another that this can't be wrong, "because we love each other." The responsible dissenter is a man who has wrestled with the meaning of the tradition that supports the present teaching and who is compelled by the evidence to say that the prohibition is not absolute. The responsible dissenter is a man prayerfully steeped in the faith, who with intuitive sureness will not water down the crucifying demands of the Gospel. The responsible dissenter is a man with a humble, self-critical sense, who has the happy faculty of being able to laugh at himself and who knows the fallibility even of his own dissent from an authentic, non-infallible teaching of the Church. Responsible dissenters are, understandably, in short supply.

"Where there is love, there is no sin" is not an argument; it is a statement. And it is eternally true. But the problem is to verify that we are dealing with love, not "luv." The pleasant feeling of being wanted and esteemed may be "luv," but it does not assure us that we are dealing with love. Love is a response to goodness. It is uncompromising and clear-sighted. It is attentive, not only to a deep affection welling up between two people, but to everyone else who is affected by them. The love that excludes sin is a love that is modeled on that love of Christ which brought him to the cross and made martyrdom the closest way to follow him in love. The true lover is attentive to what his expression of his love will mean to the person he loves, to those who might emulate him, to the feelings and hopes of parents and society, to a future that is yet merely conjecture. He will find the clearest blueprint of the actions that incarnate love in the commandments and the most beautiful analysis of the many-splendored thing love is in St. Paul's hymn to love (I Cor. 13).

Who Has the Greater Sin?

Is adultery a mortal sin still? If so, is it as great a sin or as serious a sin as failure to take an active part in the civil-rights movements? I am an older person, and I'm dreadfully confused and perplexed by many of the recent changes in the Church. Is there any hope for the likes of me?

Hope for you? Indeed there is. I wish you'd pray for us who are trying to follow after you and persevere with you in the grace of God's call to belong to his Church. Of course, you find it hard to start thinking in new ways. It almost means starting life over again for you. And you don't have to do that. You have to continue to live and grow. But it's the same life — a fully human life lived in the faith of Christ Jesus that bears fruit in the love of God and neighbor.

You ask about sin, and the tricky business of determining what sins are the more serious. A serious sin is one that cuts a person off from the love relationship that God has called us to in baptism. This means that a person sins seriously when he chooses freely and deliberately something that is incompatible with loving God. It means that he refuses to live as God's adopted son. St. John described it this way: "If anyone says, 'My love is fixed on God,' yet hates his brother, he is a liar. One who has no love for the brother he has seen cannot love the God he has not seen" (I John 4: 20).

Adultery is such a sinful choice. A person cannot remain in a love relationship with God while he is willingly reneging on that most solemn pledge of fidelity he made in marriage. By adultery, a man and woman use the language of bodily intimacy to say "We belong to each other," when, in fact, they are not free to make that gift. Their expression of affection is a stolen thing that literally "cheats" the husband or wife to whom they belong. Adultery will always be a serious sin against the virtue of marital chastity.

Is it as serious a sin as a failure to take an active part in the civil-rights movement? In itself, it is no sin to remain outside the civil-rights movement. You must love your brother. It would be a serious sin to prevent him from getting or exercising the basic rights that belong to him as a man. But few persons are seriously bound to engage actively in the civil-rights movement.

I think that the real question is this: Is adultery as serious a sin as racism? The gravity of sins can be compared from many different points of view. From a practical point of view, the more serious sin is the one that more seriously jeopardizes salvation. Racism seems to be the bigger threat. Adultery is so often a lamentable, human weakness. And the adulterer often is burdened with a sense of shame that will bring him back sheepishly to seek forgiveness and reconciliation with God. But the racist is often trapped in his sin by a smug self-righteousness. His contempt of his fellow man is masked by such plausible "good reasons" that the voice of conscience is stifled. Even God cannot break through such a shell to call him to repentance. What could be worse!

The Dimensions of Charity

In regard to the second great commandment, "You shall love your neighbor as yourself," does this mean that each one should involve himself socially with his neighbor, as well as helping him when he is in need, setting a good example, et cetera? For example, if I don't like a particular neighbor or have anything in common with him, am I breaking this commandment if I avoid becoming socially involved? It isn't aways easy to love one's neighbors in the sense of throwing your arms around them or wanting their company.

If by "social involvement" you mean the close ties of good friends, frequent visits, sharing family joys and sorrows, entertaining, et cetera — of course, the great law of Christian living does not demand this kind of thing. Imagine what it would be like if being a Christian meant that you had to throw your house and backyard open to people you just couldn't stand. And think of your poor neighbor, if you began butting into his private affairs in the name of some vague principle of "involving" yourself socially. The requirements of charity are delicate and sensitive to the needs of others. They are not naive. Even the Lord did not share his deepest self with some in Judea, for he knew what they were like (John 2:24-25).

Yet there is a measure of social involvement that genuine loyalty to Christ does require and that we have too often sinned against by slogans like "You have to love your neighbor, but you don't have to like him." We have too often hidden behind a minimizing morality to justify those deep-seated, irrational prejudices that have deprived our brothers, whose color or religious confession is different from ours, of that respect and esteem that belong to them as human beings. What I want to be careful of is the danger of having someone use the plain common sense of the preceding paragraph to justify continuing discrimination in housing and schooling and the maintaining of segregated public facilities of every kind.

These great social sins cannot be swept under the rug by appealing to the fact that "we have nothing in common." With this type of logic, too many lives have been destroyed. Fidelity to the great law of Christ in our time demands that we greatly increase whatever social and political involvement is necessary to crush the head of the demon of division.

Pity or Love?

Someone once said, "The Catholic Church preaches fear." Depressingly, I'm believing it more and more. Recently, a parish priest said from the pulpit, "God sent Jesus, not out of justice, not out of love, but out of pity." I've heard this same doctrine of despair from nuns at school and in much I read. What ever happened to John 3:16? I was raised a Protestant and taught first and foremost, "God is Love."

Who can love one whom he fears? I wish Catholicism would stress God's love more. I suspect humanity has long felt sorrow and guilt and needs now to feel protected, secure, loved. Can't the Church stop putting down its people so harshly? One cannot love others until he loves himself. He can't love himself if he doesn't think God loves him.

Amen. And let me quote John 3:16 for our readers:
  "Yes, God so loved the world
  that he gave his only Son,
  that whoever believes in him may not die
  but may have eternal life."
Pity can sound like a put-down to contemporary ears. Pity has come to look like a package of contemptuous disapproval mixed with grudging condescension. This is not the way God is toward us. Nor is it the way the authentic teaching of the Catholic Church puts it either. However, wounded people in official positions are just as prone as anyone else to project their own problems into the way they speak and act.

If pity is freighted with the overtones of the dictionary definition as "sympathetic sorrow for one suffering, distressed, or unhappy," a synonym for "compassion," then isn't it the same as the beautiful love which God shows us even when we feel most wretched and un-deserving?

God's love is always a miracle. It makes lovable all that it touches. And the supreme wonder is that it always reaches out to us and enfolds us, even when we run away from it in needless fear.

War and Peace

How are we to interpret the teaching of Christ (Matt. 5:44 and Luke 6:27) as related to war, particularly the action in Vietnam?

The passages you ask about are fundamentally the same saying of the Lord: "But I say to you, love your enemies, do good to those who hate you." They occur in the Sermon on the Mount and must be interpreted in the sense of this whole passage. The sayings of Jesus that make up this part of the Sermon (Matt. 5:38-48) are not to be seen as a repudiation of the Mosaic law of justice and self-defense. They point to the goal of the law. Christ did not require us to give up our rights in the face of unjust attack. He was proclaiming that the goal of just defense is to establish "harmony and mutual respect of men living together as brothers. Unless justice opens to love, it cannot ultimately be justified" (Jerome Rausch, O.S.C., "The Principle of Nonresistance . . ." *Catholic Biblical Quarterly,* XXVIII [1966], p. 36).

Must a Christian "turn the other cheek" and give in to anyone who is exploiting him? This is not a requirement of a new moral law that Christ is proclaiming. It is rather a forceful statement of an ideal of peace and harmony toward which we must strive as persons and as nations. We can work realistically toward this ideal only by the continual process of working in our political and social structures. There we must create the conditions of mutual brotherhood that make those who have been enemies begin to trust one another.

War is a horrible sin. No right thinking man can condone it, certainly no Christian. Family war that ends in divorce, industrial war waged by the strike or lockout, international war — all are foreign to the Christian ideal. The fact that these things happen bears witness to the deep-rooted sinfulness and selfishness that remain in the sons of Adam.

But as long as this human misery holds sway, it is certainly over-simplifying the Gospel to demand that Christians abandon the possibility of defending themselves. Pope Paul did not demand this when he spoke before the United Nations: "As long as man remains that weak, changeable, and even wicked being that he often shows himself to be, defensive arms will, unfortunately, be necessary." Nor did the Council in the *Constitution on the Church in the Modern World* (nos. 79-81).

To apply all this to Vietnam — I am at a loss. The situation is so complex, the motivations so intricate, the potential consequences so devastating that I would not presume to say that this war is so utterly without justification that we are obliged to cease all military action unilaterally. This war is horrible. Every possible approach to reconciliation should be made. But the approach will have to be made by those skilled in the hardheaded realities of political life — not by those whose facile solution to mammoth problems is always a simplistic answer.

Meanwhile, the words of the Lord do place a present burden on those who are involved in the conflict. Difficult though it be, even during the heat of battle they must continue to want to love and forgive. "Victor Charlie" is their brother. He is called to the same fullness of human life and to the same happiness of eternal life as we are. Too many fighting men battling for a noble cause have been brutalized by the experience of cruel combat. A spirit of revenge and hatred may be understandable, but revenge and hatred make men and society bad.

Conscientious Objectors

How can a Catholic be a conscientious objector? Isn't it a duty of the virtue of patriotism to serve one's country?

If the question means this: May a Catholic follow the dictates of his conscience when he objects on moral grounds to the course his government is following? — then the answer is an unqualified "Yes." The alternative is almost insulting. It would mean that the Catholic has no conscience, no personal responsibility. It would presume that the Catholic must always be an "organization man," waiting for a "party line" from above or blindly conforming to popular prejudices. Horrible!

If a Catholic, or any man for that matter, comes to the clear conviction that his country's war is unjust, then he must refuse to fight. Similarly, if a soldier is asked to cooperate in some particularly savage act of war, he must obey his conscience rather than his orders. As

Peter and the apostles told the Jewish leaders, "Better for us to obey God than men" (Acts 5:20). It is an unfortunate fact that at present the person who objects to a particular war on moral grounds cannot claim the protection of our American laws on "conscientious objection" — these define the objector as one who objects to all war "in any form." This limitation may make the law easier to administer, but it does not make it equitable.

Can there be a Catholic pacifist — one who objects to war in any form? The reason why this is a question is this: Catholic theologians teach that there can be situations where recourse to the violence of war is justifiable. If a nation honestly discovers that there is no other way in which it can defend rights of supreme value, then it can, with moral uprightness, embark on the course of war. We speak of this as a "just war." In such a case, it would seem to be the duty of citizens to serve their country in the regrettable venture — for Catholic teaching is quite clear on the responsibility of citizens to contribute to the causes that are for the common good of the people. Hence, it is assumed, no Catholic can appeal to his religious convictions as a reason for refusing to serve in his country's "just war."

I used the word "assume." There are many assumptions in all this. There is the assumption that the "just war theory" is theoretically sound and Christian, that it continues clearly to be applicable to the conditions of modern warfare, and, the biggest assumption of all, that a Catholic's obligations (and rights) of conscience can always be determined by simply applying the objective standards of the theological consensus prevailing in the Church. Are all these assumptions valid?

Personally, I cannot subscribe to the absolute pacifism that would reject even the theoretical possibility of a just war. However, the application of the theory of the just war is extremely difficult. It caused great anguish and tension at the Vatican Council, which is reflected in its *Constitution on the Church in the Modern World* (nos. 77-82). The Council reaffirmed the right of armed self-defense. But, in view of the frightful destructive power available to nations, it spoke of "an entirely new attitude" we must bring to evaluating the question of warfare. Pope John XXIII reflected this attitude when he wrote: "In this age of ours which prides itself on its atomic power, it is irrational to believe that war is still an apt means of vindicating violated rights" (*Pacem in terris*, April 11, 1963).

There is certainly an ambiguity here. In view of this lack of absolute clarity, it is normal, and to be expected, that some Catholics will see the question of pacifism in a way that is different from the view of most of their fellow Catholics. That is, some Catholics will come to the conscientious conclusion that God is calling them to bear witness to the cause of peace by refusing to fight. At present, this would be an unusual calling. While sincerely following their genuine vocation, they might also show some muddled thinking in articulating their convictions. No matter. Who will deny that the Spirit of Christ can use even stumbling prophets to call us to a greater search for peace? Among those who call themselves "conscientious objectors," there may be some fuzzy enthusiasts and some fast-talking con-men who are simply dropping out of their adult responsibilities. But isn't this the risk we face all the time in every walk of life? Who would want to suppress the civil and religious liberties of all just because some selfish or immature men abuse them?

The genuine pacifist is not a lesser patriot than the soldier. His service to his country, both by the unpopular witness of his pacifism and by the contribution he makes to the community through the alternative service provided for by our civil laws, is real. His concern and love for his country are certainly far healthier than that of the person who subscribes to the vicious principle "My country, right or wrong." He serves the real interests of the country far better than those who blindly followed orders and helped obliterate cities like Dresden or than the Nazi who exterminated Poles and Jews out of "patriotic obedience." Patriotism is a virtue of the clear-sighted. It is not a whip to be used to force uncritical submission and uniformity.

Peace and the Antichrist

On a recent television program, a Protestant fundamentalist preacher expressed his view that the present peace movement is the work of the Antichrist as predicted in the Book of Revelation. He says the Antichrist will use peace as his method of destroying Christianity. Communism, he says, will take over the world if the peace movement is successful. I would appreciate your thoughts on this subject.

It's hard to know where to begin when you hear an accusation like this. I'm amazed that anyone would imagine that he has such an inside track on the meaning of a profoundly symbolic figure in an enigmatic book of the Scriptures.

Most commentators understand the beast (or Antichrist) of the

Book of Revelation as a symbol for the Roman Empire, which is taken as a type of all the forces throughout history that are to oppose the Christian Church. The Antichrist is not a figure who is to come in the dramatic fashion of a Rosemary's Baby. The Antichrist is always at work and always under the condemnation that will issue from the victory of the risen Christ. In the Book of Revelation, the Antichrist is presented as never succeeding in impeding the coming of God's reign.

Is the present peace movement the work of the Antichrist? The present peace movement includes whole groups of marvelous people, like the Quakers, the Catholic Peace Fellowship, the veterans from Viet Nam who peacefully demonstrated their revulsion with the carnage which they had witnessed, clear-headed historians and diplomats who judge our violent approach to world problems to be political and economic folly, and dedicated Christian theologians who either are critical of the theory that any war can be acceptable to a Christian or consider war in its present dimensions to be incapable of being justified by any commensurate good purpose. Undoubtedly, there are men and groups who hope to capitalize on the peace movement for political aims that include the overthrow of our form of government. There may even be those who see the destruction of Christianity among their targets — and to that extent even the objectively noble quest for peace can be perverted into a work of the Antichrist by the intentions of those who would like to manipulate it to anti-Christian ends. But it sounds paranoic to presume that these "forces" are manipulating all the generous and dedicated men and women who are giving their lives to the quest for a speedy and just peace.

If we were to try to discover the works of the Antichrist in our society, how about looking at the war movement rather than the peace movement. Is not an event that so disrupts the normalizing influences in young men's lives that they become brutal killers, whether it be from fear or ignorance or insanity — part of the complex of forces that stand in opposition to Christ's Church? The military struggles we have been engaged in have taken a hideous toll in the lives of women and children, the maiming of bodies and minds, the mass displacement of peoples, and the destruction of land and livestock. The atmosphere of fear and boredom among our own troops has contributed to a drug problem whose dimensions are only now being made public. This hardly sounds like the fruits of the work of Christ.

It has always been easy to identify communism in its atheistic and materialistic roots as a work of the Antichrist. But was the unbridled and exploitive capitalism that spawned the communist ideology and revolution any less vicious an enemy of Christ? How about racism and bigotry and arrogance? How about the smug nationalism that glories in a standard of living that consumes the major portion of the world's wealth for a select few of the world's people, while uncounted millions subsist on the margin of human existence?

The manifestations of the Antichrist are all around us. But so are the signs of God's loving grace, which urges us to work for justice and peace.

Turn the Other Cheek

Assuming that one accepts the teaching of Christ to turn the other cheek when struck, how does one justify himself when confronted with that situation if his reaction is born of cowardice rather than of love?

Far better for a person to admit that his cowardly actions are just that than to try to justify them. To justify them to oneself is the worst kind of dishonesty. It is self-deception, and there is nothing that can make a person more spiritually blind than this. Our Lord was hated by the Pharisees because he threatened the complacent stance their continual self-deception had erected. It was the Publican who had no illusions about his need for merciful forgiveness who merited Christ's praise (Luke 18:9-14).

Good Christians are people who are honestly trying to make love dominate their lives. Saints are the only ones who notably succeed — and their success is complete only when they are already dead. Good Christians are as complex as any other good men, and daily they must confess themselves to be stumblers who are in need of God's grace. It is the hypocrite who tries to hide his weakness and failure even from himself and to make them appear virtuous.

Having said this, I want to warn against an excessively simplistic reading of the ideals presented in the Sermon on the Mount (the passage you refer to is Matthew 5:39). Our Lord's words here do not give us norms of conduct in our usual legal sense. That is, they do not express a code of minimum moral standards that we must measure up to. They show us an ideal that will always tax our capacity as we try to come close to it.

If we are to interpret these passages rightly, we must also bear in mind that they use the concrete language of metaphor. The purpose is to teach us a value and an attitude we are to cultivate. They do not give us a recipe to follow. For example, the passage you mention does not mean that every Christian who is mugged should turn the other cheek by handing over the key to his safe deposit box or that he must refuse to protect himself or complain or prosecute. The person who is ruled by the love of Christ will not always gladly suffer physical abuse or real injury. To be this kind of "patsy" would really indicate a failure to love one's assailant. True love for him would be more apt to inspire us to try to correct and stop him before his cruelty and injustice destroy him.

Finally, to say that the fullness of this ideal is beyond me is not to compromise with mediocrity. A person can and should be striving toward this goal even while he honestly feels the need to pray each day, "Forgive us our trespasses."

Thou Shalt Not Kill

The fifth commandment says, without any if's, and's, or but's, "Thou shalt not kill." To me, this is a definite statement. It makes no exceptions for the defense of your life or your country. So where is the justification for our boys' killing the "enemy" day after day? If the different religious bodies like the Quakers and the Amish are conscientious objectors, why aren't we? Are we not commanded to live up to God's commandments? Why are we Catholics making a political football out of the fifth commandment?

Your intuition is marvelous. It echoes Pope Paul's anguished plea before the United Nations, "No more war." It reflects the concern of the bishops of the world assembled at the Vatican Council. It is in harmony with an increasing number of young Catholics who are committed to the policies of non-violence, for whom military service and its inevitable involvement in killing appear as a crime against the human race and the Christian ideal of love.

However, neither the pope nor the bishops assembled in Council maintain that loyalty to the Gospel deprives a people of the right to legitimate self-defense — even though self-defense may have to be very violent and even death-dealing. These men don't hold this position as a dilution of the Gospel in order to protect their own vested interests. They are not making a political football out of the fifth commandment. Rather, they are interpreting its intent. They are holding out a realistic ideal to men who must live in an ambiguous world while striving to come ever closer to the Christian vision.

I said that they are interpreting the intent of the fifth commandment. The fact of the matter is that the fifth commandment cannot be taken as a divine prohibition of any and all taking of human life. The sacred authors of the Pentateuch fully approve of killing in battle and by capital punishment (cf. Deut. 20:1-14; Ex. 21: 12-17; Lev. 20:10). What is definitely forbidden is *murder,* not killing. The word that we have usually translated as "kill" is a form of the Hebrew word *rasah,* which is a technical term for murder. What the fifth commandment actually says is: "Thou shall not commit murder." Times change. Today, thanks to the revelation of Jesus Christ and the reflections of religious men through the ages, we have a far deeper realization of the sacredness of human life than the people of Israel did. The conditions of human life also change. Wars have become more destructive and indiscriminate, more unreconcilable with a Christian vision of life. Recourse to war's violence is far, far harder to justify today than it was a thousand years ago. In view of all this, it is to be expected that there will be some Catholics who feel obliged in conscience to object to combat duty.

Christians yearn for the day when we will live in such reasonable peace that crime will disappear, that conflicts will be resolved by dialogue, not war, that the need of self-defense and police protection will pass away. But the time is not yet. And an oversimplified reading of the fifth commandment will not hasten that day.

Hatred or Indignation?

I always seem to wind up in a job where I work hand in glove with my supervisor, but I have left my last two jobs because of my bosses' discrimination against Negroes. I am white; so is my employer.

My reasons for leaving are the same in every case. I have an intense hatred for those who treat others with scorn. I have suffered severe bouts of depression because of this. My depression stems from two things: the agony I feel for these people, and the knowledge that I am wrong in hating anyone.

I cannot seem to control my emotions. Prayer, Communion, and the rest have been no help. I ask God to forgive me for hating the

sinner more than the sin. I do fine for a time; then an incident occurs, and the hatred burns again.

Has God placed me in this position to test my charity, or should I leave employment when these practices occur?

Do you really hate? The Christ of the Gospels was not a smiling marshmallow. He saw injustice, hypocrisy, and greed. His reactions were intense. Surely his tongue-lashing directed against the self-righteous Establishment would be considered "bad form" or intemperate today (see Matt. 23:13-36). Nor was he very gentle when he made a whip to drive the buyers and sellers out of the temple (John 2:13-17). It is most unreal to say that he hated the sin but loved the sinner, if by "love" you mean that he remained in a warm, trusting relationship with these men. His love for the sinner was expressed in the anger that called his enemies to that total change of heart which is true repentance. Human life and feeling are so complex that it is simply not true to equate even strong feelings of hostility with the sin of hatred.

If you can live with the tension of your conflicting emotions, it might be better to stay where you are. You aren't contributing to the sin of discrimination. Your presence is a reproach that keeps your supervisor from being complacent in his scornful treatment of other people. Perhaps the hand in the glove will one day help the glove to bend.

Those severe bouts of depression aren't good. It is a gift to be sensitive enough to feel indignation and even anger when you are confronted with the sin of discrimination. But there is something wrong when this upsets a person so uncontrollably that it keeps him from functioning normally for any length of time. An inability to control emotions often has a deeper root that might suggest seeking the help of a physician.

A deep faith, constant prayer, and frequent use of the sacraments are often as ineffective with emotional problems as they are with broken bones. Very holy Catholics sometimes need professional help.

Euthanasia?

This seems to happen very often in the case of a person who is nearing the end of his life: the doctor comes, gives the patient a hypodermic, and within a short time the patient dies. What is the medication the doctor gives the patient? Is it something to release

the patient from life? Is it a way of hastening death? I have seen it, and I don't like it. Yet apparently it is permitted by Catholics. How come?

Physicians who observe the ethics of their profession and the laws in effect in our states do not administer drugs designed to kill or to hasten the dying of their patients. Nor would any such procedures be acceptable to Catholic moral theology.

What drugs do they give in this situation? That depends on the medical judgment of the doctor and the condition of the patient. In the cases I am most familiar with, the drugs were pain-relieving sedatives. They were given to bring relief to very uncomfortable persons, not to hasten their deaths. Did the narcotic relaxation contribute to the final stopping of the heartbeat? Perhaps. But so did the illness, the pain, and the preceding days of struggle.

For the patient who is peacefully ready to go home to God, it is a mercy to spare him some the excruciating pain of his illness. There is no reason to suspect any sinister intention to induce premature death.

Restitution

Is it the teaching of the Catholic Church that if a person is guilty of using a firm's funds for his own benefit (say to the extent of thousands of dollars), even though the person has confessed and did not realize the full extent of his guilt at the time, he must make full restitution before he can be forgiven completely? Or is it the belief that the sin is forgiven but the person who has not made restitution must pay the debt by punishment in purgatory or in some other way?

You present the case as a clear case of embezzlement. And yet you leave the puzzler of how a person could take thousands of dollars of his company's funds and not be aware that he was doing wrong.

To consider first what is clear. Catholic theology teaches that stealing is a sinful action. A person who freely and willingly takes what belongs to another without his consent is guilty of sin. The sin may be serious or light, depending on the damage done to the owner and to society and on the extent of guilty insight the thief has at the time of his theft.

In order to be forgiven any sin, a person must sincerely repent. In matters of justice, sincere repentance includes a genuine intention of paying back what was unjustly taken from another or repairing the malicious damage. It is the *intention* to pay back that is important — there may be reasons that make it impossible to make restitution for the time being, and these may continue to operate for a long time.

When a person confesses his sin with this genuine interior repentance, the sin is forgiven. God does not keep books like an accountant, waiting until the last penny is paid before entering into communion with the penitent. The completeness of forgiveness is measured by the completeness of conversion and repentance, not by the completeness of payment.

If, later on, the forgiven thief has a change of heart and decides to renege on his debt, then he is newly guilty of the sin of injustice. It is not a question of the same sin being imputed to him once more. His new decision to default is a bad human act, a sin.

Purgatory is not God's way of exacting his "pound of flesh" for bad debts. It is God's way of purifying a heart that is not yet fully turned to him.

The sleeper in your question concerns the insight the person who took the funds had into the wrongness of his action. If, in fact, there was no sin committed because the person thought that he had a right to use the funds, he does not have a strict obligation in conscience to pay back what is now long since spent. If he knew that what he was doing was shady but, through some strange quirk, did not understand that it was seriously wrong to take thousands of dollars of his firm's money, he is obligated to pay back what he took. But if he refuses to do so, it is hard to see that his sinful refusal is seriously wrong, because he lacked real insight into the extent of his wrongdoing and no longer benefits from it. (This is similar to the case of someone who did something we judge was wrong but without his appreciating its malice. When he comes to maturity of understanding, he must avoid the evil action. However, he is not morally accountable for the actions of the past done out of ignorance.)

If in the instances we mention in the preceding paragraph, the misappropriated funds are still intact, however, or if the person is significantly richer for having taken them, his new insight into the objective wrongness of keeping the money begets a serious obligation to make restitution.

Problems concerning justice can be complicated. Civil law, the conventions of the business world, and a host of other factors enter into the judgment of what is just and unjust. The severity of the obligation of making restitution and the question of whether it ought to be done immediately are colored by a number of factors pertaining to a person's own situation.

If this question is a personal one and not just a matter of theoretical information, I would suggest that you sit down with a competent moralist or confessor and give him all the facts and seek his professional advice.

Moral Obligation of Tax Laws

I work full time as a medical secretary and "moonlight" as a medical assistant three nights a week. The surgeon I moonlight for does not deduct income tax nor state tax from my salary. I will discuss the legal question with an accountant, but I would like to know if I am morally obliged to declare this part-time income. Being single, I pay very high taxes as it is, but I want to do what is morally right.

If your accountant can find a fully legal way for you to avoid declaring your part-time income, then you need not ask any further about the question of morality. Income tax is imposed by positive civil law, and your moral obligation to pay the tax is never stricter than the legal obligation.

However, I suspect that even the very best of accountants will be hard pressed to find a legal loophole large enough to permit you to leave a substantial portion of your income unreported. The moral question is whether the tax law obliges in conscience.

In general, Catholic teaching affirms the existence of a moral obligation to pay taxes. Pope Pius XII expressed this general teaching in 1956 when he wrote: "There can be no doubt concerning the duty of each citizen to bear a part of the public expense. But the state on its part, insofar as it is charged with protecting and promoting the common good of its citizens, is under an obligation to assess upon them only necessary levies, which are, furthermore, proportionate to their means."

There have been a number of moral theories concerning the exact nature of the obligation to pay taxes. But today the most commonly held view is that all just tax laws bind the consciences of individual citizens, because this is the way he contributes to the common good of society. And every member of a society is bound to contribute to the common good.

The real moral problem focuses on the question: Is this tax law just? In some countries, the tax laws might be unjust. Even today there are countries where the name of the game is deception — fraudulent tax returns are so prevalent that the state takes it for granted with a shrug of the shoulders and compensates by levying higher taxes than are really just. In these cases, the good Christian can protect himself from the unjust overtaxation by playing the game.

In the United States, however, it seems that our income tax laws are fundamentally just. They are the result of the effort of reasonable men in a representative government to provide income needed to function for the common good.

Some would argue against this justice, because so much money is wasted, goes to graft, or is used for irrational purposes (like our huge military budget). Undoubtedly, there are some inequities in the tax laws — and financial experts point out how they weigh heaviest on the middle income, unmarried wage earner like yourself.

However, these minor inequities and mismanagements are probably unavoidable in any imperfect system — and human legislation is always bound to be less than perfect. Of themselves, they do not make our tax laws unjust. Consequently, I believe that these laws, as just laws, are morally binding.

Masturbation a Sin?

What is the Church's view on masturbation, and what are her reasons? I have always thought that it was sinful. However, so many people consider it normal that I am beginning to question my belief.

The Church's view is, as you always thought, that it is sinful and seriously sinful. She sees it as a sin of impurity, and she reads in the Sacred Scriptures a condemnation of sins of impurity as serious sins. (Cf. I Cor. 6:9ff.; Eph. 5:5; Gal. 5:19; Col. 3:5.)

You ask why? What are her reasons? The basic reason why the Church declares something wrong is always her interpretation of what God asks of men. This interpretation depends on the word of God in the Scriptures and on her long experience of understanding human nature. Catholic theologians see this as wrong because it is a particularly eloquent kind of selfishness. It takes sexuality, which is designed for the total gift of self in love, and twists it into something for self-gratification.

Many people consider masturbation normal? This is true. It is normal in the sense of being very frequently committed. It is also normal in the sense that the growth process of an adolescent involves coming to terms with his sexuality, and a time of growth and learning involves mistakes and failures. But isn't the real norm the norm of learning to control sexuality rather than being controlled by it? Many mature people do learn this self-control.

This stand of the Church is not an inhuman harshness. She knows full well that a sinful action can take place without its being a sin for the particular person. Sometimes there is not enough freedom in the action for a person to be fully responsible for it. A person in the grip of a bad habit and wanting to free himself from it might find it at times overpowering. In this situation, the judgment of the Church is one of great mildness and gentleness. She does not think of God as a traffic cop hiding behind a billboard hoping to catch someone in a violation of the law. In their effort to grow in purity, some people still have some failures against the letter of the law of purity. Is each of these failures always a mortal sin? Not unless it is a free and deliberate choice, a turning away from the effort to grow.

Following this doctrine does not at all lead to neuroses or ill health. On the contrary, a person who seeks calmly to grow, to become able to live up to this norm of Christian behavior, is generally a far more mature and loving person than someone who tends to water things down to the level of what is right now easy in practice.

Nudism

In this age of miniskirts, bikinis, see-through blouses, topless waitresses, and nudity in movies, plays, magazines, and advertising, what is the attitude of the Roman Catholic Church on nudism and nudist publications?

I think that the thousands of nudists in the United States would resent anyone's bracketing their movement with the provocative styles, the degrading social phenomena, and the plain sex-ploitation you refer to in your question. They claim that the practice of nudism can contribute much to man's psychic, physical, and moral well-being. They have a certain naive enthusiasm for the physical benefits of exposing the body to the sun and the elements. They believe that the general practice of nudism would teach people that the human body is not obscene nor a necessary cause of erotic stimulation.

Nudism, they feel, would do away with the morbid curiosity and the aberrations that contemporary fashions often cater to.

However, the claim that nudism is so beneficial rests on such poor evidence that it's hard to see how anyone can take it seriously. The overwhelming majority of mankind recognizes the desirability and fittingness of clothing.

The fact that you write about nudism in connection with these other social facts of our time indicates to me that moral reflection on nudism today must take into consideration the preoccupations of our day. They are not entirely wholesome. Of course, no one will deny that the human body is the supreme work of God's artistry, in itself good and beautiful. But the question of the appropriateness of displaying or veiling it is not resolved by such a simple truism. In 1952, Pope Pius XII pointed to the problem in an unusually quotable sentence. He said, "What is of interest to the masses in this regard is not the beauty of the nude but the nudity of the beauty."

What, then, is the attitude of Catholic teachers on nudism? I think it would be fair to say that it is cautionary: there is something a bit bizarre about it which might be a source of spiritual danger for most people. The advocates of nudism seem to be unrealistic. While it may be true that some have benefited from it by shedding some unfortunate "hang-ups" with their clothing, is it really healthy to focus so much attention on a cult of health and bodily perfection? Again, the experience of mankind and the reflection of the Christian tradition have established that the good life is really possible only when there is an esteem for and practice of the virtue of modesty. This requires a certain delicacy and reserve, a wholesome sense of shame. This is not neurotic prudery. It is that quality which men consider to be missing in the person they call "shameless." While the practice of nudism may not be a serious threat to chastity for its devotees, is it really a good school of modesty?

As for the nudist publications — I find it hard to believe that they are published just to encourage others to join the sun-worshipers in jolly, chaste nakedness. There are very few well-tanned innocents ogling these magazines in the red-light district of the press on New York's Forty-second Street. Nor do the help-wanted ads in Greenwich Village newspapers inviting uninhibited models to pose for nudist magazines incline me to believe that a pure idealism, howsoever misguided, inspires their publication. These publications are a blight on our society, catering to the disturbed appetites of the unfortunate.

Standards of Modesty

I read something about the pope's banning the wearing of mini-skirts. Does this mean that the girls who wear them are all in sin? I asked my husband about a couple of dresses I've been unsure of on myself. He said that by the standard of what most girls are wearing today, he couldn't see anything wrong in the length I wear. Yet I know we judge right and wrong not by what others are doing but only by what the pope and the Church say. What should I do?

Follow your husband's judgment. Although it may happen that a man's standards for other women are regulated by a roving eye, rarely will a good husband approve a provocative or immodest style for his wife. At the present time especially, I think you should trust his opinion. It seems to me that your own is a bit too anxious right now.

I presume that you saw a reference to a decision that Vatican authorities made. They said that no woman wearing a miniskirt was allowed to enter St. Peter's Basilica. This is a question of the good manners of churchgoers in a particular cultural tradition of southern Europe. It does not imply that such a young lady is guilty of sin. Women with sleeveless dresses or uncovered heads are similarly discouraged from visiting this basilica — and the same restrictions are posted in a number of Italian churches.

I'm sure that the pope has reservations about the modesty of many things that today's fashion approves or tolerates. However, he has made no statement that means that every girl in a very short skirt is automatically guilty of serious sin. Nor is he apt to do so.

The question of what is modest or immodest cannot be settled by a papal decision on hemlines which would be applicable to every time and place. There are too many variables. A garment that is modest and acceptable on a ballet stage would be totally unacceptable and provocative in an office. A style that melts into the crowd on a Manhattan street might be exhibitionistic and offensive in a rural village in Spain. What would have been considered an occasion of sin fifty years ago because of its singularity, today would be reckoned as prim and dowdy.

I remarked that your approach to this question seems too anxious. I get this impression from the way you approach the authority of the pope in moral manners. You are right when you say that you cannot abdicate your own responsibility and simply follow the crowd. But neither should you look to the pope and bishops alone to judge what is right and wrong. This would be an abdication of responsibility.

A Catholic will always take their teaching into consideration when he is forming his own conscience. And there are times when this teaching will be presented in a way that impels the good Catholic to give it an importance that outweighs almost every other consideration. However, in the last analysis, the Catholic, like everyone else, must weigh all the elements that enter into a moral decision in the privacy of his own conscience and decide before God what is right or wrong for him to do.

This is not a view that undermines the teaching of the Church. The Catholic Church has always taught that the mature Christian is empowered to judge properly what he ought to do by the Holy Spirit, who dwells in his heart. Not that he hears voices or receives startling insights. Ordinarily, the Spirit works through the human processes of what theology calls the virtue of prudence.

The prudent follower of Christ is not an anxious compromiser. He is a decisive person who has a clear view of the present situation and the options open to him. These he considers carefully in the light of what he has learned from past experience and teaching and what the probable consequences of his choice might be. When the prudent man makes his choice, he does it with the peaceful confidence that he is responding to God's call as well as he can, that he is following the guidance of the Holy Spirit.

It is not from the statements of pope and Church alone that the Catholic can judge what is right and wrong. The pope may give us very broad guidelines concerning the value of modesty or perhaps warn us about an unfortunate tendency that is developing. The authorities of the Church in a particular locality may see fit to speak about a special local problem. But the final judgment about what is modest or immodest dress must be made by good men and women who know their own culture and are committed to the Christian teaching on the dignity of human persons. I hope that the day will come quickly when you will feel freer to trust your own judgment.

On Miniskirts

I am a teen-age boy who is a daily communicant. It isn't easy today, because of the teen-age immorality. Today's teen-agers have turned into real slobs, the girls especially. It seems like there isn't a decent girl around. They all wear such short skirts that it doesn't

even make sense for them to dress at all. One reason why the girls wear these miniskirts is because the priests don't say anything, so they think it's perfectly all right. Please say something on this grave moral problem.

You've certainly right when you indicate the difficulty there is in growing up. It is hard for a young person to learn to accept the reality of his or her sexuality and to control it and keep it in perspective. And the present emphasis on the erotic elements of human life doesn't make it any easier.

You are also right, I think, to expect guidance from us priests. We should exercise the leadership that will help our people, young and old, to maintain a wholesome attitude toward sexuality, beauty, and fashion.

However, I don't think that priests should get into the business of setting rigid standards of how many inches on a hemline are or are not moral. We might do well to remind our congregations of the need to be self-critical and our women to be aware of the impact they might have on a susceptible young man when they adopt extreme styles. While the standards and customs of a country or a decade must be considered in any judgment of what is modest or immodest — and hence there is a certain flexibility in this matter — nevertheless, in any given time and place, there are some limits beyond which dress is immodest.

The excessively short skirt, which seems to be passing out of style, is provocative and of questionable modesty. It may be of interest to note that policemen welcome the trend of the fashion moguls to phase out this style. In a recent nationwide survey, a high percentage of the police officers polled stated their conviction that revealingly short skirts are one of the factors responsible for the sharp rise in crimes of rape during the past few years. The chief of the vice squad in a large western city wrote: "Fathers and husbands are derelict in their duties when they fail to warn daughters and wives against clothing styles that some males may find provocative."

The styles that invite the attack of the violent and the deranged are sure to be disturbing to adolescent young men who are sensitive in this area. Girls should not be dowdy just because there is a possible danger; nor should they become prey to anxiety about their possible impact on men; yet they might seek a bit of advice from daddy on what is appropriate or inappropriate dress.

And for yourself, it might be good if you had a mature priest counselor or confessor with whom you can talk. It seems to me that you're overreacting, becoming too severe on others and too fearful yourself. Teen-age immorality is a problem, just as adult immorality is. But be careful not to smear all our young sisters in Christ as slobs, indecent, or half-dressed. The world is filled with wholesome and decent and lovely girls. Let yourself get to know them better. As mutual understanding and respect grow, I think you'll find less of a problem with purity.

Nudity in Films

It seems that almost every movie issued today has its obligatory nude scene. Why isn't the Church making a stronger protest against this scandalous breakdown in modesty? Does this mean that the Church no longer recognizes that this sort of thing is a real occasion of sin?

You raise a valid point, and by your question the Church is protesting. In the final analysis, the only protest that will be effective is that of the film-going public who make the point of not paying for offensive cinema. And if the Church is recognized as being much more than the clergy and hierarchy, then your protest is an element in the protest that the Church is making through its members.

The officials of the Church have not been silent on this question. The pope and the bishops have repeatedly appealed to the consciences of Catholics and the policymakers of the film industry. But it is hard for these leaders to lead effectively unless followers are prepared to follow them.

It is a fact that the approach that American Catholics took to this problem in the past is not as persuasive as it used to be. People sense that it is not accurate to label every film with a nude scene a "dirty" movie and a proximate occasion of sin for an audience. Some of these films are sensitive and artistic portrayals and seem to be free from exploitative intent. A case can be made for the appropriateness and artistic integrity of the nude scene in such a film.

Nor is it easy to maintain that a film like this is a proximate occasion of sin — something that entails a high risk of illicit sexual behavior for most normal adults. The experience of too many apparently upright people belies this affirmation.

The objection to nudity in films should be made on a sounder

basis than that of maintaining that the viewing of a nude body in
a film will ordinarily occasion a sin of impurity. Instead of using the
standards of an individualistic act-morality, it might be more
persuasive to appeal to the social consequences of the mentality
engendered by a constant exposure to these so-called adult films.

What happens to people who feed on a steady diet of films in
which occasional nudity is taken for granted? Among other things,
I suggest that they go through a kind of brain-washing. Their outlook
on the meaning of human life and sexuality begins to shift. There
is an erosion of a wholesome sense of reticence and modesty. Genital
sexuality begins to be vastly overrated. As a result, young people
become intimidated and find themselves apologizing for trying to
maintain an ideal of premarital chastity. The idea of personal fulfillment fudges into oneness with that of sexual fulfillment. The possibility of living a normal human life as a celibate begins to be
doubted even by those dedicated to it by holy orders or religious vow.

It is, of course, excessive to blame all this on the motion pictures.
But they are a very powerful force that interacts with and reinforces
the excessively erotic elements in our society.

If my suggestions have any merit, I think that Christians should
object to the regular introduction of nudity in the cinema. Even
though many persons know that these films are not an occasion of
personal sin for themselves, do these films not subtly distort a
Christian vision of human life? A distortion of this kind is a condition of sin that is more deadly than an occasion of personal sin.
We are responsible not merely for maintaining personal control of
sexuality. We owe it to mankind to work for a genuinely wholesome
attitude to it in the whole of society.

Is Abortion Negotiable?

**In our son's sociology senior high-school class, one day the topic
of discussion was abortion and the Catholic Church's attitude
toward it. The teacher led the students to believe that at no time
would an abortion meet with approval of the Church. We, his parents, tend to differ with this, as in cases of incest and criminal rape.**

We would appreciate a clarification on this subject.

I agree with your son's high-school teacher. That is, I believe that
abortion is something that will never meet with the approval of the
Church. By abortion, I mean the intentional expulsion of a nonviable,

living fetus from the mother's uterus. The Church has always been the defender of the right of the unborn child to life. She has looked on abortion with the same horror as she looks on murder. While the Church has always been aware of, and deeply concerned with, the human suffering and the emotional anguish of carrying a child that is the product of incest and criminal rape, she has felt that her anguish should be expressed in her effort to support the unwilling mother and provide a good home for the child rather than by taking the life of the child so conceived. Once conception has taken place, the Church acts on the probability that the fertilized ovum is already a human person and already has a right to life.

Now there are a couple of refinements I might put on this position. The first is: If there has been a rape, during that time in which medical science supposes that conception has not yet been able to take place (roughly, up to sixteen hours after the fact), Catholic moral theologians commonly approve of a physician's taking whatever means are possible to prevent conception.

The second point is only theoretical at present. It concerns this question: At what point does the fetus truly become a human being? The practice of the Church is closely linked with the assumption that we have *human* life from the moment of conception. Some are questioning this on the basis of biology and philosophy. If the question were ever resolved in a way that demonstrated that the newly conceived remains distinctly subhuman for a matter of some weeks or months, then there would be possible grounds for reassessing the absolute prohibition of all abortions. However, as things stand at present, I think that the outlook for even this kind of change is extremely remote.

You mention your own feeling that abortion should be legitimate in cases of incest and criminal rape. I wonder if you have thought this through or if you have perhaps been reading some of the literature urging a total change and reform of the present abortion laws in our states. The reason I ask is that I find much of this propaganda highlights these extremely rare and extremely heart-rending cases. Thus they seek to create a climate in which, with our hearts, we want to find an exception. The impression is given that many of the back-alley, unhygienic, illegal abortions that do take place are a solution to these desperate problems. Yet, as a matter of fact, most of the criminal abortions that happen in our country nowadays are the result not so much of these unfortunate conceptions as they are the result of unwanted conceptions by married women. It seems to many observers that there is a great conspiracy on to create a climate favorable to abortion by pulling on these heartstrings. But the abortion path, once it is legally open, will be trod not so much by these unfortunate young women as by those evading responsibility at the expense of unborn human life.

Is It a Human Being?

On a recent television program, a Catholic doctor, opposing abortion, stated that when the fertilized ovum becomes implanted in the uterus, it is a human being and may not be aborted. Since this occurs some days after conception, is this the beginning of a discrete human life, or is the full human being present from conception?

There is something mysterious about the exact moment when human life begins and the exact moment when it ends in death. Religious authority has no definitive word to say on either of these subjects. The question is biological and philosophical.

From the first moment of conception, the being that is living is already human and distinct from its mother and father. It is not an undifferentiated piece of protoplasm (as if there could be such a thing). It already has the genetic characteristics that are found in no living thing but a human being. And the geneticists tell us that in this tiny cell are the codes that will determine the features, pigmentation, temperament, sex — the things that distinguish one human being from another. From this information, it would seem that the living being is, from the moment of fertilization, a human being with the sacredness and the rights of every human person.

However, there is also the phenomenon of identical twins to reckon with. The embryologists believe that identical twins result when the zygote, the fertilized ovum, divides into two. Both share the identical genetic information. But each develops into a distinct human being.

This raises the philosophical question concerning the nature of the zygote prior to twinning. Was it a single human being? Was it already two human beings, even though apparently only one? Does this phenomenon indicate that there was a time in the life of this zygote (the time prior to twinning) when the being was human without being a distinct human being? Does the biological possibility of twinning mean that there is a time when every fertilized egg is more than the sum of its parts but less than the distinct human being it will become? One cannot find the answer to these questions by examination and experimentation. Nor can one appeal to a religious revelation for answers. We have no such revelation. Yet the questions are real ones.

I'm sure that the physician you refer to spoke the way he did in order to bypass questions of this sort. In effect, he was saying that after implantation, there can be no question but that we're speaking about a human being. I doubt he meant to imply that before implantation, the fertilized egg is less than a human being or could be aborted.

The Church's approach is to preserve the sacredness of human life from its inception, not to settle technical problems of genetics and embryology. What the Church teaches is that the product of human conception is to be treated as a human being from the moment of conception. It considers procedures that prevent implantation to be the moral equivalent of those that destroy the life of the implanted zygote or the developed fetus. Morally, it is abortion, the taking of human life at its most defenseless.

On Abortion

How do you convince our Catholic teen-agers that abortion is wrong? Believe me, I have tried.

It is especially difficult to convince a person by the logic of reason or faith if strong feelings about either the subject matter or the manner of arguing stand in the way. The communications barrier you have experienced is often one of feeling. It seems to me that you must begin with a clear understanding of your own conviction that abortion is wrong and why. You must also have some understanding of what makes young people hesitate to take the conviction of their Church as adequate for them. Then, starting from where the youngsters are, you can proceed by stages to try to show them that abortion violates some of the deepest sentiments the young people live by. Your argument may not be the most cogent demonstration, but if it succeeds in opening their minds to new considerations, you may be able to go much further.

Catholics and, up until recent times, large segments of mankind have reckoned abortion to be wrong (both a sin and a crime) because it is the snuffing out of the most defenseless and innocent human life. The Vatican Council expressed this conviction when it bracketed abortion and infanticide together as "unspeakable crimes"

(*Constitution on the Church in the Modern World,* no. 51).

None of the research that has been conducted in modern times has demonstrated that the human fetus is something less than human. Theoreticians speculate on distinguishing between a "human organism" and a "human person" — denying inviolable human rights to the former. But a Christian cannot form his conscience on tentative theories, especially when the eventual disproving of such a theory would leave in its wake the slaughter of unborn human persons.

Why are young Catholics rejecting this conviction of their Church? We have to remember that they have been brought up in a period of revolutionary change, a period that has placed an unparalleled emphasis on experience and feeling at the expense of thought. Our cultural revolution has made it easy for them to call into question any conviction, religious or humane, inherited from the past. They have seen our hitherto intransigent Church become flexible in other areas, and they fancy themselves in the wave of the future, merely a few steps ahead of the next inevitable change. They lack the ability to distinguish carefully between the changeable and the changeless in doctrine and moral thought.

They have also been bombarded by a propaganda campaign that seems so plausible — we all have. It appeals effectively to youth's feeling for the person they can see — the anguished pregnant woman. It is hard to *feel* as strongly for the unseen being as for one who has rights that are quite independent of its mother, and the abstract thought that could lead to such a conviction is not easy to come by.

However, young people are quite caught up in a beautiful concern for life. It shows up in their revulsion against war, and in their concern for the preservation of the earth as the environment of life. Does this not give us leverage to have them consider the fetus as a living thing? Whether it be described by an embryologist or a theologian, there is no denying that the human fetus is an organic part of the total life cycle of the universe. At a time when we are conscious of the balance of nature and the sacredness of life, does it make any sense to snuff out the highest form of life at any stage in its development? Are we sufficiently aware of the consequences of removing the moral strictures against abortion that we can take such a shift lightly?

Again, young people are sensitive to the need of defending the underdog. Who in this case is more the underdog — the woman who feels cornered into the need for an abortion or the unborn human being who cannot live outside her body? I submit that a persuasive person can make a very strong case for the fetus.

These approaches are not foolproof. They can even be turned around. But in the hands of one who has earned the respect of the young and who uses these approaches as persuaders rather than as proofs, they may help to prepare a young person to question his own position and to be more open to the real arguments and to the teaching of his Church.

Children—Fruit of Personal Love

The Church has become so "broad-minded." I'm anxious to know the ruling on artificial insemination.

We have not become so "broad-minded" as to approve artificial insemination. The Church sees children as the supreme gift of marriage. They are the fruit of the personal, conjugal love of a couple. While one can sympathize with the anguish of a childless couple, there seems to be something abhorrent about the idea of artificial insemination, especially "donor" insemination, as a means of bringing a child into the family.

The last "ruling" on this matter is that given by Pope Pius XII (October 29, 1951). He declared that artificial insemination is "absolutely to be rejected." In God's plan, the conception of a child must be the result of a personal involvement of the parents. And this act of mutual self-giving ought to be a loving cooperation with the love of God, the Creator — which is hardly very evident in artificial insemination.

Sex-Change Surgery

How does the Church regard a man who has surgery to change his sex and become a woman, or a woman who is surgically changed into a man?

The Church regards them as dearly beloved sons and daughters of God who may be even more in need of the help and support of the Church than most other persons.

The frustration and anxiety of these men and women must have been well near intolerable to bring them to seek medical help in providing for them the secondary characteristics of the opposite sex. They are people who are very much in need. And it is for the needy that Christ came. His Church exists to help them find peace in Him.

The Catholic theologian's appraisal of the surgery is different from the Church's regard for the persons. The surgery is unacceptable on moral grounds, inasmuch as it is an unjustifiable mutilation and sterilization.

Purity for the Engaged

Please tell me the Church's feeling on the sexual intimacies of an engaged couple. I ask this question because we find it quite impossible to refrain from petting, and the young lady is extremely anxious about this.

The Church's "feeling" is strongly in favor of upholding the special sacredness of marriage. Since human sexuality finds its full meaning only in marriage's unbreakable bond of love, the Church is concerned that a very high ideal of self-control be held up to the unmarried and also to the engaged. In your long letter it was good to see that you recognize this and are trying so successfully to control your normal desire to consummate your love.

The Church's feeling about lesser intimacies is one of gentle understanding and guidance toward self-control. She understands that a person cannot avoid all occasions that constitute for him or her some danger of sexual excitement. The noted moral theologian Bernard Häring has this to say in his book *Shalom: Peace* (New York: Farrar, Straus and Giroux, 1968): "It would be ridiculous, for example, to maintain that engaged couples may not embrace or caress each other if this provokes some sexual urge and pleasure. If this restriction were imposed and carried out today, no girl following such advice would ever get married. Notwithstanding, a betrothed couple should avoid occasions which they know will constitute proximate dangers of experiencing full sexual pleasure and giving free consent to it" (p. 192).

A couple will know whether what they speak of as "petting" is something that goes beyond tender affection and becomes a counterfeit of the intimacy of the married. If it goes this far, it is excessive and wrong, even for the engaged.

I said that the Church's understanding is gentle. No confessor who is conscious of acting in the place of Christ will "throw the book" at a young couple whose love for one another occasionally leads them into an excessively intimate caress. Don't stay away from confession if your conscience reproaches you. Many couples find it helps them to grow in love of God and each other, if they go very regularly to the same priest for confession and help.

Sterilization—One Mortal Sin?

I am now in my fifth pregnancy. I have chosen not to take the pill, and other forms of rhythm or contraception have not worked well for us. We have found it impossible to maintain a happy, harmonious home — if we abstain from marital relations. I am contemplating sterilization after the birth of this baby. If this is not feasible, my husband may have a vasectomy. With overpopulation, finances, and the situation of the world, we feel we have had enough children. Will we be excommunicated if we choose sterilization, or will it be one mortal sin?

The authorities of the Church have not considered the sin of sterilization reason for declaring the guilty parties excommunicated — as they have for everyone involved in an abortion.

You ask a very poignant further question: "Or will it be one mortal sin?" I know that you are upset and that you are using a churchly vocabulary that may not express your true feelings accurately. But what you ask raises a couple of points that are very important for Christian living.

Mortal sin is a far more terrible thing than excommunication. And we should not think of mortal sin as a single indiscretion. It can never be compared to the calculated violation of a parking regulation that we might allow ourselves in an emergency, knowing that we will pay the fine and return to normal good citizenship. A Christian cannot set out to choose "one mortal sin" as a regrettable necessity and expect to quickly turn around, confess it, and make everything right again.

Mortal sin is a deliberate act which breaks the bond that joins man to God in a relationship of friendly intimacy that the New Testament speaks of as "sonship." It is a refusal to live in accordance with God's designs in the way a child of God should. Such an act deals a mortal blow to this vital relationship. The relationship is restored only when we consent to love once more in harmony with our heavenly Father. This means that we stop sinful action, are genuinely sorry for it, and do our best to undo the consequences of our rebellion.

Catholic moral theology has always considered sterilization to be so opposed to God's design for human living that it strikes a death blow at this relationship — presuming, of course, that the step is taken by a person who has clear insight and is quite free in making the decision. While it takes place in a single act, and so may be considered a single sin for the purpose of classification and confession, it has enduring consequences that make real repentance difficult.

When a person repents his sin, he tells God in effect, "I am sorry *that I offended* you." This is not the same thing as saying, "I'm sorry *that I had to offend* you." The first expresses a genuine regret and the sinner's desire to make his will be one with God's. The second implies a regret that God's will does not coincide with the sinner's, but he is still set on his own.

Genuine repentance for the sin of sterilization is psychologically quite difficult. Will the husband and wife who chose this procedure after a good deal of reflection be able to be sorry for their sinful choice? It's possible, of course, but not easy. Will they regret it enough to be willing to repair the surgical damage if it is possible to do so? You see how complicated it is for a person to return to God in a humble repentance and confession after "one mortal sin" like this.

I hope that you and your husband will reconsider this step very carefully. It is indeed your right and your responsibility before God to decide how many children your love and resources can support. But the way you achieve this goal is not a matter of indifference. It is one thing to recognize that artificial contraception, while never a good thing, is not always a serious sin. It is something else to choose irreversible surgical mutilation as a way to achieve your legitimate purposes.

The pressure of the times can quickly break down the moral attitudes that made sacred new life and the sources of life. Propagandists are beginning to speak of a new chemical procedure, by which a woman can abort her one or two-month-old fetus, as "birth control." We can let ourselves become blind to the responsibilities of what it means to follow the cross-bearing Christ. Please don't let that happen to you.

On Sterilization

The reply you gave to the woman who was contemplating sterilization because she found it impossible to maintain a happy home

otherwise irritated me. The only reply you gave her was, in substance, "Catholic moral theology has always considered sterilization to be opposed to God's design for human living." I reply to
this that Catholic moral theology has often been composed by
reasoning bordering on the idiotic. It has been mainly thought up
by male, celibate priests alone, without sufficient consultation with
the lay person in the Church, particularly lay women. It is my view
that the whole theology of marriage should come from married
people and not from celibate priests, who have a very limited
knowledge of what it means to be married. I cannot see that sterilization interferes at all with "God's design for human living," particularly when it is undertaken with a view to making a family
happier.

I agree with you that one of the weaknesses of Catholic moral
theology has been its failure to probe deeply enough into the lived
experience of Christians. It has tended to be excessively rational and
objective. It did not always take sufficiently into account the fact
that God manifests His design for human living also in the lives of
people who are doing their best to live in the light of the gospel.
A moral theologian can ignore this personal and living data only at
the risk of becoming irrelevant.

However, I can't agree with your assumption that the only valid
theology of marriage and sexuality can come from married people.
Nor can I agree with what you seem to be implying, that this experience of the reality of conjugal love is the only source, or even
the principal source, for theological reflection and conclusions on
the subject of marriage.

Moral theology is a science that searches out the principles of
human living appropriate for the redeemed man who is called to a
destiny of union with God. It seeks to discover what God wants us
to do, in the light of the revelation given in Christ on how He
wants us to be.

The first source to which the moral theologian must look is Christ.
He is God's self-revelation. He is also God's revelation of what man is
to become. To be Christ's disciple and to love God and neighbor
in the likeness of Christ's own self-emptying love are the supreme
moral demands incumbent on every man. The moral theologian has
the task of helping his brethren understand what it actually means
to love totally and responsibly, in view of the various relationships
and commitments we have that make us be persons in different walks
of life.

To do this, the theologian must reflect on the nature of the human person and his acts. It is a fundamental premise of traditional Catholic moral theology that, despite the uniqueness of each person and each personal relationship, there are recognizable constants in which every human person shares. In a sense, these stable and enduring elements precede the person's uniqueness, and they are the root of that law, grounded in his being, which indicates what is good or bad. It is reflection on these "natural" elements that has given rise both to Pope John's enthusiastically received encyclical *Pacem in Terris* and to Pope Paul's unpopular *Humanae Vitae*.

A Catholic moral theologian also assents to the truth that his discipleship to Christ commits him to hear and follow the movement of the Holy Spirit in the Church. He does not have the office of authoritatively deciding what is the genuine movement of the Spirit and what is its counterfeit. (This office belongs to the pope and the bishops according to the ancient tradition of the Church reaffirmed by Vatican II.) But he does have a role of discernment. By his studies, he shows us more clearly what in the past teaching of the Church are the constants and values that manifest God's abiding design for human living and what are the variables that reflect a mentality conditioned by a particular place and time.

If the theology of marriage is to be whole, it cannot be worked out solely from the reflection of a married couple on what it means to be married. Reflection on the mystery of Christ, on the nature of the human person, on the teaching of the Church, and on the data of other sciences and experiences must also be called upon if such a theology is not to be partial and distorted.

It is as a result of an honest wrestling with all this data that Catholic moral theology has concluded that contraceptive sterilization is never a good thing in itself.

This is not a dogma of the Church, infallibly proclaimed and binding the faith of all Christians. No teaching on the morality of particular kinds of human action has ever been so proclaimed. But it is a constant teaching that binds the consciences of loyal Catholics. A person is not free to decide to ignore this teaching in the name of "freedom of conscience," on the grounds that he knows more about the reality of happy marriage than the celibate official teachers of the Church.

Does this mean that every person who chooses contraceptive sterilization is always personally guilty of mortal sin and effectively cut off from the grace-giving love of God? Not necessarily. It is impossible for someone to decide in general the degree of responsibility and imputability each person will have for actions and decisions that occur in individual contexts and under individual pressures. Again, while I cannot conceive of the act of contraceptive sterilization as ever being something that is morally good in itself, I can conceive of a person's being in a situation where some consent to sterilization is given blamelessly. It can happen that a person is placed in a dilemma of either consenting to sterilization or seeing the marriage fall apart. The decision to protect the greater value — that of the marriage and family — may be able to be carried out only by tolerating the surgical loss of bodily integrity. I presume that such a situation would occur very rarely.

Inevitably, there will be difficulties and ambiguities in the effort to keep in balance the values of Christian marriage and parenthood. When we are tempted to oversimplify, I think we ought to meditate on a few sentences from Vatican II's *Pastoral Constitution on the Church in the Modern World*: "Therefore, when there is question of harmonizing conjugal love with the responsible transmission of life, the moral aspect of any procedure does not depend solely on sincere intentions or on an evaluation of motives. It must be determined by objective standards. These, based on the nature of the human person and his acts, preserve the full sense of mutual self-giving and human procreation in the context of true love" (no. 51).

Impossibility Excuses

Next June I will be graduating from college and I have already applied for the Peace Corps. I asked to be assigned to Iran, which is 98 percent Shiah Moslem. Suddenly I realized that there would probably be no provisions made for Catholics (Mass, et cetera). I was wondering what the Church's view is on such situations and if she grants dispensations for volunteers.

The obligation to participate in the Eucharistic Sacrifice on Sundays and holydays comes directly from a human law of the Church. Like all human laws, it obliges ordinarily and in normal circumstances. But it does not bind the conscience of a person who is truly unable to observe it. If you are assigned to a part of the world that is deprived of the Eucharist, the law of Sunday Mass simply will not apply. There is no need to be dispensed from a law that cannot be observed. Impossibility excuses.

The Church established the Sunday obligation as a way of spurring her people to give regular, conscious expression to their indispensable need to serve and worship God. Worship is a hallmark of the Christian life. "Whether you eat or drink — whatever you do — you should do all for the glory of God" (1 Cor. 10:31), St. Paul told the early Christians. It is a normal instinct of the Christian faith to want to gather up the implicitness of these "whatevers" and explicitly join them with our Lord's supreme act of worship that is made present in the Mass. There is something wrong with the quality of a Christian's life and worship if he deliberately neglects this weekly opportunity.

Should you volunteer to serve in a place where you will rarely, if ever, have this opportunity? That depends. Suppose your own commitment to Christ and the Church is shaky? If in this state you were needlessly to separate yourself from the external supports of a Catholic community, you might risk having the whole thing crumble tragically.

On the other hand, if your faith is strong and your loyalty is solid and your life is prayerful, your presence in a Moslem culture might be thought of as a solitary witness to the ultimate values of Christianity.

8
Christian
Miscellany

The Widow's Mite

If a person gives at every chance to charity and wishes he had more to give but doesn't, can it be said that he can't merit as much of a reward as the wealthy person who can give more? And what about the extremely poor person who wishes to do all of this but, of course, can't? By his desire, does he merit just as great an amount of grace?

The basic and eternally true answer to your question was written down by the Evangelist St. Mark (12:41-44). "Taking a seat opposite the treasury, he [Jesus] observed the crowd putting money into the collection box. Many of the wealthy put in sizable amounts; but one poor widow came and put in two small copper coins worth a few cents. He called his disciples over and told them: 'I want you to observe that this poor widow contributed more than all the others who donated to the treasury. They gave from their surplus wealth, but she gave from her want, all that she had to live on.'"

You speak of meriting "as much of a reward" and "as great an amount of grace." This is a traditional Catholic way of speaking. But don't forget the limitations of human language. When we speak of an amount of grace, we are not talking about a bank book, in which there can be more or less money; we are really referring to a personal relationship with God, to the degree of personal closeness with him. God sees our hearts and our intentions. A human father will be more moved by the token gift of his child that expresses a great love than he is by the more expensive gift of a business associate which means little more than that it's gift-giving time again. Our heavenly Father is no less perceptive. The genuine desire of the very poor person will deepen his personal relationship with God more than will the begrudged million of the harried rich man. And if their sincere desire and compassion and charity are equivalent, the rewards of the one who can give and of the one who can't will also be equivalent. The greater closeness is the greater reward. It is the greater amount of grace.

283

Why Brilliant Atheists?

Why are so many scientists and intellectuals atheists?

There are all kinds of disbelieving attitudes that are lumped together under the name of "atheist." They range from a militant assault on God to a simple unsureness that man can know anything one way or the other about God. The latter category is the more prevalent, and it would seem that many in the scientific and intellectual community hold this view.

Why? We could appeal to the mysteriousness of God's gift of faith. But this would be dodging the question. It seems that there are two factors that make it easy for these men to set aside the question of God.

One is the nature of the method science uses in its investigation. The scientist isolates a problem, observes its phenomena, experiments with multiple possibilities, and arrives at a working solution. Generally, he is not concerned with the absolute truth of his solution but with its probability, with its workable practicality. He is not concerned with the question of ultimate causes, but with the correlation of phenomena. In its own sphere, this method works wonderfully well. It has shaped the world as we know it. It has made space travel possible. It has unlocked the secrets of the material universe and seems to have penetrated the secrets of biological life. The question of God doesn't enter this whole process; God is not a phenomenon which interacts with other phenomena. Now, a man can be so caught up with the processes of the scientific method that he ignores, as meaningless, any question that does not relate to it, or he can try to apply these processes to the hopeless task of trying to ascertain God's existence. This is bound to be a blind alley.

The other factor that seems to open the way to the atheism of so many of our learned contemporaries is their passionate belief in man. They see that the idea of God has been used in the past to explain purely natural mysteries that are better explained by men of science. They find that God and religion have in fact been used as "the opium of the people" to keep men contented with political and economic misery. Twice bitten, twice shy, they feel that if they confess the existence of God, Lord and Savior of the universe, they will thereby diminish the nobility of man and of the world.

Vatican II considered atheism to be "among the most serious problems of this age." The Council turned its attention to this problem in several places — especially in the *Constitution on the*

Church in the Modern World (nos. 19-21). It called on believers to examine their own consciences to discover their own responsibility for some of this atheism. It asked us to develop a mature faith, free from superstition, to strive to manifest the face of God through a genuine charity, and to work together even with the atheists for the betterment of the world. The work of Christian scientists like Teilhard de Chardin has helped many of these brilliant men to break through to the recognition of the God who made them and who ennobles the world and man who is its crown.

The Wealthy Vatican

The enclosed clipping, estimating the world-wide financial holdings of the Vatican at about 5.6 billion dollars, left me stunned. If there is so much wealth, why keep collecting for the poor? I know that parents who have five and six children find it most difficult to give, give, give.

If you or I had billions of dollars invested and went around trying to beg more money to be able to give to the poor, people would certainly have a right to complain and to tighten their purse strings. But do the same standards apply when we speak of a great public-service organization? The Church should be, and to a large extent is, the poor Church of Christ's poor.

But it must also be a very expensive operation. The Vatican maintains official representatives and their office staff in about *seventy* countries to facilitate the contact of the local Church with the center of unity. It has a network of offices in Rome to handle the affairs of our international Church, and each of them has a sizable quota of clerical and lay employees. It underwrites some of the expenses of our missionaries. The Vatican is also a tiny state with a population of about one thousand people, and the goods and services required in any municipality must be provided. All of this costs a great deal of money, and that money comes both from the donations of the faithful and the investment income of the Vatican holdings.

Actually, the Vatican has never issued a financial report. It has, however, stated that the estimate you refer to is wildly inflated.

Suppose, for the sake of argument, that the report were fairly accurate. Would financial holdings like these be scandalously excessive? I think it would be illuminating to consider the wealth of the Vatican as an endowment fund and compare it to other endowments. Several years ago, the Ford Foundation had assets of almost two and a half billion dollars, and it laid out in grants almost 350 million. Harvard University has a generous endowment of more than a half-billion dollars to provide for research, salaries, and the educational needs of its 13,562 students and 6,014 faculty. And it also receives income from tuition and the gifts of benefactors of the university. Because the Vatican provides services that affect the lives of the almost 600 million Catholics in the world, it is not surprising that the income from the Vatican's invested billions would have to be supplemented by regular appeals to the generosity of the faithful who do not have much to spare.

Pomp and Circumstance

Why don't the bishops and cardinals stop having their rings kissed?

I imagine that they will stop the custom as soon as the word gets out that it is "turning people off" and as soon as the bishops get a breather from their far more pressing problems in which they can find the time to consider this one. As Lorelei Lee said, "A kiss on the hand may be quite continental. . . ." And this is a continental custom that was entirely natural in another age. It expressed reverent love and adult submission to the person who stands in the place of Christ and is the source of the unity of the local Church. Reverent love and submission to our bishops are attitudes that we should find in every time and place. If the sign we use to express these attitudes no longer signifies, or seems to mean obsequiousness, or bewilders our contemporaries, then it is time to let it go and look for a new kind of sign. I think we're getting close to a middle road in this time of reassessment. I know of no bishop who makes a big thing of having his ring kissed. And I know of many lay Catholics who are happy to show their reverence in this way.

Three Wishes

When I was a girl, I understood that whenever you enter a church for the first time, you have the privilege of making three wishes. Not just saying a prayer, but something nice you could do in addition. Is this correct?

My mother taught me the same thing when I was a boy. I don't know where the custom comes from, but I think it's nice. It reminds us that there is something special about a visit to a sacred place that is new, at least new to us. It focuses our attention on the childlike attitude that is proper for a person who comes before God. It reminds us of the irreplaceable value of the prayer of petition — for a wish presented to God is a prayer. And there is very little chance that the whole thing will degenerate into superstition. There is no reason why we can't hold on to the customs of simpler times, as long as they help us to lift our minds and hearts to God and to remember the needs of our brethren.

Money in the Church

Is it a matter of faith or morals, rules or regulations of the Church that a fee be paid before the sacrament of confirmation can be administered?

As I'm sure you anticipated, the answer is "No." The sacraments of the Church are Christ's free gift to the Church, and they are to be bestowed on the faithful as a free service by those who minister in the Church.

Most parishes consider it quite appropriate to offer a generous gift to the bishop when he comes to confirm. The generous gifts of a parish are made up of the small donations of the faithful members of the parish. I know only too well that communications can break down to such an extent that the gathering of funds to make up this may begin to look like charging a fee. Under the pressures of deficit spending, a particular priest or parish might even be tempted to ask outright for a fee.

Your very brief letter, in which I can read an admixture of indignation and hurt, is an eloquent reminder to us priests of the need to be discreet and sensitive whenever we request monies of this kind.

Religious Education without Schools

All this talk about abolishing the Catholic schools is fine except for one thing. What about me — the parent? What am I supposed to do?

Everything I know and feel about God I have learned from the

nuns. How can I convey to my children the benefit I received from attending daily Mass with my playmates and teachers or the insights I gained when the entire class got on their knees and prayed for a sick friend?

I loved the nuns that taught me religion, and I learned my love of God from them. I know I can never give my children the foundation in religion that I received. What can I, as a parent, do about my responsibility to bring my children and God closer together?

I hope your nuns read your letter. When they begin to wonder "Is it all worth while?" — and being human they probably do — it helps to get such a sincere love letter.

You put your finger on the right spot. The greatest value of Catholic education is not the religion class but the total environment. Leon Bloy begins one of his novels with the startling phrase, "This place stinks of God." A successful Catholic school does, too, and in a good sense. But so should a good Catholic home and a good Christian society.

There are some hard facts we have to reckon with when we are considering the problem of maintaining Catholic schools. The most obvious are the mounting costs of education and the shortage of personnel. The cost per pupil is skyrocketing, and the end is not in sight. If we are going to give the children in Catholic schools an education that is equal to that available in public schools, we have to continue investing in extremely expensive buildings and equipment. The number of religious to staff the schools is not increasing in proportion to the demand. Dedicated lay teachers are doing a marvelous job, but they deserve a salary that will let them live with dignity.

Economic facts and changing social situations are sometimes the ways God uses to show us that he wants us to launch out onto new and deep waters. If he is, in fact, telling us that the day of the parochial school is coming to an end in some places, it should be seen as an invitation to something equally as rich for the Church and our children. To have the children of our Catholic families in the public schools might be an enriching of these schools. It might also help parents to assume more conscientiously their role as the first educators of their own children. Sometimes parents develop an unnecessary sense of inferiority about their ability to share with the children those things that are most important to them. They leave that to the professionals at school who can do a "better job."

You who care as much as you do already have everything going for you as the one to convey to your children the benefits you received from the Sisters. Don't sell yourself short. At the same time, you do need help. Some parishes that are perforce without a school are conducting programs to help people like you do a more effective job. Would that they were everywhere available. Many of the newer religion textbook series (like the Paulist Press *Come to the Father Series* and the Benziger *Word and Worship Program*) have Parents' Guides worked out for parent-teacher cooperation in religious education. You will find the books of Mary Reed Newland helpful: e.g., *Homemade Christians* (Dayton, Ohio; Pflaum) and *We and Our Children* (New York: Doubleday). Both are inexpensive paperbacks.

Catholic Education

What is the position of the Catholic Church in regard to sending children to Catholic schools? Recently I read in a book that parents are obliged to send their children to Catholic schools. Is this rule in effect any longer?

The Catholic Church strongly maintains that parents have the principal right and duty to provide for the education of their children. The school exists to help the parents accomplish their very serious duty of bringing their children to full development as mature persons.

Mature personhood, in the Christian vision of life, includes everything that the social and behavioral sciences describe of natural psychological and cultural development. But besides this, and thoroughly permeating it, are the special dimensions of the human person that belong to the one who has been reborn to the new life in Christ through baptism.

The Catholic parent can never be satisfied with an education which ignores this supernatural dimension or which is based on a purely materialistic vision of life, nor with an education that merely adds a dose of religious information to a general curriculum. The purpose of Catholic schools is to help parents give their children this integral Christian education.

Are parents obliged to send their children to Catholic schools? That depends. If it is quite likely that attending another school would entail a serious risk of destroying the youngster's faith, then there is a serious obligation to send him to a Catholic school. In the early decades of this century, a number of American bishops judged this risk was present, and they commanded their people to use the parochial schools.

On the other hand, if the danger does not seem to be so threatening and the reality of a genuine Christian family life and a vital religious education program are cooperating in the child's growth as a Christian, parents may weigh other considerations and decide to send their children to other public or private schools. Perhaps they find a better quality of secular education elsewhere than is available in the Catholic schools of a particular area. A family may find the cost of Catholic schooling beyond their means. Parents might decide that their children need more contact with people of various backgrounds to prepare them for life in a pluralistic society. Any of these can be good and sufficient reasons for sending children to a school other than a Catholic one.

Still, there is some obligation for parents to send their children to Catholic schools. It is a conditional one, recognizing that there can be many variables that have to be taken into account. The Vatican Council expressed it this way: "As for Catholic parents, the Council calls to mind their duty to entrust their children to Catholic schools, when and where this is possible, to support such schools to the extent of their ability, and to work along with them for the welfare of their children" (*Declaration on Christian Education,* no. 8).

More important than the question of legal obligation is the question of the welfare of the school-age children. The Catholic schools have served generations of American children well and enabled parents to exercise their conscientious duty to have their faith's vision pervade their children's total development. It is our hope that future generations will have the same advantage available to them — not as a financial luxury, but as a cherished right.

High-school Reading

A nun in our parish who teaches CCD classes to the Junior class of high-school girls told them to read "The Graduate," 'Rosemary's Baby," and "The Valley of the Dolls" so that they may be better able to cope with what's going on in the world today. This seems to me like saying that you have to rob a bank to know better how a robber thinks and acts. What do you think of this approach?

I'm sure that Sister had no problem holding the attention of her girls. She probably got them to do their homework, too. The chances are that sixteen- or seventeen-year-old girls would be passing these books around anyway, and it might have been a stroke of genius on her part to bring them into the open and make them the subject of discussion. A perceptive teacher steeped in a Christian view of life can use material even as inept and contrived as *The Valley of the Dolls* to impress her students with Christian and human values.

If these titles were selected as wholly appropriate reading for high-school girls, I would have a number of reservations. They contribute to a somewhat unhealthy fantasy life in young people at a time when this needs little encouragement. A steady diet of books like this can dull a person's critical sense and spoil his taste for really good literature. These books reflect the values of a good life only indirectly, and unless there is an uncommon degree of mutual openness between the teacher and her students, the chances are that the distorted values of the fictional characters will come through more strongly than those of the teacher.

The teacher who takes this approach would have to be, I think, either caught in a situation where this seems the only way out or extraordinarily gifted or extremely naive. I hope your nun was a gifted woman of profound faith.

Don't Push

I'm eleven years old and I have a friend (the friend is more than just someone I know; he doesn't just use me to bring him pleasure). The boy is a Lutheran but not very devout; nor is his family, from what I understand. I would like to get him interested in the Catholic faith and reform him. So far, he said he's reading a revised children's Catholic Bible, a bit every night when he has time. He recently started a conversation about religion instead of my having to do it, although it was about the walls of Jericho, not about taking part in Catholic practices. Please help me to go on from here.

You are already doing well. You have a friend — a person whom you value for himself and with whom you want to share things of greatest value to yourself. It saddens you to find that our Lord is not an important person in his life. What you are doing is introducing him to Christ and to the depths of meaning that knowing and loving him bring to your own life.

At this stage in your friend's life, this is far more important than getting him to take part in Catholic practices. Even though you think that his religious allegiance is not very strong, he is very young to make any switch. And trying to get him to change over right now might cause problems with his family that could stand in the way of any future decision he might want to make.

As things are, you've enriched the boy's life by encouraging him to read God's word each day. You've brought him to the point of beginning to see the value of religion in his life — even if, like the Samaritan woman in the Gospel (John 4:19-20), he's focusing on secondary things like the story of Joshua's battle rather than on the one thing necessary, the Person of Jesus Christ. But don't worry, and don't push. If you are his friend, if he finds you fun to be with and at the same time one whose life is fuller because of his faith, you may be setting the stage for God, in his own good time, to touch his heart and show him what he should do.

Do I Have a Religious Vocation?

How can a person know what God wants him to do after he has failed to follow through in the first call? After six months as a postulant, I just came out of the convent. It was almost impossible for me to adjust to that way of life. Is there a possibility that I may still have the call? I feel so bad about the whole thing. Do I have to try again?

It is a mistake for a young lady to feel that the "call" to religious life is something that hangs over her head as a threat — as if God had mapped out a single path which she must follow and that otherwise she will fail to do what God wants.

We use the words "vocation" and "call" to express the theological truth that God is active whenever a person makes a lifetime decision to follow Christ in a special way. In a real sense, this decision is a response to God's call. But the only way we can be sure of the call is through the person's decision. We know God's graces and invitations only through signs. And the only sure sign of a religious vocation is the prudent, free decision of a candidate, which is ratified by the superiors of a religious order.

I think it is a shame when a girl enters a community because she feels that she *has* to become a Sister. God has left you free. No one can tell you that you have to enter the convent, any more than he can tell you that you have to marry Jack rather than Frank.

Sometimes we meet girls who are "afraid they have a vocation."

Then it's most important to clear the air. A question like this is helpful: If the choice were completely up to you and you were sure that any choice you might make would be equally pleasing to God, would you choose to marry and raise a family or would you choose to be a Sister? If the spontaneous reaction is "Oh, I'd get married!" then there's no need to go any further into the question of a vocation. But if she is not sure, if she feels that she wants to follow Christ more explicitly than she could in the lay vocation, if love is drawing her to want to enter a religious community, then there should be a follow-through. She should talk the matter out with an experienced vocational counselor to find out if her motives and qualifications are enough to warrant testing her decision.

You have tested your decision. That's what postulancy is for. And you found that you did not want to decide to stay. Leaving in these circumstances does not usually mean "failing to follow through in the first call." Rather, it usually means discovering that there was no "call" and, therefore, no failure. However, I do not think that you will be settled and content until you go personally to some competent priest or religious to get some help.

The Lowest Way of Life

When only fifteen years of age, I made a vow of virginity. I decided to make this just overnight and without any advice from anyone. I was never instructed on marriage and I had the idea marriage was the lowest way of life, because no one wanted to answer any questions I would ask about it. I'm now twenty-one, and I see how beautiful it is to really love someone. I want to be married this summer but fear I might have to remain faithful to the vow I made when I was fifteen, after Communion one morning. Before I ever dated anyone, when I was eighteen, I asked a priest, and he told me this vow wasn't binding in any way. But I know a friend of mine who was asked if she had ever made such a vow before she was married. Will this in any way hinder my marriage, Father, and will God be very displeased with me because I did not keep such a sacred vow?

The advice you received three years ago was good. The priest you consulted undoubtedly judged that your precipitous "vow" lacked the qualities of mature deliberation and knowledge that would have to be present in a true vow. Your friend is right. There is a question on many marriage forms asking if a vow of virginity was made. I think you can simply answer "No." There was a moment of enthusiasm, perhaps, but not a mature, lifetime commitment to a way of life — and that's what a vow is.

Forget the worry about God's displeasure. If we can talk about God's "displeasure," I think it applies more to the climate of embarrassed silence that afflicted an older generation and that made too many Catholic young people grow up with the impression that marriage is "the lowest way of life." Thank God you are now free from this taboo. And thank God for the love you have found and the call to share it with him in the sacrament of marriage.

Devotion to the Passion

I often read that saints, passing by a crucifix, wept. Others making the Stations are really disturbed by the thought of Christ's suffering. I cannot feel like this about the Passion. It seems to me that it is over. Easter was always the most wonderful day of the year for me. I cannot feel sorrow at his dying. I am rather proud that our Lord was a man (such a man!) and that he lives.

I like what you write. Don't try to become a sad Catholic. Being devoted to the Passion of our Lord does not mean imagining that the Resurrection never took place. Suffering together with our Lord in his Passion does not mean being upset, as if our Lord himself were still dying. Christ is risen — his death has been swallowed up in victory.

The saints who wept at the sight of the crucifix also knew this. Their tears were tears of grateful wonder that God would so love them as to lay down his life for them, tears of anguish that so many continue to refuse to accept this mercy, tears of contrition that their own sinfulness was responsible for the horrible suffering and death of Christ.

Through their meditation on the Passion, they learned something of the path along which the Risen Lord would bring them to himself — there is no other path to our resurrection with him than the way of the cross. It is only by losing our lives that we will gain life. There is nothing morbid about those who consciously set out to live a life crucified with Christ. It is not a sick quest of suffering for its own sake, but a willing acceptance of life's diminishments as something whose meaning appears most clearly in our Lord's own suffering and dying. It was only through the cross that he entered his glory. The cross is also our only way to the fullness God has prepared for us.

Rosary Blessings

Years ago, my rosaries were blessed with what I was told was the Crosier blessing. I would be very much obliged if you could give me some information regarding this blessing — the indulgences attached to it, et cetera.

The Crosier blessing gets its name from the Order of the Holy Cross, whose members are often called Crosiers.

Years ago, priests of this religious order were given the privilege of blessing rosaries so that special indulgences would be attached to the recitation of each prayer. Their privilege was, in time, shared by other priests, so that many rosaries had the Crosier indulgences attached to them even though there was no Crosier Father available.

As you know, our Holy Father has reorganized the whole discipline of indulgences. Today there is no difference between one rosary and another, no matter who the priest was who blessed it. This does not really mean that anything has been lost. All blessed rosaries are indulgenced. A person who devoutly says the rosary gains an indulgence whose extent is limited only by the degree of faith and love with which he prays. In addition, a plenary indulgence may be gained once a day if the rosary is recited in a church or public oratory or in a family group, a religious community, or a pious association.

I find the above information in the recently published English translation of the *Enchiridion of Indulgences* (New York: Catholic Book Publishing Co., 1969). This is the revised edition of the *Raccolta* which was ordered by Pope Paul in January, 1967. It is not the same kind of collection of indulgenced prayers that the old *Raccolta* was. One reason for the change seems to be that the Church has extended a partial indulgence to any prayerful invocation of the faithful.

The Praise of Mary

Why do we think of Mary as being noteworthy only for her vir-

ginity? Jesus said we would all be judged on love. Surely, his mother wasn't "judged" solely on the merits of her virginity! Why can't we extol Mary for her charity, compassion, hospitality, and tender motherly virtues instead of her chastity? This has been something of a bother to me for some time now. Because of the emphasis, which is probably misplaced, Mary and I have long since "parted company," and I used to be able to talk to her all the time.

I just can't identify myself with the "we" who think of Mary as noteworthy only for her virginity. It is true that some recent theology (the kind that reaches the newspapers) has concentrated on the question of her virginity. The only reason for this is that the teaching has been challenged in certain circles. However, neither those who raise the challenge nor those who defend the tradition think of her virginity as the principal reason to praise and revere Mary. All will subscribe to the judgment of the ancient Father of the Church who declared, "Chastity without charity is damnable."

The Church's praise of Mary has been a long, joyful fulfilling of the Gospel word, "All ages to come shall call me blessed" (Luke 1:48). Why blessed? Because he who is mighty has done great things for her. He found her one whose unspotted, selfless love made her perfectly open to receive his word and his Word. Everything that Israel had been called to be was realized in her who was its most perfect daughter. Everything that the Church would ever become in the greatest of its saints was already a fact in her who is its first member, mother, and model.

She stands out among the poor and humble of the Lord who confidently hope for and receive salvation from him. Her divine Son's supreme praise of her had nothing to do with the biology of either virginity or motherhood. Rather, he praised her as the woman of faith who heard the word of God and kept it (Luke 11:27-28). We may think that when he described the characteristics of those who are blessed and in whom God reigns, he was thinking of her who was poor and meek and merciful and who yearned for God's Kingdom (Matt. 5:3-12).

Since she was a woman totally responsive to God, there can be no doubt that she was fully attuned to the needs of others. We cannot even imagine the delicately balanced perfection in her of all those human qualities that made her the paragon of mothers, the tenderest of wives, and the best of neighbors.

So, get to know her again. Read the beautiful pages of Chapter VIII, "The Role of the Blessed Virgin Mary, Mother of God, in the

Mystery of Christ and the Church," in Vatican II's *Dogmatic Constitution on the Church*. It is heavy reading — every sentence is food for a lifetime of prayerful reflection — but it will show how modestly the mystery of her virginity fits into the panorama of those realities that make her noteworthy for the "we" who are the Church.

The Nuclear Disarmament Symbol

What is the meaning of the symbol that is used so much in the Peace Movement: the circle with the "bird's foot" inscribed?

Some people have been making a fuss about this symbol. It has been suggested that a diabolical fraud has been perpetrated on a hoard of naive doves. Some have claimed that the symbol is a mark of the anti-Christ, or a carry-over from the practices of witchcraft: the broken cross.

However, the groups who have taken this design as the standard of their organizations offer a far simpler explanation.

In February, 1958, the Direct Action Committee against Nuclear War was preparing in London for a great demonstration. It was to take place on Easter Sunday. Its purpose was to call for unilateral nuclear disarmament. The demonstration has come to be known as the first Aldermaston March.

The Committee worked to create a symbol that would communicate its message. The symbol grew through a number of sketches. The first sketch showed a white circle against a black square. In the circle, various forms of the Christian cross were drawn — and these finally gave way to the central motif we are all familiar with.

The central design is a stylized composite of the basic form of the semaphore signals for the letters *N* and *D* — standing for "nuclear disarmament."

Like any symbol, this one is evocative. It stimulates the imagination to find several levels of meaning. The *N-D* quickly came to be read as a gesture of man's despair under the threat of nuclear annihilation.

In my opinion, I see no reason why we ought to question this version of the origin and meaning of the nuclear disarmament or peace symbol.

Even if a careful search of the literature of black magic should succeed in showing that a design like this had a sinister meaning once upon a time, this wouldn't change things substantially. Artificial symbols have the meanings that people give them. They have no power or meaning apart from this. And all over the world today, the *N-D* symbol stands as an expression of a wish for peace.

A person may have a difficulty accepting the philosophy of some of the groups that have made the design their own. He may consider their schemes woolly-headed and unrealistic. I'm not arguing this. But I think it is irrational, even sick, to consider the existence of the symbol as a demonic plot to foist an anti-Christian design on the world — as if the design had a magical power and life all its own.

The Silence of Heaven

Why is it that today, when communications are so much to the fore, we have practically no communications from heaven? The last authenticated word received from us here on earth was in the year 1917 at Fatima. Why all the silence now?

I have received a number of letters from concerned Catholics along the same lines. Obviously a number of people are looking for striking signs to reinforce their faith in the reality of God and the hereafter.

No man can say with certainty why God does not choose another way to communicate with us than the way he chooses. God is a mystery. He reveals himself to us, but he does not promise to clear up all our problems. Centuries ago, when the Christian Church was faced with the enigma of the refusal of the Chosen People to accept the fulfillment of its history, St. Paul wrote these lines: "How deep are the riches and the wisdom and the knowledge of God! How inscrutable his judgments, how unsearchable his ways!" (Rom. 11:33). There is wisdom in not trying to give a clear answer to the question, "Why all the silence now?"

Yet one reason for the silence is that there is nothing new. God has already said everything when he spoke the Eternal Word, co-equal with himself, who became flesh and dwelt among us. Christ is God's full and adequate communication to mankind. He is the same yesterday, today, and forever.

The religious experiences of Lourdes, Fatima, and the rest are in no way a new word. They add nothing to the perfect communication given in the beginning. They highlight an aspect of the message — they do not change or extend it. As Cardinal Ottaviani wrote in

1951, they "can furnish us with new motives for fervor, but not with new elements of life and doctrine."

Sometimes we feel that these extraordinary and miraculous interventions are the proof of our faith. Actually, it's the other way round. Our assurance of the authenticity of these phenomena comes, in large measure, from their conformity to the original Word spoken once and for all.

Lourdes and Fatima are props for the faith. They are like good advertising copy that forces us to see the value of the product or that focuses our attention on a particular aspect of it that is especially important for our time. They are not, nor ever were, the proper object of faith.

Today men all over the world are conscious of the silence of God. Might not this silence be the very way he is speaking to us? Might he not be echoing the words of the Savior: "An evil and unfaithful age is eager for a sign! No sign will be given it but that of the prophet Jonah" (Matt. 12:39). In other words, I suggest that the silence of God, the absence of any compelling new "signs," can be seen as a divine pedagogy leading us to entrust ourselves to him rather than to search for signs of his presence.

The spiritual journey of the saints has always been marked by a rather frightening negative side. They always experienced a gradual stripping away of much of the comfort and assurance that supported their effort to serve God. But they came to see this not as a diminishment but as a growth. It was the "crutches" that were taken away. But they were not snatched as a cruel prankster might take them from a cripple. They were taken as an understanding physician might take them in order to get a fearful patient to begin to walk on his own.

The saints found that they no longer could hear God in the complicated ways of a former time; yet he still spoke to them in a Word that called on all the resources of their faith to grasp. What had formerly seemed as light to them was eclipsed, but the apparent darkness was like the blindness a person feels in the presence of a light too brilliant to grasp.

I suggest that God may be calling the world to repeat the experience of the saints. His apparent silence may be designed to wean us away from the milk of spiritual infancy to accept the meat and potatoes of mature and simple faith.

St. John of the Cross, who wrote so penetratingly of the way of spiritual growth to the full maturity of faith, noted that many who are called to this richer life with God refuse to let go of the past and launch out into what seems like silence and darkness. There is always a risk in growing! And it may well be that our age will not have the courage to respond to the apparently silent Word of God. It may be that we will continue to substitute one felt experience for another and never commend our spirits into the hands of God. By way of parenthesis, it seems to me that this is the danger of our search for ever more meaningful liturgies and experiences that will "turn us on."

If our age refuses to grow, I believe that God will come to us where we are, even if that means that he will come through new extraordinary manifestations. But ultimately our assurance of the reality of God and of an eternal life with him does not rest on any vision or on any word from a loved one who has gone before us. It rests on the Word of God, who became Man for us, who died for our sins, who was raised from the dead as the firstborn among many brothers. We hear this Word and share his lot as his brothers only through the dark medium of faith.

More—The Silence of Heaven

Shame on you for your response "The Silence of Heaven." It is difficult for me to believe that you are really ignorant of the recent apparitions of our Blessed Mother in Spain and elsewhere. Why cover up the facts? In my opinion, you owe your readers an apology for your paternalism and your untruthfulness.

You put it quite directly and forcefully. I was surprised at the number of letters I received from people reacting to this item. One person wrote of messages our Lord had entrusted to her personally that she is trying to get to the attention of the pope. Most referred, as you did, to the alleged apparitions of Our Lady that are supposed to have occurred in Garabandal, Spain, during the four years between 1961 and 1965. Certainly this is the occurrence that has had the most publicity. I presume that it is my silence about this that strikes you as a suppression of the facts.

Actually, I don't feel that I suppressed any facts. I question whether there is any fact to report. Is Garabandal, in fact, like Lourdes and Fatima — an instance of an extraordinary manifestation of the Blessed Mother's care for her wayward children, one that we may prudently believe? To answer this question we ought to go to qualified investigators rather than to enthusiastic propagandists, however sincere.

Garabandal is located in the diocese of Santander. The diocese conducted just such a detailed and prolonged investigation. In 1967, on the basis of this report and all available information, Bishop Vincente Puchol Montiz came to the conclusion that he could not declare the "visions" as being so probably from God that they were credible. His successor, Bishop Joseph Cirarda Lachiondo, has recently reiterated the judgment and reminded his people that all devotions based on the supposed apparitions are absolutely forbidden in his diocese. He added that "it is also the evident desire" of the Vatican's Congregation of the Doctrine of the Faith that the rest of the world follow suit.

This judgment doesn't come from enemies of the Blessed Mother. Neither the investigating committee nor the bishops are persons who are trying to sweep genuine supernatural occurrences under the rug. They are as interested as any devotee to inspire people to a renewed spirit of prayer and sacrifice. However, they cannot in conscience encourage people to get involved in a devotional enterprise based on such a questionable foundation.

I'm sorry if you thought I was being paternalistic or condescending. But I was not concealing the truth.

Fatima 1960

I would like to know what happened to the letter that was supposed to be opened in 1969 or 1970, a letter that the Blessed Virgin Mary gave to one of the children of Fatima. This letter supposedly had to do with the future of the world. Can you tell me why nothing has been said about it?

I believe that you are referring to the letter that was written by Lucy to the Holy Father with the request that it was not to be opened before 1960. Whether it was opened or not is really the business of the Holy Father. If he did in fact open it, he chose not to make its contents public.

Personally, I cannot help thinking of the parables of the rich man and Lazarus when I find people anxious to learn the contents of the famous Fatima letter. To the rich man's plea to send Lazarus back to warn his brothers, Abraham replied: "If they do not listen to Moses and the prophets, they will not be convinced even if one should rise from the dead" (Luke 16:31).

Our era has received the good news of Christ. This gospel has been made practical and urgent for us by the tremendous grace of an ecumenical council. The Holy Spirit is constantly appealing to us through the signs of the times to change our way of life: to live by a vision of faith, to become more prayerful, to exorcise the demon of violence that terrorizes our cities and makes us be a warrior people, to become reconciled with all men as our brothers, to stem the tide of lust and avarice. . . . If we will not listen to this impelling call from God, we will not be convinced even should a messenger from heaven preach to us.

Superstition

A member of my family has a copy of a letter claiming to be a "true letter of our Saviour Jesus Christ" signed by Pope Leo XIII on April 5, 1890. He fears letting anyone have it even long enough to make a copy of it. He believes that his life has been saved on two occasions by having it in his possession. Do you know of any writings by Jesus Christ, signed by Pope Leo XIII?

There is not a single authentic word written by our Lord that has come down to us — not even in the form of a copy. Pope Leo never authenticated any such document. It would be well to consign this paper to the circular file — the wastebasket.

I do not for one minute question the sincerity of your relative's faith. However, in this instance it is that form of misplaced faith that fades over into superstition. Faith is both a belief in the truths about God and man that have been revealed in Christ and a handing over of one's whole life to the Lord. Superstition is the counterfeit of faith which imagines God to be one who can be manipulated into helping us by the use of charms, prayers, or special letters.

Faith accepts God as he is, and the man of faith is glad to be made in God's image and likeness. Superstition fashions its own god, and the superstitious man makes a god in the image and likeness of his own fears and anxieties.

It is quite easy for a person to fall prey to superstition in a time of personal crisis. The danger of superstition is that it can eat away at the roots of real faith. The superstitious man's god will inevitably disappoint him — his luck will run out, literally. And in his disillusionment, the victim of superstition may find himself rejecting the true God of love and mercy and every religious service of him.

The path to true faith and confident trust in the providence of

God may lead some people through the byway of superstition. But once superstition is unmasked for what it is, the searcher for God will fearlessly wrench it out of his life.

Even authentically sacred things can be misused in a superstitious way. It happened in ancient times with the bronze serpent that Moses had made when his people were plagued in the desert (Numbers 21:8-9). The bronze serpent had been the instrument of God's healing power. St. John saw in it a foreshadowing of the cross of Christ (John 3:14f.)

But about seven hundred years before Christ, the people of Israel had perverted their sacred relic and come to revere it as a magical thing, offering sacrifice to it. The purity of Israel's belief in God was threatened. So King Hezekiah, in his fearless reform of the religion of his people, smashed the bronze serpent (II Kings 18:4).

Be it bronze serpents or words said to be written by Jesus Christ — when they come to be regarded as magical shields from all harm — they must go.

St. Malachy's Prophecy

Could you tell me something about the prophecies of St. Malachy concerning the popes? I would check in the public library, but I hesitate even to ask, as I don't even know where they are contained. I was educated in Ireland, and they were mentioned often, but people in this country never seem to have heard of them.

I hope they said more about St. Malachy in Ireland than they did about his so-called prophecy. St. Malachy was a great reforming archbishop of Armagh, who lived during the first half of the twelfth century. He left a tremendous impact on Catholic life in Ireland during his lifetime of fifty-four years. He introduced the Roman liturgy into Ireland, worked at the renewal of monastic life, and acted as papal legate to Ireland. He was the real article. His prophecy is a fake. An unknown author forged it under his name during the sixteenth century. It lists the 111 successors of Pope Celestine II (elected in 1143) not by name but by a short epithet. For the period from 1143 to 1590, the epithets are perfectly fitting — these popes, after all, were known figures of history. After 1590, the titles become very vague. Knowledge of the "prophecy" of St. Malachy is but frosting on the cake of religious information. Believing in it is sheer foolishness.

Automatic Writing

What is the Catholic opinion or attitude regarding automatic writing? A Catholic woman I know recently had this experience. We had been having fun reading the unimportant writings. Suddenly a message came through from her deceased father asking for a Mass to be said for him. Now she refuses to go on with the writings. She is afraid she may be violating a Church rule. I feel she should continue to develop this. It is a form of science, is it not?

By the term "automatic writing," I take it that you refer to the sort of thing that is done with a Ouija board or the use of a pendulum suspended above the alphabet or something similar. What is it that accounts for the so-called "messages"? Parapsychology is the young science that seeks to find the answer to this and other similar questions. It attempts to distinguish between the phenomena that are produced by fraud or illusory autosuggestion and those which can be explained only by some force outside the usual area of sense perception and communication.

The founder of French parapsychology, Charles Richet (1850-1935), gave this judgment on the subject of automatic writings: "One would need a culpable dose of credulity to see anything in them but aesthetic projections of the unconscious." In other words, there is nothing that goes beyond the sphere of ordinary psychology in this, any more than there is in our most extravagant dreams or in the delirium of fever. It is most probable that the "messages" are the creation of the practitioner's subconscious, of his hopes and fears and guilts. In this light there is nothing unusual in the fact that a Catholic would subconsciously associate having a Mass celebrated with the thought of her deceased father.

What is the Catholic attitude on automatic writing? It would be safe to say that the Church frowns on it as something that smacks of superstition. The Church has repeatedly forbidden the faithful to attend and actively participate in spiritualistic séances that attempt to communicate with the spirits of the dead. This does not prevent competent investigators from doing research to discover the scientific explanation of the spiritualist phenomena. Nor does it deny that, under the special providence of God, the spirits of the deceased may communicate with the living. However, efforts to communicate with the dead by anxious people can hardly be called scientific research into spiritualistic phenomena. Nor is it to be expected that God's providence will make use of such inept means as automatic writing to convey his messages to men.

When I hear about things like this, I am reminded of our Lord's parable of the rich man and Lazarus (Luke 16:19-31). The rich man begged Abraham to send a messenger back from the dead to warn his five brothers. Abraham replied, "They have Moses and the prophets, let them hear them." "No, Father Abraham," said the rich man, "But if someone would only go to them from the dead, they would repent." Then Abraham said to him, "If they do not listen to Moses and the prophets, they will not be convinced even if one should rise from the dead." God's ordinary dealings with us are just that — ordinary.

The Rage for Astrology

Why does Christianity reject astrology? If astrology is false and our destiny is not predetermined in the stars and planets, how can you account for the fact that the future can often be correctly foretold by it — and the designated signs of the zodiac are so accurate in revealing people's dispositions, character, and personality traits according to respective birth months?

As I was preparing to answer your letter, I took time out to look up my horoscope for the day. I'm a Capricorn, and the four-line item in the local paper reminds me: "Little gifts expressing personal feeling are welcome, and friends can be generous. Keep combativeness out of the picture." So I'll try to be gentle.

Astrology, like alchemy, is a pseudoscience. It has a highly complicated and technical structure requiring considerable knowledge of mathematics and astronomy in its practitioners. Men of many cultures and civilizations have practiced the art of astrology, beginning with the men of ancient Babylonia. They believed that the heavenly bodies exert a preponderant influence over the world and its inhabitants. Eventually, astrologers came to think that man's fate is fixed in advance, at least partially, and can be predicted by carefully observing the positions of the heavens at the time of birth or conception.

The Church opposes astrology as she opposed the magical and the occult. She opposes it as she does every fatalist doctrine or any kind of determinism that tends to empty human liberty of meaning. Christianity's objection is based on the fundamental belief that God rules the universe by a personal providence and that each man is free and responsible for his own actions.

For all her objections, the Church has never been entirely successful in stamping out astrology. There has always been something fascinating and mysterious about the stars, and astrology has left its stamp on Western culture. A great deal of the art and literature of the Western world is unintelligible without some knowledge of the ancient myths and the signs of the zodiac. Kings and emperors made use of court astrologers to help them with their decisions of state. In the time of the Renaissance, Pope Julius II used astrology to set the day of his coronation, and Pope Paul III consulted the horoscope to determine the proper hour for every consistory. The leading astronomers at the dawn of the scientific age were also astrologers.

Today we are seeing a resurgence of astrology in the United States. It is a curious phenomenon. At a time when many are giving up a belief in the living God, people are embracing a belief in a star-dominated fate. At a moment when the world of reason is undermining many of our ancient assurances, our contemporaries are clinging to the dreams that promise them a glimpse of their own destiny.

Perhaps it is proof of the ultimate need men have to depend on powers beyond them, evidence of the unquenchable instinct to believe that is part of the human spirit. But a belief in the rule of the stars is a poor substitute for a belief in the God and Father of us all.

Irish Fable

Wasn't there a period when we had no pope? I recall reading years ago that it was the Irish who kept the faith going at that time.

Although I am of Irish extraction and I have a great respect for the faith of my ancestors, I'm afraid (or happy) that it is not true. There was no time in which the Church had so collapsed that the center of faith and unity shifted from Rome to Dublin. It is true, of course, that whenever a pope dies, there is a period in which we have no pope. That period may be longer or shorter, depending on the method used at a particular moment in history to choose a successor.

As far as I can discover, the longest period that the Church was without a Bishop of Rome was during the three years from 1268 to 1271. The cardinals couldn't agree on naming a successor to Pope

Clement IV, until the people of Viterbo hastened the process. They removed the roof from the palace and put the electors on bread and water. A committee quickly chose Pope Gregory X.

A deadlock like this does not interrupt the papal succession. And there was no occasion for the sons of Erin to leap into the breach.

Theresa Neumann

Has the Church accepted Theresa Neumann's life as that of a living saint?

The Church hopes she lived as a saint, as she hopes you are doing. The test of her holiness will be in the way in which her faith, hope, and charity made her a true follower of Jesus Christ. Whether the extraordinary things that surrounded so much of her life were natural phenomena or special gifts of God is of wholly secondary importance to the question of holiness.

The Church accepted her as a beloved daughter at her baptism. She rejoices in her fidelity until her death in 1962. I don't know if any official investigations have been begun to determine the genuine heroicity of her Christian life. But certainly she has not yet been canonized.

Catholic Feminists

I would appreciate it if you can give me any information on St. Joan's Social and Political Alliance, which was founded in England in 1911 and established here in 1965.

This organization is now officially known as St. Joan's International Alliance. Originally it was known as the Catholic Women's Suffrage Society and worked actively at the beginning of this century to obtain the right for women to vote. The United States section of the alliance states its objectives thus: "to secure political, social, and economic equality between men and women in all fields and the full participation of women in the Church and the State."

The alliance now has consultative status with the United Nations, where it has worked effectively in sponsoring resolutions for the elimination of slavery, for the education of women, and for equal pay for equal work. In the area of Church affairs, it lobbies for women's full participation in liturgy with a view to their ordination as deaconesses and priests, and for the elimination of anti-feminist tendencies in Church law and practice.

It is not an official Catholic organization. Membership is open to all Catholic women who approve the objectives of the alliance — and associate membership to men and women of other denominations. Headquarters are at 15 Carlisle Street, London, W 1, England, where the organization publishes *The Catholic Citizen*. If you are interested in more information, you can contact the U.S. Section at 435 W. 119th St., New York, N. Y. 10027.

Index

INDEX